Igor Okunev and Petr Oskolkov (eds.)

TRANSFORMING THE ADMINISTRATIVE MATRYOSHKA

The Reform of Autonomous Okrugs in the Russian Federation, 2003–2008

With a foreword by Vladimir Zorin

Bibliografische Information der Deutschen Nationalbibliothek
Die Deutsche Nationalbibliothek verzeichnet diese Publikation in der Deutschen Nationalbibliografie; detaillierte bibliografische Daten sind im Internet über http://dnb.d-nb.de abrufbar.

Bibliographic information published by the Deutsche Nationalbibliothek
Die Deutsche Nationalbibliothek lists this publication in the Deutsche Nationalbibliografie; detailed bibliographic data are available in the Internet at http://dnb.d-nb.de.

Cover illustration: Photo taken by Dr Igor Okunev in Naryan-Mar

ISBN-13: 978-3-8382-1721-5
© *ibidem*-Verlag, Stuttgart 2022
Alle Rechte vorbehalten

Das Werk einschließlich aller seiner Teile ist urheberrechtlich geschützt. Jede Verwertung außerhalb der engen Grenzen des Urheberrechtsgesetzes ist ohne Zustimmung des Verlages unzulässig und strafbar. Dies gilt insbesondere für Vervielfältigungen, Übersetzungen, Mikroverfilmungen und elektronische Speicherformen sowie die Einspeicherung und Verarbeitung in elektronischen Systemen.

All rights reserved. No part of this publication may be reproduced, stored in or introduced into a retrieval system, or transmitted, in any form, or by any means (electronic, mechanical, photocopying, recording or otherwise) without the prior written permission of the publisher. Any person who does any unauthorized act in relation to this publication may be liable to criminal prosecution and civil claims for damages.

Printed in the EU

Soviet and Post-Soviet Politics and Society (SPPS)   Vol. 253
ISSN 1614-3515

General Editor: Andreas Umland,
Stockholm Centre for Eastern European Studies, andreas.umland@ui.se

Commissioning Editor: Max Jakob Horstmann,
London, mjh@ibidem.eu

EDITORIAL COMMITTEE*

DOMESTIC & COMPARATIVE POLITICS
Prof. **Ellen Bos**, *Andrássy University of Budapest*
Dr. **Gergana Dimova**, *University of Winchester*
Dr. **Andrey Kazantsev**, *MGIMO (U) MID RF, Moscow*
Prof. **Heiko Pleines**, *University of Bremen*
Prof. **Richard Sakwa**, *University of Kent at Canterbury*
Dr. **Sarah Whitmore**, *Oxford Brookes University*
Dr. **Harald Wydra**, *University of Cambridge*

SOCIETY, CLASS & ETHNICITY
Col. **David Glantz**, *"Journal of Slavic Military Studies"*
Dr. **Marlène Laruelle**, *George Washington University*
Dr. **Stephen Shulman**, *Southern Illinois University*
Prof. **Stefan Troebst**, *University of Leipzig*

POLITICAL ECONOMY & PUBLIC POLICY
Dr. **Andreas Goldthau**, *Central European University*
Dr. **Robert Kravchuk**, *University of North Carolina*
Dr. **David Lane**, *University of Cambridge*
Dr. **Carol Leonard**, *Higher School of Economics, Moscow*
Dr. **Maria Popova**, *McGill University, Montreal*

FOREIGN POLICY & INTERNATIONAL AFFAIRS
Dr. **Peter Duncan**, *University College London*
Prof. **Andreas Heinemann-Grüder**, *University of Bonn*
Prof. **Gerhard Mangott**, *University of Innsbruck*
Dr. **Diana Schmidt-Pfister**, *University of Konstanz*
Dr. **Lisbeth Tarlow**, *Harvard University, Cambridge*
Dr. **Christian Wipperfürth**, *N-Ost Network, Berlin*
Dr. **William Zimmerman**, *University of Michigan*

HISTORY, CULTURE & THOUGHT
Dr. **Catherine Andreyev**, *University of Oxford*
Prof. **Mark Bassin**, *Södertörn University*
Prof. **Karsten Brüggemann**, *Tallinn University*
Dr. **Alexander Etkind**, *University of Cambridge*
Dr. **Gasan Gusejnov**, *Moscow State University*
Prof. **Leonid Luks**, *Catholic University of Eichstaett*
Dr. **Olga Malinova**, *Russian Academy of Sciences*
Dr. **Richard Mole**, *University College London*
Prof. **Andrei Rogatchevski**, *University of Tromsø*
Dr. **Mark Tauger**, *West Virginia University*

ADVISORY BOARD*

Prof. **Dominique Arel**, *University of Ottawa*
Prof. **Jörg Baberowski**, *Humboldt University of Berlin*
Prof. **Margarita Balmaceda**, *Seton Hall University*
Dr. **John Barber**, *University of Cambridge*
Prof. **Timm Beichelt**, *European University Viadrina*
Dr. **Katrin Boeckh**, *University of Munich*
Prof. em. **Archie Brown**, *University of Oxford*
Dr. **Vyacheslav Bryukhovetsky**, *Kyiv-Mohyla Academy*
Prof. **Timothy Colton**, *Harvard University, Cambridge*
Prof. **Paul D'Anieri**, *University of Florida*
Dr. **Heike Dörrenbächer**, *Friedrich Naumann Foundation*
Dr. **John Dunlop**, *Hoover Institution, Stanford, California*
Dr. **Sabine Fischer**, *SWP, Berlin*
Dr. **Geir Flikke**, *NUPI, Oslo*
Prof. **David Galbreath**, *University of Aberdeen*
Prof. **Alexander Galkin**, *Russian Academy of Sciences*
Prof. **Frank Golczewski**, *University of Hamburg*
Dr. **Nikolas Gvosdev**, *Naval War College, Newport, RI*
Prof. **Mark von Hagen**, *Arizona State University*
Dr. **Guido Hausmann**, *University of Munich*
Prof. **Dale Herspring**, *Kansas State University*
Dr. **Stefani Hoffman**, *Hebrew University of Jerusalem*
Prof. **Mikhail Ilyin**, *MGIMO (U) MID RF, Moscow*
Prof. **Vladimir Kantor**, *Higher School of Economics*
Dr. **Ivan Katchanovski**, *University of Ottawa*
Prof. em. **Andrzej Korbonski**, *University of California*
Dr. **Iris Kempe**, *"Caucasus Analytical Digest"*
Prof. **Herbert Küpper**, *Institut für Ostrecht Regensburg*
Dr. **Rainer Lindner**, *CEEER, Berlin*
Dr. **Vladimir Malakhov**, *Russian Academy of Sciences*

Dr. **Luke March**, *University of Edinburgh*
Prof. **Michael McFaul**, *Stanford University, Palo Alto*
Prof. **Birgit Menzel**, *University of Mainz-Germersheim*
Prof. **Valery Mikhailenko**, *The Urals State University*
Prof. **Emil Pain**, *Higher School of Economics, Moscow*
Dr. **Oleg Podvintsev**, *Russian Academy of Sciences*
Prof. **Olga Popova**, *St. Petersburg State University*
Dr. **Alex Pravda**, *University of Oxford*
Dr. **Erik van Ree**, *University of Amsterdam*
Dr. **Joachim Rogall**, *Robert Bosch Foundation Stuttgart*
Prof. **Peter Rutland**, *Wesleyan University, Middletown*
Prof. **Marat Salikov**, *The Urals State Law Academy*
Dr. **Gwendolyn Sasse**, *University of Oxford*
Prof. **Jutta Scherrer**, *EHESS, Paris*
Prof. **Robert Service**, *University of Oxford*
Mr. **James Sherr**, *RIIA Chatham House London*
Dr. **Oxana Shevel**, *Tufts University, Medford*
Prof. **Eberhard Schneider**, *University of Siegen*
Prof. **Olexander Shnyrkov**, *Shevchenko University, Kyiv*
Prof. **Hans-Henning Schröder**, *SWP, Berlin*
Prof. **Yuri Shapoval**, *Ukrainian Academy of Sciences*
Prof. **Viktor Shnirelman**, *Russian Academy of Sciences*
Dr. **Lisa Sundstrom**, *University of British Columbia*
Dr. **Philip Walters**, *"Religion, State and Society"*, *Oxford*
Prof. **Zenon Wasyliw**, *Ithaca College, New York State*
Dr. **Lucan Way**, *University of Toronto*
Dr. **Markus Wehner**, *"Frankfurter Allgemeine Zeitung"*
Dr. **Andrew Wilson**, *University College London*
Prof. **Jan Zielonka**, *University of Oxford*
Prof. **Andrei Zorin**, *University of Oxford*

While the Editorial Committee and Advisory Board support the General Editor in the choice and improvement of manuscripts for publication, responsibility for remaining errors and misinterpretations in the series' volumes lies with the books' authors.

Soviet and Post-Soviet Politics and Society (SPPS)
ISSN 1614-3515

Founded in 2004 and refereed since 2007, SPPS makes available affordable English-, German-, and Russian-language studies on the history of the countries of the former Soviet bloc from the late Tsarist period to today. It publishes between 5 and 20 volumes per year and focuses on issues in transitions to and from democracy such as economic crisis, identity formation, civil society development, and constitutional reform in CEE and the NIS. SPPS also aims to highlight so far understudied themes in East European studies such as right-wing radicalism, religious life, higher education, or human rights protection. The authors and titles of all previously published volumes are listed at the end of this book. For a full description of the series and reviews of its books, see www.ibidem-verlag.de/red/spps.

Editorial correspondence & manuscripts should be sent to: Dr. Andreas Umland, Department of Political Science, Kyiv-Mohyla Academy, vul. Voloska 8/5, UA-04070 Kyiv, UKRAINE; andreas.umland@cantab.net

Business correspondence & review copy requests should be sent to: *ibidem* Press, Leuschnerstr. 40, 30457 Hannover, Germany; tel.: +49 511 2622200; fax: +49 511 2622201; spps@ibidem.eu.

Authors, reviewers, referees, and editors for (as well as all other persons sympathetic to) SPPS are invited to join its networks at www.facebook.com/group.php?gid=52638198614
www.linkedin.com/groups?about=&gid=103012
www.xing.com/net/spps-ibidem-verlag/

Recent Volumes

244 *Rumena Filipova*
Constructing the Limits of Europe
Identity and Foreign Policy in Poland, Bulgaria, and Russia since 1989
With forewords by Harald Wydra and Gergana Yankova-Dimova
ISBN 978-3-8382-1649-2

245 *Oleksandra Keudel*
How Patronal Networks Shape Opportunities for Local Citizen Participation in a Hybrid Regime
A Comparative Analysis of Five Cities in Ukraine
With a foreword by Sabine Kropp
ISBN 978-3-8382-1671-3

246 *Jan Claas Behrends, Thomas Lindenberger, Pavel Kolar (Eds.)*
Violence after Stalin
Institutions, Practices, and Everyday Life in the Soviet Bloc 1953–1989
ISBN 978-3-8382-1637-9

247 *Leonid Luks*
Macht und Ohnmacht der Utopien
Essays zur Geschichte Russlands im 20. und 21. Jahrhundert
ISBN 978-3-8382-1677-5

248 *Iuliia Barshadska*
Brüssel zwischen Kyjiw und Moskau
Das auswärtige Handeln der Europäischen Union im ukrainisch-russischen Konflikt 2014-2019
Mit einem Vorwort von Olaf Leiße
ISBN 978-3-8382-1667-6

249 *Valentyna Romanova*
Decentralisation and Multilevel Elections in Ukraine
Reform Dynamics and Party Politics in 2010–2021
With a foreword by Kimitaka Matsuzato
ISBN 978-3-8382-1700-0

250 *Alexander Motyl*
National Questions
Theoretical Reflections on Nations and Nationalism in Eastern Europe
ISBN 978-3-8382-1675-1

251 *Marc Dietrich*
A Cosmopolitan Model for Peacebuilding
The Ukrainian Cases of Crimea and the Donbas
ISBN 978-3-8382-1687-4

252 *Eduard Baidaus*
An Unsettled Nation
State-Building, Identity, and Separatism in Post-Soviet Moldova
With forewords by John-Paul Himka and David R. Marples
ISBN 978-3-8382-1582-2

Contents

Vladimir Zorin
Foreword 7

Igor Okunev & Petr Oskolkov
Introduction 11

PART I: Merger of Regions as a Part of the Federative Reform of the Russian Federation in the 2000s

Igor Okunev
Composite Regions as an Element of Russian Federalism 23

Emma Bibina
The Merger of Perm Oblast and Komi-Permyak Autonomous Okrug 29

Emma Bibina
The Merger of Taymyr Dolgano-Nenets Autonomous Okrug, Evenk Autonomous Okrug and Krasnoyarsk Krai 35

Rostislav Shilovskiy
The Merger of Koryak Autonomous Okrug and Kamchatka Oblast 43

Rostislav Shilovskiy
The Merger of Ust-Orda Buryat Autonomous Okrug and Irkutsk Oblast 53

Rostislav Shilovskiy
The Merger of Agin-Buryat Autonomous Okrug and Chita Oblast 63

Petr Oskolkov
The Attempt to Merge Nenets Autonomous Okrug and Arkhangelsk Oblast 71

PART II: Assessing the Consequences of Merging Regions of the Russian Federation

Petr Oskolkov
The Institutional Aspect 77

Emma Bibina
The Electoral Aspect.. 87

Maria Tislenko
The Socio-Economic Aspect 125

Petr Oskolkov
The Ethnic Aspect.. 147

Maria Tislenko
Analysis of Media Messages 157

Maria Tislenko & Igor Okunev
Analysis of Opinion Polls 175

Petr Oskolkov & Igor Okunev
Analysis of In-Depth Interviews 203

Igor Okunev
Conclusions and Recommendations.. 217

Bibliography.. 223

Appendix 1: Questions for the Sociological Survey..................... 243
Appendix 2: In-Depth Interview Questions 247

Foreword

Vladimir Zorin

There is a common understanding in modern political science that federalism in Russia is designed to ensure state unity and territorial integrity, the development of self-governance and the ethno-cultural self-determination of peoples within a single state, and the protection of the rights of national minorities and small-numbered peoples. The Strategy of the State National Policy of the Russian Federation for the period until 2025 has set the dual challenge of achieving the formation of the Russian nation and the ethno-cultural development of all the peoples inhabiting it.

It is this aspect of the federal structure of Russia that the authors of this work address, as it has remained almost completely unexplored until now. This is a process that has been called the "parade of associations." Scientific developments in the issue we are exploring certainly offer us a great deal in terms of our analysis of the features of the formation of the national policy of the Russian Federation and in terms of identifying ways to improve and develop it. As a result of the referendums that took place in Russia in the 2000s, only four of the ten autonomous *okrugs*, along with the country's numerous republics and the autonomous *oblast*, remained.

In the years that have passed since they were merged into larger entities, I have yet to come across a single comprehensive empirical study of these reforms based on a comparative analysis of all the mergers and their fallout. The authors took a comprehensive approach to the issue: the monograph covers almost all the important aspects of the reforms of the autonomous regions – historical, institutional, electoral and socioeconomic. The ethnic component, which is of particular interest to me as an ethnopolitical scientist, has also been explored. It should be noted here that this monograph is the result of a three-year study carried out with the support of the Russian Science Foundation, during which time the authors proved themselves to be more than purely theoreticians, but also experienced field researchers. What is more, the project can be considered one of the most logistically challenging in the modern history of Russian political science: a total of eight exhaustive visits were made to some of the remotest and hardest-to-reach areas of the country, in difficult climatic and infrastructural conditions. The successful pairing of questionnaires and in-depth interviews, conducted both in the centres of the former autonomies and in the capitals of the *krais* and *oblasts*, made it possible for us to present a complete picture of public opinion on the reforms. There was a wealth of opinions both "for" and "against" the reforms, so we cannot say that the study yielded one-sided results.

There is also a practical dimension to the study. Russian public discourse has frequently touched upon the need for a radical transformation of the country's territorial structure that would consist in either the significant reduction in the number of constituent entities or the elimination of national regions altogether. Economic or manageability reasons are typically cited – a grid-like restructuring of the country will improve the standard of living and make the functioning of the state apparatus more efficient. Or so they say. The present monograph demonstrates that Russian territory is far more dispersed and multifaceted than it would seem in Moscow. The complex territorial structure of the Russian Federation took shape during the Soviet period of the country's history, and now there is talk of the need to revise it. The authors of this monograph arrive at the conclusion that there is nothing intrinsically wrong with reforming the territorial organization of the Russian Federation, but it should be done more carefully, not according to some arbitrary schemes thought up by those "above," taking the specifics of each region into account. Most importantly, it should be carried out on the basis of fundamental field research and following consultation with experts. This will ensure that ethnologically sound decisions are made at the legislative level.

As someone who had a direct hand in the complex sociopolitical processes that took place in the Russian regions in the 2000s, I would say that it was extremely important that the gap that had appeared in the study of Russian federalism be filled. Moreover, I would say that the present study has done just that, as a qualitative, empirical and interdisciplinary work that combines political science and sociological methods and is capable of standing on a par with the classic works on federalism.

It is profoundly symbolic that it was a young team that undertook this most important of projects, a team that did not recoil at the scale of the tasks they faced and the numerous difficulties they faced on the way to achieving their goal. The only thing left is to thank the authors for their work and wish them further success in their scientific endeavours.

Vladimir Zorin,
Doctor of Political Sciences, Professor, Chief Research Fellow,
Institute of Ethnology and Anthropology of the
Russian Academy of Sciences,
Minister of the Russian Federation (2001–2004)

Introduction

Igor Okunev & Petr Oskolkov

The administrative division of a state is often seen as a tool for building relations between the centre and the regions, which allows us to define and construct a configuration of centre–periphery relations. Accordingly, any change in administrative division – even more so a large-scale reform – can lead to a fundamental transformation of federal relations. This carries significant political and economic risks, while it is always safer to maintain the established status quo.

In the mid-2000s, the decision was taken in the Russian Federation to reform the administrative structure of the country, which consisted in the merger of certain constituent entities of the Russian Federation, specifically:

- Perm Oblast and Komi-Permyak Autonomous Okrug were merged into Perm Krai
- Taymyr Dolgano-Nenets and Evenk Autonomous Okrugs were merged into Krasnoyarsk Krai
- Kamchatka Oblast and Koryak Okrug were merged into Kamchatka Krai
- Ust-Orda Buryat Autonomous Okrug and Irkutsk Oblast was merged into redesigned Irkutsk Oblast
- Chita Oblast and Agin-Buryat Autonomous Okrug were merged to form Zabaykalsky Krai

According to Sergey Artobolevsky and Evgeny Gontmakher, administrative reforms are nothing new for the Russian Federation, and, with the exception of short political fluctuations, the redrawing of the country's internal borders has always been initiated by the state (2010). Such decisions were thus mostly spur-of-the-moment, although they were justified by political or economic reasons, urgent tasks facing the state administration, or the need to ensure control over territories and borders. In the case of the transformations of the 2000s, the reasons cited were economic (so that successful regions could pull less successful regions out of their economic backwardness, as in the case of Perm Oblast and Komi-Permyak Autonomous Okrug) and administrative (for example, Koryak Okrug was frequently described as the constituent entity most bogged down in red tape until it was merged into Kamchatka Krai). That notwithstanding, another important but unspoken reason for the administrative and territorial reform was to increase the "governability" of regions that had seen a surge of independence in the 1990s – something that the centre actually condoned following Boris Yeltsin's famous statement to Russia's regions in Kazan in August 1990, "take as much sovereignty as you can." Thus, according to Vladimir Gel'man, the "parade of sovereignties" was replaced by a "parade of associations," with the aim being to build a power vertical, increase subordination and build solidarity in the regions (2001).

The reasons for the transformations we have noted demonstrate that administrative reforms are often evaluated in terms of institutional and socioeconomic impact only: in the first case, researchers focus on the restructuring of federal institutions and changes in relations between the regional and federal elites; and in the second case, they note the economic feasibility of reform, the possibility of improving living standards and optimizing migration and financial flows. Consequently, the study of reforms to the administrative structure is reduced either to an analysis of the interactions between the elites in the centre and the regions undergoing transformations, or to an assessment of the possibility that reform could act as a driver for the socioeconomic development of the regions. What this means is that the national and cultural component is often overlooked, especially if the transformation was not aimed at resolving existing ethnic, religious or cultural contradictions.

On the one hand, cultural contradictions can be nothing more than a tool in the hands of the local elites in the struggle for financial and political compensation in exchange for loyalty. On the other hand, the ability of the establishment to impose its will on the population should not be overestimated, even with strong guarantees from the centre. There are a number of risks associated with how the population will react: flight from the region, voting against the discredited elites who carried out the reforms; as well as growing discontent and social tension, which are cumulative and may "detonate" years later. What is more, while the first two consequences can be studied using socioeconomic and electoral statistics, the third cannot be examined from official sources. That said, an analysis of the transformations of territorial identity in the regions affected by the reforms may help the scientific community and the political leadership understand not only what the people affected by the reforms think about the changes, but also what adjustments need to be made to the administrative decision-making process and how the risks mentioned above can be managed in the regions. These challenges are especially significant in the run-up to the 2018–2021 electoral cycle.

These circumstances have permitted the authors to put forward the hypothesis that the constituent entities of the Russian Federation that lost their political autonomy did not lose their special territorial identity. Having lost the institutional basis of their identity and the political actors who supported it, the population retained specific ideas about the special significance of these territories and the unique nature of their spatial position, which demands special attention from both the federal and new regional centres. Accordingly, according to residents, these territories cannot be treated as ordinary districts of *krais* and *oblasts*, even though the tendency in the centres of these enlarged *krais* to group them together with other districts remains. The recognition of territorial identities and their formalization within a general model will thus allow us to evaluate the progress of the reform of the administrative structure of the Russian Federation and the development of institutions of federalism over the past ten years at the local level, and to subsequently manage part of the regional risks.

To test the hypothesis, eight expeditions were carried out to the former administrative centres of the constituent entities that had been merged into other entities, as well as the administrative centres of the constituent entities that incorporated them, specifically:

1. Perm and Kudymkar (about the former Komi-Permyak Autonomous Okrug)
2. Chita and Aginskoe (about the former Agin-Buryat Autonomous Okrug)
3. Irkutsk and Ust-Orda (about the former Orda Buryat Autonomous Okrug)
4. Dudinka and Norilsk (about the former Taymyr Dolgano-Nenets Autonomous Okrug)
5. Krasnoyarsk and Tura (about the former Evenk Autonomous Okrug)
6. Petropavlovsk-Kamchatsky (about the former Koryak Okrug)

The project methodology involved overt observation, with researchers keeping diaries of what they had observed; in-depth interviews with local officials and people employed in the education, cultural and tourism sectors as carriers of a standardized discourse on territorial identity; blitz surveys of people on the streets; the collection of written, oral and audio-visual materials, national symbols; and the creation of a corpus of relevant texts for content and discourse analysis.

A total of 555 telephone surveys were completed, and a further 48 partially completed, all of which were collected and processed. A total of 3383 telephone calls were made as part of the survey. The number of completed questionnaires was roughly equal in all the cities being studied: Irkutsk (50 questionnaires), Ust-Ordynsky (former Ust-Orda Buryat Autonomous Okrug; 51 questionnaires), Chita (51 questionnaires), Aginskoe (former Agin-Buryat Autonomous Okrug; 50 questionnaires), Perm (51 questionnaires), Kudymkar (former Komi-Permyak Autonomous Okrug; 50 questionnaires), Krasnoyarsk (51 questionnaires), Dudinka (former Taymyr Dolgano-Nenets Autonomous Okrug; 63questionnaires), Tura (former Evenk Autonomous Okrug; 38 questionnaires), Petropavlovsk-Kamchatsky (50 questionnaires), and Palana (former Koryak Okrug; 51 questionnaires). The small population of the village of Tura meant that it was impossible to collect 50 questionnaires there, so the difference was made up in another region that joined Krasnoyarsk Krai – Dudinka. In addition, a total of 125 in-depth interviews were conducted at 95 organizations during the expeditions.

The role of territorial identity and "centre–periphery" relationships is one of the key topics of political geography. Modern ideas about identity in political science, social geography and other social sciences are based on the close interpenetration of culture, economics and the social sphere. In this regard, identity, including regional identity, is one of the most important concepts. The subject of territorial identity has been explored by a number of Russian and foreign geographers: O. Vendina (Vendina and Zinoviev 2022), D. Vizgalov (2011), A. Gritsenko and M. Krylov (2015), D. Zamyatin (2014), N. Zamyatina (2012), V. Kalutskov, V. Kolosov (Kolosov, Galkina, and Krindach 2001), A. Manakov (Manakov and Evdokimov 2013), I. Mitin (2015), S. Pavlyuk (2007), N. Petrov, K. Puzanov (Puzanov 2013), M. Ragulina (2012), L. Smirnyagin (2005), V. Streletskii (2008), A. Tkachenko (1995), R. Turovsky (1999), U. Zelensky, E. Relph (1976), Yi-Fu Tuan (1979), H. Hale (2005), and others. Several political scientists and other researchers have also touched upon the issue: V. Gel'man, A. Goncharik (2011), M. Nazukina (2014), V. Pantin (Pantin and Lapkin 2015), I. Prokhorenko (2012), I. Semenenko (2016), S. Rokkan and D. Urwin (1983), P. Berger and T. Luckmann (1967), P. Bourdieu (1989), V. Gasilin (Gasilin and Riazanov 2016), M. Guboglo (2017), L. Drobizheva (2002), L. Ionin (2005), P. Krastev, I. Malygina (2011), A. Panarin (2005), M.-A. Robert, A. Sofronov, T. Stefanenko (2009), F. Tilman (Robber and Tilman 1988), V. Tishkov (2008), N. Fedotova (2015), V. Yadov (1995), V. Yarskaya (Yarskaya et al. 2004), and others.

Many researchers consider the issue of the formation of regional identity in the context of the "centre–regions" relationship. This is connected with the specifics of the "centripetal" image of Russian space. They are interested in the causes of these processes, as well as the mechanisms and methods of interaction between the centre and the regions and the content of centrifugal and centripetal processes (A. Miller (2003), M. Nazukina and O. Podvintsev (2009), V. Nechaev (1998), N. Petrov (2000), R. Turovsky (2006b)). In political geography, regional identity is often correlated with administrative division and the general principles of building federalism. Rostislav Turovsky has examined the role of administrative division in the manifestation of regional identity in great detail, pointing to a higher degree of "bureaucratization of the regional structure" in Russia, since even at the level of official toponymy, Russian regions are named after their respective administrative centre (2006a).

An equally common subject is the study of territorial community as a specific social formation and the treatment of territorial identity as a criterion of territorial community. The works of the following researchers deal with these issues: I. Beloborodova (2008), L. Bogdanova (2005), J. Gold (Hirschon and Gold 1982), E. Goryachenko (Mosienko and Goryachenko 2010), Z. Grunt (1982), M. Dobriakova (1999), A. Zavalishin (Riazantsev and Zavalishin 2009), T. Zaslavskaya (Zaslavskaya and Yadov 2008), M. Krylov, T. Kuveneva (Kuveneva and Manakov 2003), A. Manakov, G. P. Murdock (1949), O. Oracheva (1999), A. Poplin, R. Ryvkina (Zaslavskaya, Aganbegian, and Ryvkina 1991), R. Redfield (1947), R. Warren (Ostrom, Tiebout, and Warren 1961), J. Szczepański (1964), A Shchukina (Bogdanova and Shchukina 2002), and others. Of particular interest is the study of administrative reforms in the context of regional identity, which is effectively what the present project is all about. In their book *Integration of the Constituent Entities of the Russian Federation: For and Against*, E. Gontmakher, S. Artobolevsky, O. Vendina, N. Zubarevich and A. Kynev touched upon the relationship between administrative reforms of any kind and territorial identity, and how they influence each other. The authors argue that when carrying out territorial reforms and changes the ethnocultural characteristics of the region in question must always be taken into account.

The role of regions and "centre-periphery" relations in the formation of nation states is a key topic in political geography. A surge of interest in the subject was witnessed in the 1980s in connection with the emergence of a new regional geography in which regions within countries started to be studied as independent actors in the political process. The role of the region in state (nation) building is covered in detail in the works of the following researchers: J. Agnew, T. Barnes and M. Farish (Barnes and Farish 2006), A. Jonas and I. Pincetl (2006), D. Clayton (2004), M. Keating (1998), A. Lagendijk (Lagendijk and Cornford 2000), M. Jones and G. MacLeod (Brenner, Jessop, Jones, and Macleod 2008), A. Marcusen (1987), A. Paasi (2001), H. Hans, J. Harrison (2007), D. Henley (1995), and B. Yack (1996). Russian experts who have dealt with this topic include I. Busygina, A. Makarychev (2000), A. Treivish (Gritsai, Ioffe, and Treivish 1991), S. Artobolevsky, R. Turovsky, M. Fadeicheva, and others.

Despite this impressive list of researchers, the problem of the territorial identity on the course of administrative reforms remains insufficiently studied. The authors of this book use the extensive empirical material they collected to carry out a comprehensive study of the consequences of the merger of regions of the Russian Federation in the 2000s.

The research was carried out by a group of MGIMO scholars: Igor Okunev, Petr Oskolkov, Maria Tislenko, Emma Bibina, and Rostislav Shilovskiy. *Dr. Igor Okunev* was responsible for the overall management of the project, developed the theoretical and methodological framework of the research, organized fieldwork to collect the empirics and an opinion poll. He studied composite regions as an element of Russian federalism, as well as transformation of territorial identity in the course of the reform, formulated general conclusions and recommendations. *Dr. Petr Oskolkov* designed in-depth interview questionnaires and respondent samples, organized interview data collecting and processing, described in detail the (failed) reform attempt in Nenets Autonomous Okrug, wrote chapters on institutional and ethnic aspects of the reform and a chapter presenting the results of in-depth interviewing. He also conducted the overall management of the final manuscript writing and editing. *Maria Tislenko* wrote chapter on the socio-economic aspect of the reform, as well as analyzed media messages and the results of the opinion poll. *Emma Bibina* wrote case-study chapters on the developments in Komi-Permyak, Evenk and Taimyr Dolgano-Nenets Autonomous Okrugs and analyzed the electoral aspect of the reform. *Rostislav Shilovskiy* described in detail the reform process in Koryak, Ust-Orda Buryat and Agin-Buryat Autonomous Okrugs.

The intermediate results of the research were presented in a book in Russian and in a number of research papers in Russian and English:

1. Okunev I. Y., P. V. Oskolkov, M. I. Tislenko, E. S. Bibina, and R. S. Shilovskiy. 2020. *Ob'edinenie regionov Rossiyskoy Federatsii: sotsiologicheskie dannye, glubinnye interview, sravnitel'nyy analiz.* Moscow: Aspekt Press.
2. Okunev I. Y., and E. S. Bibina. 2019. "Ob'edinenie Taymyrskogo (Dolgano-Nenetskogo) i Evenkiyskogo avtonomnykh okrugov v sostave Krasnoyarskogo kraya: istoriya izmeneniya statusov i otsenki v SMI." *Pskovskiy regionologicheskiy zhurnal,* no. 1 (37): 46-55.
3. Okunev I. Y., and P. V. Oskolkov. 2019. "Posledstviya ob'edineniya rossiyskikh regionov v hode federativnoy reformy 2000-h godov (sravnitel'nyy analiz na osnove ekspertnykh interview)." *Politiya: Analiz. Khronika. Prognoz (Zhurnal politicheskoy filosofii i sotsiologii politiki),* no. 1 (92): 149-166.
4. Okunev I. Y., P. V. Oskolkov, and M. I. Tislenko. 2019. "Transforming the Matryoshka: Merger of Russian Regions." *Regions and Cohesion* 9, no. 3: 29-57.
5. Okunev I. Y., and R. S. Shilovskiy. 2018. "Posledstviya ob'edineniya Kamchatskoy oblasti i Koryakskogo avtonomnogo okruga." *Vestnik Rossiyskogo universiteta druzhby narodov. Seriya: Politologiya* 20, no. 4: 484-495.
6. Tislenko M. I., and I. Y. Okunev. 2018. "Posledstviya ob'edineniya sub'ektov Rossiyskoy Federatsii: analiz obshchestvennogo mneniya." *Regional'nye issledovaniya,* no. 4 (62): 118-125.
7. Okunev I. Y., M. I. Tislenko, and E. S. Bibina. 2018. "Otsenki posledstviy ob'edineniya Permskoy oblasti i Komi-Permyatskogo avtonomnogo okruga." *Istoricheskaya i sotsial'no-obrazovatel'naya mysl'* 10, no. 2-2: 133-147.

8. Okunev I. Y., and R. S. Shilovskiy. 2018. "Reformy ob'edineniya Ust'-Ordynskogo Buryatskogo avtonomnogo okruga s Irkutskoy oblast'yu i Aginskogo Buryatskogo avtonomnogo okruga s Chitinskoy oblast'yu: motivy i posledstviya." *Pskovskiy regionologicheskiy zhurnal*, no. 1 (33): 10-23.
9. Okunev I. Y., P. V. Oskolkov, and M. I. Tislenko. 2018. "Ob'edinenie regionov Rossiyskoy Federatsii: institutsional'nye i sotsial'nye posledstviya." *Polis. Politicheskie issledovaniya*, no. 2: 8-28.
10. Oskolkov P. V. 2020. "Merging Russia's Autonomous Entities: Ethnic Aspect." *ICELDS*, June 15, 2020. https://www.icelds.org/2020/06/15/merging-russias-autonomous-entities-ethnic-aspect/.

The research project was supported by Russian Science Foundation under Grant 17-78-10053 and realized at the MGIMO University. For their valuable and constructive comments and friendly support, the authors are indebted to Prof. Dr. Irina Busygina, Prof. Dr. Vladimir Zorin, Sardana Avksentyeva, and Prof. Dr. Andreas Umland.

Igor Okunev,
Petr Oskolkov

July 2022

PART I

Merger of Regions as a Part of the Federative Reform of the Russian Federation in the 2000s

Composite Regions as an Element of Russian Federalism

Igor Okunev

Today, almost every country and even dependent territories are divided along administrative borders at one level minimum. Few exceptions include the Vatican without administrative or municipal division and Monaco, Liechtenstein and Qatar, which have only municipalities. The administrative division seeks to meet two basic criteria, regularity and hierarchy, in any state. The regularity implies that, on the one hand, the division refers to the entire territory of a state, and on the other hand, not a single part of the same hierarchical level refers to different administrative units at the same time. The hierarchy means there exist several levels of units of government, with units of a higher order divided into subregions of a lower order. In other words, the emerging political and territorial organization presupposes that a unit of a higher order cannot include the units of a lower order, which are not hierarchically subordinate to it.

When applied, both basic administrative division criteria have a few exceptions. Take, for example, the Taymyr (Dolgan-Nenets) Autonomous Okrug, which existed in Russia for a few decades after the dissolution of the USSR. The unit had a complex structure as it was simultaneously subordinate to the federal center and another region (the Krasnoyarsk Krai), while Norilsk, its largest city, was not part of the Okrug and was directly subordinate to the Krai.

The administrative division differs across the globe in accordance with such variables as fractionalization, heterogeneity, and congruence. The required degree of fractionalization remains a key debatable issue related to the administrative division. There exists a dilemma of the state's fractionalization. By reducing fractionalization, the state gives impetus to stronger centripetal forces and promotes more consistent management. However, it may disregard separatist sentiments. At the same time, by increasing fractionalization, the state authorities take heed of territorial heterogeneity and allow taking into account peculiar regional factors, which increase centrifugal forces but impedes regional management. Thus, there is no one-size-fits-all solution depending on the size of the territory or the population of the region. Fractionalization is a compromise between the need to make some aspects congruent and consider territorial heterogeneity, which is unique in every state.

According to Rostislav Turovsky's calculations, a state has on average 18 first-order administrative divisions, with the average territory size of 40,000 km² and the average population 1.8 million people. Although these parameters may differ a lot across countries, they should be taken as a reference point. From this perspective, North Macedonia, Slovenia, Greece, France, and Turkey have the highest degree of fractionalization, with the number of territorial units exceeding 50 and being close to 100. Pakistan and Bangladesh are the least fractionalized states and have only 4 and 6 regions, respectively, despite the large population. However, when studying fractionalization, one must realize that a country can be divided into units which differ in size and population. For instance, Yakutia, Russia's largest region, is over 3,500 times larger than the smallest one, and Moscow, the most populated city, is home to 300 times more citizens than the Nenets Autonomous Okrug, the least populated unit. The parameter of heterogeneity describes the discrepancy between territorial units. It is especially pronounced in countries with directly administered cities.

The analysis of congruence turns out to be by far more complicated than computing the other two parameters. It describes to what extent internal fault lines (political, historical, economic, ethnic and cultural, etc.) coincide with the territorial division and must be assessed qualitatively rather quantitatively. Thus, the administrative division in Russia, which is debatable in terms of fractionalization and heterogeneity, is largely congruent, as it has evolved over time and reflects a long history of border formation in both ethnic and economic regions.

In federal states the local level of government authority has final jurisdiction over a broad range of policy areas. While unitary states rely on the principle of subordination, which envisages the dominant role of higher levels of government in determining what powers to preserve and what decisions to "devolve" to lower levels, federal states are characterized by the principle of subsidiarity, which holds that issues are dealt with at the most immediate (or local) level that is consistent with their resolution, with the tasks requiring vaster resources performed at higher levels. For example, municipalities have enough resources to manage a school but lack what is needed for a college. That is why the regional level government is tasked with managing it. The region can run a college but cannot open a university, which necessitates the national level of government. In case of subordination, the subordinate is accountable to the superior while in case of subsidiarity, the subordinate sets the superior tasks, which it cannot handle on its own.

Thus, power can be exercised at two or three levels in a federal state. In case of dual federalism, the center is responsible for the federal level while local authorities are entrusted with the local one. In case of cooperative federalism, there is a third level where federal and local governments interact cooperatively and collectively to jointly address some issues. Federal states have a bottom-up structure. They can be either highly decentralized (the loose federation of Bosnia and Herzegovina) or, on the contrary, highly centralized (like Russia or Canada). Moreover, they can be symmetric, that is having constitutionally equal-status regions (Russia and Germany), and asymmetric (or federalist), that is having regions with different powers (the USA and Canada). Being a source of authority, regions in federal countries, however, do not enjoy full sovereignty, which is a property of federal government. According to their genesis, federations are divided into classical and contractual. Classical federations arose when independent units merged into a single entity pooling in their sovereignty and creating a new level of central government (Switzerland and the USA). Contractual federations used to be unitary but at some stage the center and regions agreed on the division of powers (Russia and Belgium) (Okunev 2021).

Russia is a constitutionally symmetric contractual federation. Although the names of the regions differ, the country's Constitution accords the equal status to them. The republics have only one peculiar feature, which is the right to select official languages to be used on their territory together with the state one (Article 68 of the Constitution of the Russian Federation). Thus, Russian federalism is basically not just ethnic. Russia includes 22 republics, 9 krais ("territories"), and 46 oblasts ("regions"), three cities of federal importance, one autonomous region, four autonomous districts, and Baikonur, a region which is equated to a city of federal significance under the international treaty.

In the 2000s, Russian federalism increased a rare phenomenon in its history – the number of constituent entities actually decreased, instead of the other way around. So-called composite regions were merged.

Composite regions are territorial unites of both the first (N-1) and second (N-2) order in the administrative structure of the state. On the one hand, they are equal subjects of the main territorial network and, as such, they can build relations with the centre directly. On the other hand, they are part of regions of the first order, and thus share powers with them. The phenomenon of composite regions is the result of the evolution of a purely Russian style of federalism, and they are sometimes referred to as Russian *matryoshkas* in the literature.

The emergence of these unique territorial entities occurred in three stages: 1) the consolidation of territorial units in the Russian Soviet Federative Socialist Republic (RSFRF) in the 1920s that produced special units called *krais*, which included autonomous regions; 2) the creation of national (later autonomous) *okrugs* of small-numbered peoples as part of certain regions in the 1930s; and 3) the decisions made in the early 1990s with regard to determining the basic parameters of the federal structure of the new Russia on giving the autonomous *oblasts* and *okrugs*, which until then had been part of the territories and regions, equal status as constituent entities of the Russian Federation that retained the right of parallel entry into the parent constituent entity and the sharing of powers with it.

The political model of composite regions assumes, on the one hand, that they enjoy the rights of full-fledged and equal as constituent entities of the country (for example, they are represented in the same proportion in the regional chamber of parliament), and, on the other, that – due to their small populations, transport inaccessibility and unique natural features – they will delegate some of their powers, including in terms of determining the appropriate budget items, to parent regions.

The number of composite regions has been declining ever since. The first wave of reduction in 1991–1992 saw them leave their parent regions, while the second wave in 2005–2008 stripped them of their status as constituent entities of the Russian Federation (Table 1). Interestingly, both waves affected significantly the Nenets Autonomous Okrug, which was denied the right to a referendum on withdrawal in 1994, and ran a successful campaign against merger with Arkhangelsk Oblast in 2009.

Three composite regions remain today: the aforementioned Nenets Autonomous Okrug (part of Arkhangelsk Oblast), and Yamalo-Nenets Autonomous Okrugand Khanty-Mansi Autonomous Okrug (both of which are part of Tyumen Oblast). All of the rest composite regions outstrip their parent regions in terms of economic indicators.

Now let us take a look at the circumstances surrounding the merger of each of the composite regions that were involved in the federal reform of the 2000s.

Table 1: Composite Regions of Russia that Became Territorial Units

Year	Composite Region	Parent Region	Status Following Separation from Parent Region	Administrative Centre
First Wave				
1991	Adyghe Autonomous Oblast	Krasnodar Krai	Republic of Adygea	Maykop

1991	Karachay-Cherkess Autonomous Oblast	Stavropol Krai	Karachay-Cherkess Republic	Cherkessk
1991	Gorno-Altai Autonomous Oblast	Altai Krai	Altai Republic	Gorno-Altaysk
1991	Khakas Autonomous Oblast	Krasnoyarsk Krai	Republic of Khakassia	Abakan
1991	Jewish Autonomous Oblast	Khabarovsk Krai	Jewish Autonomous Oblast	Birobidzhan
1992	Chukotka Autonomous Okrug	Magadan Oblast	Chukotka Autonomous Okrug	Anadyr
Second Wave				
2005	Komi-Permyak Autonomous Okrug	Perm Oblast	Komi-Permyak Okrug of Perm Krai	Kudymkar
2007	Taymyr Dolgano-Nenets Autonomous Okrug	Krasnoyarsk Krai	Taymyr Dolgano-Nenets Region of Krasnoyarsk Krai	Dudinka
2007	Evenk Autonomous Okrug	Krasnoyarsk Krai	Evenk Region of Krasnoyarsk Krai	Tura
2007	Koryak Autonomous Okrug	Kamchatka Oblast	Koryak Okrug of Kamchatka Krai	Palana
2008	Ust-Orda Buryat Autonomous Okrug	Irkutsk Oblast	Ust-Orda Buryat Autonomous Okrug of Irkutsk Oblast	Ust-Ordynsky
2008	Agin-Buryat Okrug	Chita Oblast	Agin-Buryat Autonomous Okrug of Zabaykalsky Krai	Aginskoe

The Merger of Perm Oblast and Komi-Permyak Autonomous Okrug

Emma Bibina

For the purposes of our analysis, the roots of the modern Perm Krai can be traced back to the 18th century, when the future internal contours of Russia were determined. The Perm Governorate – the cradle of the Perm Oblast and the Komi-Permyak Autonomous Okrug – was established in 1781 by decree of Catherine II. As for the geography of Perm, its location was clearly defined – the city was the capital of the *uyezd* of the same name. The case with Kudymkar, the centre of Komi-Permyak, is open to debate. Most likely, its ancestral home is the Cherdynsky Uyezd. Some sources mention Invensky Krai, named after the river that flows through the region. The Perm Governorate was abolished in 1923 and the territory was included in Ural Oblast, which also included the Yekaterinburg, Chelyabinsk and Tyumen governorates. In 1934, Ural Oblast was divided into three regions – Sverdlovsk Oblast (with Sverdlovsk as the capital), Chelyabinsk Oblast (with Chelyabinsk as the capital) and Ob-Irtysh Oblast (with Tyumen as the capital). Four years later, Perm Oblast was separated from Sverdlovsk Oblast and existed in this form all the way up until 2005.

Komi-Permyak Autonomous Okrug was established on February 26, 1925, as the Komi-Permyak National Okrug, part of Ural Oblast, located in the lower reaches of the Ural Mountains and the upper basin of the Kama River, with an area of 32,770 square kilometres. It was the country's first national *okrug*, and the city of Kudymkar was named its capital in 1925.

For many centuries, Komi-Permyak people lived in this territory, making up more than half of the Indigenous population. Komi-Permyaks are a Finno-Ugric people with their own language (the Komi language) and a rich cultural heritage – Komi folk art is particularly well known.

After the dissolution of Ural Oblast in 1934, Komi-Permyak National Okrug was made a territorial unit of Sverdlovsk Oblast.

Later, when Perm Oblast was split from Sverdlovsk Oblast, it fell under the jurisdiction of the former. Komi-Permyak Autonomous Okrug was granted autonomous status in 1977 with the adoption of the newest Constitution of the Soviet Union. During Boris Yeltsin's "sovereignization" in the early 1990s, the Komi-Permyak Autonomous Okrug leadership announced its fiscal separation from Perm Oblast and refused to obey the regional authorities. This was reflected in the 1993 Constitution of the Russian Federation, when Komi-Permyak Autonomous Okrug was made a full-fledged constituent entity of the Russian Federation while remaining part of Perm Oblast. Now Perm Oblast has itself become one of the so-called composite regions.

The foundations for the merger of Perm Oblast and Komi-Permyak Autonomous Okrug were laid during the deep demographic, financial, economic and social crisis of the 1990s, which hit the Okrug particularly hard. This was the first time since the adoption of the 1993 Constitution that two regions had been merged.

The official website of Komi-Permyak Okrug presents its stance on the merger of the two constituent entities. Komi-Permyak Okrug was supposed to benefit in a multitude of ways from the merger and receive economic support (Komipermyatskiiao.ru n.d.). The fact of the matter is that for decades Komi-Permyak Autonomous Okrug had a failing economic system, serving primarily as a supplier of timber for Perm Oblast. What is more, various social organizations in the Okrug were subordinated to higher instances in Perm Oblast. Komi natives would move to Perm to receive their vocational education and training and retraining. The centre would also allocate subsidies to aid in the development of the social sphere in Komi-Permyak Autonomous Okrug, which did contribute to the region's development somewhat.

A referendum on the merger of Perm Oblast and Komi-Permyak Autonomous Okrug was held in both regions on December 7, 2003, where people were asked to answer the question: "Do you agree on the merger of Perm Oblast and Komi-Permyak Autonomous Okrug in a single constituent entity of the Russian Federation, as part of which Komi-Permyak Okrug will be an administrative and territorial unit with a special status determined by the region's charter in accordance with the legislation of the Russian Federation?" Voter turnout in Komi-Permyak Autonomous Okrug was 64.17% (60, 472 people), with 89.76% of those (54,281 people) voting in favour of merger. The turnout in Perm Oblast was 62.33% (1,241,434), with 83.81% (1,040,446) responding positively (Zinoviev n.d.).

As a result, the Federal Constitutional Law "On the Creation of a New Constituent Entity of the Russian Federation Following the Merger of Perm Oblast and Komi-Permyak Autonomous Okrug" was adopted at the initiative of the President of the Russian Federation. The goals of the new law were almost identical to those set out in the previous text: "The formation of a new constituent entity of the Russian Federation in order to accelerate the socioeconomic development of Perm Oblast and Komi-Permyak Autonomous Okrug and improve the standard of living of the population in these constituent entities of the Russian Federation."

The law pronounced the creation of a new constituent entity of the Russian Federation, Perm Krai, as well as the dissolution of Perm Oblast and Komi-Permyak Autonomous Okrug. A new territorial unit, Komi-Permyak Okrug, was also established. Oleg Chirkunov was named first Governor of Perm Krai.

Changes often bring about all kinds of disputes. And the creation of Perm Krai was no exception, causing a lot of heated discussion in society. Perhaps the most well-documented response to the merger of the two regions was the report "Integration of the Constituent Entities of the Russian Federation: For and Against" presented at the Institute of Contemporary Development on April 7, 2010 (Artobolevsky and Gontmakher 2010). Its authors, S. Artobolevsky, E. Gontmakher, N. Zubarevich and A. Kynev analysed integration projects in details, outlining their advantages and disadvantages. In their critique of the merger process, the researchers noted that the population in Komi-Permyak Okrug was in constant decline, approximately half of the local elite were unhappy with the changes, and many people had lost their jobs as a result of the reduction of red tape.

In addition, the experts believed that many of the tasks that had been set as part of the merger of the regions had not been achieved. For example, they expressed their belief that if a crisis were to appear, any problems facing Komi-Permyak Okrug would fade into the background and the regional centre would concentrate its efforts – primarily financial – on other issues. Artobolevsky et al assumed that governance of the new *krai* would become more complicated due to the increased area of the territory and the growth in the number of municipalities. Finally, the researchers claimed that it would not be possible to improve governance of territories as planned while at the same time reducing spending for these purposes in the federal budget.

The work relies heavily on the results of surveys of the population, although it contains no information about the number of respondents, when the surveys were carried out and where. According to the survey, the leadership of Komi-Permyak Autonomous Okrug was, according to respondents, strong-armed by senior officials. In addition, those who opposed merger were not granted access to the media, and the local elite was replaced by political technologists from outside the region who took over the campaign. The report repeats the opinion of the local elites – the leadership of the former autonomous *okrug* are not given the opportunity to promote their interests, as they have lost their jobs and thus cannot influence decisions that affect them directly. That said, the local political elites highlighted some positives: the deepening of ties between the two regions, the reduced administrative costs, and the provision of one-time assistance. The researchers conclude that the overall impact of merger processes on the quality of life of the population of the Komi-Permyak Autonomous Okrug has been close to neutral. For example, the average per capita income of the population in Komi-Permyak Autonomous Okrug in 2002–2007 was almost equal to the living wage. In addition, the share of people with an income lower than the living wage decreased by 4% over the same period, while the unemployment rate (according to the International Labour Organization's methodology) did not fall.

Naturally, the report did not go unnoticed, and responses were quick to come. In 2010, Chairman of the State Duma Committee on Construction and Land Relations Martin Shakkum said that there were "practically no arguments in favour of the report," and that "the focus was solely on the negative consequences of the merger" (2010). He gave the following arguments: the merger processes are aimed at eliminating national and territorial animosities, and they open up new paths for fruitful development. Moreover, all these transformations are welcomed by the people, since they form a single social space between the territories that have been unified, which means ease of access to and use of common hospitals, schools, cultural facilities and much more. The merger of regions will also help increase their investment attractiveness and reduce the administrative burden on businesses, which will undoubtedly improve the socioeconomic indicators of these territories. Shakkum also cites the following arguments – the merger of legislation, the planning and implementation of joint infrastructure and development projects, an improved tariff policy, the creation of uniform tax regimes, and more extensive social support for the population.

Mikhail Milchakov also offered his view on the events of the early 2000s (n.d.). He believes that the new law on quotas of representatives from Komi-Permyak Okrug in the Legislative Assembly of Perm Krai limits the access of deputies from the *okrug* to executive positions compared to the previous period. What is more, the provision in the Agreement between Perm Oblast and Komi-Permyak Autonomous Okrug on the Legal Status of the Okrug as Part of Perm Krai regarding the creation of a twenty-seat duma for the *okrug*, has not been executed. Milchakov also believes that large regional business structures will not make large-scale financial injections into the *okrug* due to its poorly developed infrastructure.

In addition, Milchakov points out that the infrastructure development programme for Komi-Permyak Autonomous Okrug adopted on the eve of the referendum has proved ineffective. For example, Decree No. 1283 "On Measures to Ensure the Social and Economic Development of Komi-Permyak Autonomous Okrug and Perm Oblast" signed by the President in November 2003 tasked the region's leaders with implementing a series of measures to develop the transport infrastructure in Komi-Permyak Autonomous Okrug and provide gas to the region, but it was never carried out by the authorities.

Finally, consolidating the budgets of Perm Oblast and Komi-Permyak Autonomous Okrug could have an adverse effect on the development of other areas in the *oblast*, since the *okrug* requires significant financing to improve the quality of life of the population.

Milchakov comes to the following conclusions. First, the establishment of Perm Krai as a region in which economically strong territories would help the weak did not work out as expected. Second, the economic situation in this particular constituent entity will depend on financial support from the centre. Third, the national elite of Komi-Permyak Autonomous Okrug failed to achieve significant representation in any representative body, and could not formulate a coherent plan for the social and economic development of the *okrug*.

Of course, many of the statistics from back then are irrelevant today. But what do the updated figures for the 2010s say?

According to the official website of the Ministry for the Affairs of Komi-Permyak Okrug of Perm Krai, the Okrug's population as of January 1, 2017, was 109,642 people (4.2% of the population of Perm Krai), including 31,265 urban and 78,377 rural dwellers. The total population of the Okrug has decreased by 20,200 people (16%) over the past ten years, yet population decline was just 9%. The population density is 3.4 people per square kilometre, which is over 4.8 times lower than in Perm Krai, and more than 2 times lower than in Russia as a whole. Komi-Permyak Okrug has a low level of urbanization: Kudymkar, the only city in the *okrug*, is home to just 28.5% of its population. Representatives of over 60 national groups live on the territory of Komi-Permyak Okrug, with 97.1% being either Komi-Permyak (54.2%) or Russian (42.9%).

Data on the dynamics of the main socioeconomic development indicators for 2005 and 2010–2016 show a slight decrease in the unemployment rate (from 3.9% in 2005 to 3.0% in 2016), and a significant increase in emigration (67 people left the *okrug* in 2005, compared to 681 in 2016). Production of livestock, poultry and dairy products also decreased. Wood production decreased, although not significantly, while logging actually increased. The average growth in investments in fixed capital between 1999 and 2005 was 50%, dropping to almost half of this figure by 2016. The average salary in Perm Krai in 2005 was 7748.9 roubles per month, compared to 4595 roubles per month in Komi-Permyak Okrug (which is 40.7% lower). The average salary for the region in 2015 was 28,527.9 roubles per month, and 23,892 roubles per month in Komi-Permyak Okrug (16.3% lower), indicating an impressive increase in the salaries of Komi-Permyak people (Sayt Ministerstva po delam Komi-Permyatskogo okruga Permskogo kraya).

The Merger of Taymyr Dolgano-Nenets Autonomous Okrug, Evenk Autonomous Okrug and Krasnoyarsk Krai

Emma Bibina

It is well known that the 1920s–1930s in the Soviet Union were marked, among other transformations, by the creation of national *okrugs* with a view to increasing the level of support for Soviet power among the Indigenous minorities. Another reason for establishing the *okrugs* was to address the problems of building socialism: collectivization, industrialization and cultural transformations.

The most suitable starting point for our study of these regions would be the beginning of the 1930s, when the Taymyr National Okrug was established as part of East Siberian Krai, which included four districts – Dudinsky District, Khatanga District, Ust-Yeniseysky District and Avamsky District. As a result, the Dolgans, Nenets, Nganasans, Evenks, Enets, Kets and Selkups were united under common administration. The traditional activities of these peoples are hunting, reindeer herding and fishing (according to the Taymyr Okrug Executive Committee, a total of 7650 people lived in the *okrug* as of January 1, 1932) (Taimyrskiy Dolgano-Nenetskiy munitsipal'nyy rayon n.d.).

The exploitation of the Northern Sea Route played an important role in the development of the *okrug*. In the 1930s, the village of Norilsk was established as a settlement for the recently created Norilsk Mining and Metallurgy Combine, and seaports were built in Dikson and Dudinka to support the company's activities, and they continue to be of great importance today (the wealthy Norilsk industrial region would later become a sore spot in relations between Krasnoyarsk Krai and Taymyr Autonomous Okrug). The literacy rate in the *okrug* increased following the appearance of Soviet power in the country thanks to the emergence of schools, institutions of local culture and educational centres. Health facilities were also built. The fishing industry on the peninsula blossomed (five motor fishing stations were built in the early 1940s), and geological exploration of oil and gas was carried out in Ust-Yeniseysky District, Nordvik and Ust-Port (the Taymyr municipal district is the only gas-producing region in the north of Eastern Siberia today).

Taymyr National Okrug was included as part of Krasnoyarsk Krai in 1934 by decree of the All-Russian Central Executive Committee, and in 1977, it was renamed Taymyr Dolgano-Nenets Autonomous Okrug. In 1992, following the signing of a Federal Treaty, the *okrug* was given the status of an independent constituent entity of the Russian Federation, while remaining an administrative and territorial part of Krasnoyarsk Krai. The Duma of Taymyr Dolgano-Nenets Autonomous Okrug was made the highest legislative (representative) body of state power, and its administration acquired the status of the highest executive body of state power. The first head of the administration was Gennady Nedelin, who took office in December 1991, and would later go on to serve as governor of the *okrug* from 1996 to 2000. Nedelin failed to win a second term as governor, however, receiving just ca. 36% of the votes cast in the January 28, 2001 gubernatorial election, losing out to Norilsk Nickel General Director Alexander Khloponin (who won ca. 63% of the votes).

It is impossible to be completely impartial when assessing the results of Gennady Nedelin's work. On the one hand, he had a wealth of experience in government and a deep knowledge of the specifics of life in Taymyr: he spent almost ten years as the head of the administration, and around 20 years before that as deputy chair of the *okrug*'s executive committee. Nedelin could have reasonably expected to be voted back into office, since the local residents were used to seeing him at the helm, and his achievements were undeniable: reduced unemployment, the introduction of social programme, and increased industrial production. However, the 1990s was a difficult period for the entire country. The abrupt transition to a market economy triggered a profound financial crisis. In socioeconomic terms, and according to numerous macroeconomic indicators, Taymyr Dolgano-Nenets Autonomous

Okrug remained one of the most backward regions of the Russian Federation until early 2000.

The success of the young and energetic Alexander Khloponin in the elections can be put down to a strong election campaign, promises of a prosperous future, and the critical role that Norilsk Nickel played as a major sponsor in numerous areas. And the situation on the peninsula naturally improved after he came to power: the number of unprofitable companies decreased, industrial production continued to grow, and debts on wages, social benefits and other obligations of the district budget were eliminated completely. In addition, social programmes were introduced for low-income residents of Taymyr Dolgano-Nenets Autonomous Okrug, war and labour veterans, retirees and young people. The infrastructure in the *okrug* has also been improved, with the construction of housing, schools, hospitals and cultural centres having been resumed.

Before turning to the history of the development of the status of the Evenk region, it is important to make sense of what it means to be part of the Norilsk industrial region in Krasnoyarsk Krai, which is geographically located on the territory of Taymyr Dolgano-Nenets Autonomous Okrug (Norilsk enclave). Norilsk Nickel is the largest taxpayer in Krasnoyarsk Krai (for example, its tax payments in 2004 accounted for over 70% of the *krai*'s budget in 2004). For a long time, this was the source of fierce disputes between the authorities of Taymyr Dolgano-Nenets Autonomous Okrug and in Krasnoyarsk Krai, as the former did not reap any economic benefits from the use of its rich mineral resources due to the "extraterritorial" nature of Norilsk, which is directly subordinate to Krasnoyarsk Krai, with a significant part of its tax payments going to the regional budget. These disagreements quietened down in 2002 when Alexander Khloponin was voted Governor of Krasnoyarsk Krai and Taymyr's attempts to bring Norilsk back to its own jurisdiction ceased.

The history of the formation of Evenk Autonomous Okrug in many respects mirrors what happened in Taymyr. In December 1930, the Evenk National Okrug was established, with the city of Tura acting as its administrative centre. The collectivization of the

Evenk fishing industry started in the early 1930s with the creation of simple production associations, which later became arteries that helped the Indigenous population transition to a settled way of life. Literacy projects were launched, schools and outpatient clinics were opened, an educational program for people working on collective farms was introduced, and a college specializing in first aid and obstetrics was established. Collective farms, state-owned farms and fur farms started springing up everywhere.

Industrial development of ore deposits began in the late 1930s, as did the production of salt. The extremely unfavourable geographical location of the Evenk region meant that there was no large-scale industrial production there for a very long time. It is a well-known fact that Russia's "gold" reserves – large deposits of graphite, coal, oil and gas – are concentrated in the mines and quarries of this territory. The reserves here are huge, and industrial development is only just beginning. The Yurubcheno-Tokhomskoye oil and gas condensate field was only discovered in 1982.

Evenk National Okrug was renamed Evenk Autonomous Okrug in 1992. It remained a part of Krasnoyarsk Krai, while at the same time being an independent constituent entity of the Russian Federation, just like Taymyr Dolgano-Nenets Autonomous Okrug. The then President of the Russian Federation Boris Yeltsin appointed Anatoly Yakimov as head of the Okrug's administration in March 1997, before the first gubernatorial elections were held. In December 1993, the Legislative Assembly (*Suglan*) of Evenk Autonomous Okrug became the highest legislative (representative) body of state power.

The political processes taking place in Russia at the end of the 20th century could not but affect the socioeconomic situation in Evenk Autonomous Okrug. The long-standing budget shortfall led to a collapse of economic ties, the stagnation of production, and the impoverishment of the people living in the territory, despite Yakimov's best efforts (the internet is full of nothing but praise for his work on the part of the people of Evenk Autonomous Okrug). The first democratic elections for Governor of Evenk Autonomous Okrug were held in December 1996, with Alexander Bokovikov being elected to the post. Unfortunately, the period of Bokovikov's governorship was marred by a series of crises connected with the provision of heating to the *okrug* and a number of corruption scandals revolving around the misuse of budget funds that had been earmarked for the purchase of fuel. It was at this time that the Evenk people started to talk about the ineptitude of the local government and the need for the federal authorities to step in and take direct control.

Life in Evenk Autonomous Okrug started to improve following the election of Boris Zolotaryov as governor in 2001 (his appointment was in many respects thanks to the leadership of Yukos Oil Company, which was interested in developing the region's oil and gas fields). Regular electricity and heat supply was established, with supplies being provided through the Northern delivery system. In addition, internet cables were installed and the infrastructure of the villages was improved.

The merger of a number of Russian regions started in 2003. According to the amendments to the Federal Law "On the General Principles of the Organization of the Legislative and Executive Bodies of State Power of the Constituent Entities of the Russian Federation" adopted at the time, a significant part of the powers, as well as the revenues of *okrugs*, was transferred to the jurisdiction of the so-called "head" regions to which they belonged. Up to 85% of the powers of the Taymyr and Evenki okrugs was transferred to Krasnoyarsk Krai. The okrugs were left with the upkeep of their respective administrations, maintaining archives and managing expenses related to the promotion of their national cultures.

There were some clear prerequisites for the merger of Krasnodar Krai and the Taymyr and Evenk autonomous okrugs: the historical unity of the Yeniseysk Governorate; Norilsk Nickel, which is extremely important for both the peninsula and the mainland; and large interregional projects (oil and gas fields in Evenk, diamond placers on the border of Krasnoyarsk and Evenk, and the Vankor oil and gas field in Turukhansky District). However, the so-called Council of Governors – a supra-regional executive body made up of the Governor of Krasnoyarsk Krai Alexander Khloponin and the governors of the Taymyr and Evenk autonomous okrugs, Oleg Budargin and Boris Zolotaryov – initially ruled out the possibility of uniting the three regions. The Head of Evenk Autonomous Okrug was steadfast in his disapproval of the abovementioned amendments to the Budget Code and the potential merger of the regions, mentioning in an interview with *Kommersant* that this would lead to catastrophic consequences ("I don't think that Krasnoyarsk Krai will find those 2 billion roubles that Evenk needs") and that "merger for the sake of merger is pointless" (Kommersant 2004).

By 2004, Alexander Khloponin had changed his tune completely on the issue of merger (possibly due to his desire to win another term in office in the upcoming elections for Governor of Krasnoyarsk Krai). Whenever he was interviewed, he would reel off arguments in favour of merger, suggesting that those who are against it are more concerned with their own future, rather than what with what will happen to their territories under their current jurisdiction (REGNUM 2004b). What is more, the decision was widely supported both by the federal authorities and by a number of major business entities (Interros, Norilsk Nickel, Rosneft, etc.). Zolotaryov would eventually go on to approve the reform as well, since Yukos curtailed its activities, and it would be unprofitable for Gazprom to develop the hard-to-reach deposits in Evenk Autonomous Okrug. However, according to opinion polls at the time, 70% of Siberian population opposed merger, so the main task of those calling for it was to convince the people that reform was necessary.

On April 17, 2005, a referendum on the merger of Taymyr, Evenk and Krasnoyarsk Krai was held. The people voted "for" by a large majority in all territories (Table 2).

Taymyr and Evenki autonomous okrugs were dissolved on January 1, 2007, and replaced with administrative units of the Taymyr and Evenk municipal districts, which were incorporated into Krasnoyarsk Krai. Elections to the Legislative Assembly of the newly created constituent entity of the Russian Federation took place on April 15, 2007. The Krasnoyarsk Krai Legislative Assembly included 52 deputies, 26 of whom are elected from a list, 22 are elected from single-member districts, and two are elected from the former autonomous okrugs.

Table 2: Results of the Referendum on the Merger of Krasnoyarsk Krai and the Taymyr and Evenki Autonomous Okrugs

Region	Turnout, %	For, %	Against, %
Taymyr	62.9	69.95	29.10
Evenk	79.92	79.00	20.00
Krasnoyarsk	60.71	92.25	7.80

What arguments did those in favour come up with to convince the majority of the population to vote for the reform? According to the report "Three in One: A United Krasnoyarsk Krai" by Andrey Gradetsky (lead researcher, Expert Analytical Center), and Grigory Marchenko (Expert RA), the purpose of the merger of Krasnoyarsk Krai and the Taymyr and Evenk autonomous okrugs was to create a large region with an effective system of administrative management and a strong economy based on an understanding of the strategic advantages of the region's territories. Instead of one donor region (Krasnoyarsk Krai) and two recipient regions (Taymyr and Evenk), the idea was to form a single powerful donor constituent entity of the Russian Federation in order to increase the region's economic potential, which would provide significant Gross Regional Product in the medium term (four to six years) (Gradetskiy, Marchenko and Shmarov n.d.). The geopolitical aspect was also important: the creation of an economically strong region that occupies a large area in the centre of Siberia would allow Russia to act as a central link the economic integration of the European Union, the countries of Central Asia and the Asia-Pacific region.

The researchers argued that the domestic political effects of merger would include the modernization of regional public administration and the elimination of administrative barriers between the three regions, while the economic effects would include the restoration of the historical economic community, the accelerated implementation of investment projects in the newly united region, the preservation of the region's economic competitiveness, and the development of small and medium-sized businesses.

It would thus seem that the merger brought nothing but good to the three regions. However, remember that the people of Taymyr were not happy with the living conditions on the peninsula. Those who opposed merger argued that Evenk and Taymyr would once again be treated as nothing more than suppliers of raw materials, the quality of public services would go down, and it would become increasingly difficult to defend the rights and interests of the Indigenous small-numbered peoples of the North. Previously, both Taymyr Dolgano-Nenets Autonomous Okrug and Evenk Autonomous Okrug were directly represented in the Federation Council: L. Bindar, A. Zabeyvorota, G. Nedelin, L. Roketsky, V. Sitnov and A. Filatov from Taymyr; and A. Amosov, N. Anisimova, A. Bokovikov, M. Odintsov, V. Sturov, A. Uss, Y. Sharandin and A. Yakimov from Evenk.

More than ten years went by before some of the fears about the merger turned out to be true: respondents in polls taken at the time claim that life in Taymyr has become worse, as the regional authorities do not understand the ins and outs of the life of the people of the North, and many have lost their jobs. Perhaps the biggest source of displeasure is the fact that government agencies that once resided in Dudinka, the administrative centre of Taymyr Dolgano-Nenets Region, have moved to Krasnoyarsk and Norilsk, meaning that residents have to travel to these cities to obtain official documents (with a few exceptions, a passport being one of them). A review of media messages in recent years also shows that "mortality in the villages has increased to 7% of the population per year. Villages themselves are being liquidated – more than twenty settlements have disappeared from the map of Taymyr, and another ten are likely to go the same way." "There are no roads, no transport links, and no medical stations in the villages..." "Twelve years have passed since we became part of Krasnoyarsk Krai, and we have been left with nothing. No money – oil-worker taxes go to the region, where they are divvied up between the districts at their own discretion." In addition, a survey of the local population asked participants to answer the question: "Should Taymyr Dolgano-Nenets Region be reorganized as Taymyr Dolgano-Nenets Autonomous Okrug, with the return of all the federal public services that residents of Taymyr Dolgano-Nenets Autonomous Okrug received before joining Krasnoyarsk Krai?" A total of 1197 of the 1200 polled answered "yes."

The Merger of Koryak Autonomous Okrug and Kamchatka Oblast

Rostislav Shilovskiy

Kamchatka Oblast was established as part of the Far Eastern Territory in 1932, and became an independent constituent entity in 1956. In economic terms, the *oblast* was successful: it had a relatively robust timber industry that satisfied both domestic needs and the needs of partners outside the country; a meat and dairy industry that provided the population with meat and milk; fur trade and fisheries were especially developed here. In addition, large quantities of various minerals were mined in the region's mineral-rich area. The economy of Kamchatka Oblast thus developed successfully, which was in large part due in part to government control.

The situation changed dramatically following the collapse of the Soviet Union: all the economic areas listed above fell into decay, causing a large outflow of the working population from the region. This was exacerbated by the lack of housing, the high mortality rate, the underdeveloped and even declining transport infrastructure, and the fact that one fifth of the population had been left almost penniless (Dorogin 2003). Governance was the only area in which everything was running smoothly, with the real power in the region resting in the hands of the governor of Kamchatka. Thus, the economic, social and demographic dimensions suffered greatly in the 1990s and early 2000s.

Was the situation in Koryak Autonomous Okrug better than the situation in the oblast as a whole?

Koryak National Okrug was established in 1930. The majority of the population was made up of indigenous peoples – Koryaks, Itelmens, Chukchi and Evens. In 1934, Koryak National Okrug was made part of Kamchatka Oblast. Palana was named the centre of the okrug in 1937, and remains so to this day. The region was particularly hard to reach and could only be accessed by air or sea transport. The region lived mainly on fishing and deer farming.

The 1977 Constitution of the Soviet Union renamed Koryak National Okrug Koryak Autonomous Okrug, which in 1993 became an independent constituent entity of the Russian Federation following the collapse of the USSR (it was a *matryoshka* subject of Kamchatka Oblast at the time). The okrug was one of the most backward in the Russian Federation, a fact that is supported by a number of metrics: deer farming, one of the foundations of the okrug's economic development, had all but ceased to exist; no progress had been made in the development of the transport infrastructure, with road construction being extremely slow, and air traffic often being interrupted due to adverse weather conditions and technical issues; the okrug ranked first in terms of the incidence of tuberculosis, and healthcare was in a sorry state, as almost every single hospital was an old wooden building; the region also ranked first in unemployment (although its population did shrink by 40% during this period), and more than three quarters of the population was living below the poverty line, with prices for goods and services being among the highest in Russia. High morbidity rates, wretched living conditions and the massive flight of people from the okrug have led to a reduction in the population of indigenous small-numbered peoples, which negatively affects the national and cultural heritage of the region, and of Russia as a whole. In addition, the territory was extremely difficult to govern: a two-tier system of self-governance existed in the okrug (which was made up of diffusely populated districts dispersed widely across the territory) whereby the heads of districts and village councils operated independently of the governor of the okrug. Alexander Kynev referred to the situation as "democracy in poverty," which is true in every sense of the term (Kynev 2004). Thus, the deeply subsidized Koryak Autonomous Okrug was in dire need of measures to overcome economic, social, demographic, cultural and political problems.

It was in these conditions that a referendum on the merger of Kamchatka Oblast and Koryak Autonomous Okrug was held in 2005. According to official data, approximately 85% of the inhabitants of Kamchatka Oblast, and over 89% of Koryak Autonomous Okrug residents, voted in favour of the merger.

Kamchatka Krai was established in 2007, with Petropavlovsk-Kamchatsky serving as its administrative centre.

The merger has had mixed results for the various groups it affected, all of which pursued different goals. It is thus worth addressing each group separately: the federal authorities, the authorities of the two regions, and the electorate.

In all cases of merger, the federal authorities pursued two goals: increasing the level of socioeconomic development of the territories and improving the governability of the regions, with greater attention being paid to those autonomous regions that were less economically developed and less governable. In the case of Kamchatka, the goal was to improve the socioeconomic indicators and governability of the Koryak Autonomous Okrug, but this was quite difficult to implement due to the many problems inherent to Kamchatka Krai itself.

A decree was issued in 2005 (i.e. not long before the merger took place) "On Measures for the Socioeconomic Development of Kamchatka Oblast and Koryak Autonomous Okrug" that set out the tasks for the development of energy, the transportation infrastructure, the social sphere, and housing in the territory (Ukaz Presidenta Rossiyskoy Federatsii No. 1227 'O merakh po sotsial'no-ekonomicheskomu razvitiyu Kamchatskoy oblasti i Koryakskogo avtonomnogo okruga' 2005 (Russia)). The implementation of this programme brought unimpressive results: on the one hand, hospitals, kindergartens and schools, as well as transport infrastructure facilities, were built or renovated (although this has only happened in the past four years, that is, 7–11 years after merger); on the other hand, housing prices continued to be high and the energy sector is still underdeveloped (construction of the Sobolevo–Petropavlovsk–Kamchatsky Gas Pipeline, as well as a thermal power plant in Palana, both launched before the merger, was completed, although the remaining four thermal power plants mentioned in the decree remain unfinished).

That said, the merger did have more positives than negatives for other sectors of the economy. Gold deposits in particular are being actively developed, new mining and processing plants have been built, and geological exploration is moving along at an impressive pace (Vladimirova and Korostelev 2017). The meat and dairy industry and fisheries have also demonstrated growth (Territorial'nyy organ Federal'noy sluzhby gosudarstvennoy statistiki po Kamchatskomu krayu. n.d.). Deer farming has also started to bounce back following the introduction of the programme "Support for and Development of Deer Farming in Kamchatka Krai" in 2010 with funding from the Government of Kamchatka Krai. Deer farmers have been provided with cutting-edge technology, medicines and special equipment, veterinary measures have been improved, and the gene pool of deer increased, all with the support of the regional authorities (Vladimirova 2014). Only the timber industry demonstrated negative dynamics, with figures falling by almost a third between 2009 and 2016 (Territorial'nyy organ Federal'noy sluzhby gosudarstvennoy statistiki po Kamchatskomu krayu. n.d.). On the whole, despite a myriad of issues, merger contributed significantly to socioeconomic growth in the region.

The merger of the two constituent entities also helped improve administrative efficiency in Koryak Okrug: the transfer of the regional centre from Palana to Petropavlovsk-Kamchatsky led to the dissolution of administrative structures there and a sharp reduction in the number of local officials, with Koryak Okrug falling completely under Kamchatka Krai jurisdiction (nothing was indicated in the "special status" regarding the spheres in which the independence of the okrug's administration would be preserved). The officials that had been in power until then represented the educated classes, they knew their okrug, its strengths and weaknesses, and the people trusted them. Now, the people would have to make the long journey to Petropavlovsk-Kamchatsky for help and advice, as it simply was not available in the former regional centre, with unemployed officials and their families starting to leave the okrug. In addition, the issue of the fragmentation of the socio-political space in the okrug was never resolved. In fact, it was only made worse by the chronic underdevelopment of the road system between settlements.

Koryak Autonomous Okrug and Kamchatka Oblast did not initially want merger. Both faced a number of serious problems, and neither could see the benefits of such a move. The regional authorities showed almost no initiative when it came to developing the project, which was in any case ultimately devoid of any real socioeconomic content, meaning that "the main motivation for merger was the expression of the willingness of the regional elites to comply with the decree of the federal government" (Artobolevsky and Gontmakher 2010, 61-62). Chairman of the Committee on Fisheries and Fishing Fleet of the Oblast Council Anatoly Shashkun called it a dilemma of the "merger of the poor and the naked" (Kravchenko 2005).

Why were the regional authorities, especially those in Koryak Autonomous Okrug, categorically against merger given the deteriorating socioeconomic and demographic situation?

Deputies in Kamchatka Oblast council were worried about the budget issue, since the region was deep in debt, and Koryak Autonomous Okrug even more so (Kravchenko 2005). The Kamchatka authorities were thus worried that they would not be able to cope if they were handed even more debt upon merger with Koryak Autonomous Okrug. And these fears extended beyond budgetary issues (Artobolevsky and Gontmakher 2010, 61).

Despite all these difficulties, no one in Koryak Autonomous Okrug was in favour of merger with Kamchatka Oblast. Promises of greater subsidies and increased investments in the okrug failed to sway people: Koryak deputies were convinced that the budget would be distributed according to the residual principle, which would hurt the already problematic socioeconomic situation in Koryak Autonomous Okrug. The authorities also saw the futility of a merger that formally sought to achieve socioeconomic development when the constituent entities in question were both heavily subsidized by the state, meaning that nothing would really change in practice. The argument about supporting indigenous small-numbered peoples of the North was not convincing either, as it had been used in 1993 when Koryak Autonomous Okrug was established, yet the indigenous people continued to live in poverty (RIA Novy den 2005). Finally, the most serious danger was the crippling reduction in the number of officials in Koryak

Autonomous Okrug following the liquidation of the relevant institutions there.

That said, some arguments in favour of merger turned out to be very attractive to the regional authorities in both constituent entities. For example, some deputies in Kamchatka Oblast pointed out that the regions had been artificially separated back in 1993 (RIA Novy den 2005). The revival of a united Kamchatka without administrative barriers would restore socioeconomic contacts between representatives of the two regions, which would in turn improve the socioeconomic situation. Moreover, the creation of a single region could help solve transport problems, particularly the joint development of the transport infrastructure and the reduction in ticket prices, which are extremely high for residents of both constituent entities. The same arguments were used by deputies in Koryak Autonomous Okrug, who also pointed out the potential benefits in education and healthcare (Artobolevsky and Gontmakher 2010, 61-62): in a unified region with a developed infrastructure, residents of the okrug would be able to register with medical centres or apply to the educational institutions in Kamchatka Oblast, which were objectively of a higher quality.

Merger thus had a positive impact on the development of the two former regions. Almost all the socioeconomic benefits the regional authorities had hoped the merger would bring did indeed appear: administrative barriers to the development of economic relations between the former constituent entities were removed, reindeer breeding experienced a resurgence, air travel subsidies were introduced in 2008 (residents pay 30–40% of the real cost of air tickets (Kamchatskiy Kray. Ofitsialnyy sayt 2018)), and the transport infrastructure has been developed over the past four years, although a number of dirt and forest roads remain in the *krai*. What is more, some of the fears of the regional authorities turned out to be unfounded: budget revenues increased by 2.3 times between 2007 and 2016 (the Krai's revenues increased too); the share of federal transfers decreased from 64% to 54%; expenditures increased 2.6-fold; the budget deficit fell sharply; credit debt fell from 1.5 billion roubles in 2007 to 48 million roubles in 2017; and state and municipal debt decreased by 26% (Vladimirova and

Korostelev 2017). In other words, the budget situation did not worsen as a result of merger. On the contrary, it only improved it: the Kamchatka Krai government went to great lengths to reduce debt, increase its budget revenues, reduce subsidies and increase spending.

Merger was also positive in terms of governance for Kamchatka officials: they had gained another constituent entity, and the oblast was made a krai, boosting their economic and political status among the regions of the Russian Federation.

As for Koryak bureaucracy, merger was a double-edged sword. On the one hand, "*okrug*'s court, procurators, militsiya… and other federal structures," were dissolved, meaning that many Koryak officials were left without work and had to leave the okrug (Artobolevsky and Gontmakher 2010, 65). The okrug's special status does not actually give any independence to the Koryak authorities: the chapter on the special status of Koryak Okrug in the Kamchatka Krai Charter – the only official document that mentions the issue – is the smallest in terms of length and content among the other documents on the special status of the former autonomous okrugs and does not give any specific details about what makes Koryak Okrug "special" (aside from mentioning that the indigenous small-numbered peoples of the North live in the okrug). On the other hand, Koryak deputies received the most seats in the Legislative Assembly (20%).

Like any political decision, the referendum of the merger of the two constituent entities of the Russian Federation had it supporters and opponents. However, while those who opposed merger presented arguments for why it should not happen, those who supported it were not particularly invested in the processes – they just realized that a referendum was inevitable and could not be cancelled (REGNUM 2005). We can thus conclude that the majority of the population was not actively looking to become a part of a single region and could not see the benefits that would come of it. The low voter turnout in Kamchatka Oblast (barely surpassing 50%) proves this.

First of all, the inhabitants of Kamchatka Oblast were concerned that incorporating Koryak Autonomous Okrug would only make their situation worse, as the government had been unable to solve many of the oblast's problems as it was. To start with, there would have to be a common budget, an unpopular notion given the high level of debt, numerous unprofitable companies and declining production in Koryak Autonomous Okrug, which could have a negative effect on the socioeconomic situation in the oblast. The population was particularly concerned about this because the increased size of the territory meant that less money would be directed towards ensuring the uninterrupted supply of heat and power to the oblast (Sokolov 2006).

Representatives of Koryak Autonomous Okrug were not enamoured with the merger project. *First*, they believed that unifying the regions would not bring about an economic breakthrough or offer a way out of the problems the okrug had traditionally suffered – problems they believed should be dealt with first before any talk of merger could take place (REGNUM. 2005). *Second*, they were concerned that the life of the indigenous population, which was slowly dwindling in number, would become even more complicated. Some thought that this could become a serious obstacle to a positive outcome in the referendum (Sokolov 2006).

But the referendum did take place and the regions were unified. Ten years later, the population continues to view the merger predominantly in a negative light: 50% are against the merger, while 39% support it (Kam 24 2017).

If we compare what the population expected from merger with what actually happened, then at first glance the results would appear to be exclusively negative because, despite the improved budgetary situation, the worsening socioeconomic situation caused many to take to the street in 2017–2018. However, it is difficult to gauge the real effect of the reform due to the problems caused by the Western sanctions and the appreciation of the dollar since 2014, which are superimposed onto the real pros and cons of the merger. For example, the residents of Kamchatka Krai complain about the high prices of goods, but this is true of people across the country since 2014. Before 2014, the purchasing power of the population was growing at a rapid rate (Territorial'nyy organ Federal'noy sluzhby gosudarstvennoy statistiki po Kamchatskomu krayu n.d.). The same applies to real wages, which only started to drop in 2014 (Territorial'nyy organ Federal'noy sluzhby gosudarstvennoy statistiki po Kamchatskomu krayu n.d.), and the poverty rate, which had been falling until 2014, after which it returned to the 2010 level (Territorial'nyy organ Federal'noy sluzhby gosudarstvennoy statistiki po Kamchatskomu krayu n.d.). The most noteworthy problems directly related to merger include the increased morbidity rate (Territorial'nyy organ Federal'noy sluzhby gosudarstvennoy statistiki po Kamchatskomu krayu n.d.), which the people of the region put down to medical incompetence and the fact that there are fewer health workers in general, rather than to the state of healthcare facilities (Demidenko 2018a). What is more, the problems getting the heating on at the start of the cold season persist, and the region's roads are in an unsuitable state, with most being forest roads (Demidenko 2018a). The problems of merger, coupled with the socioeconomic challenges brought about by the events of 2014, led to significant population decline due to growing flight from the region.

Certain positive trends have appeared after the referendum: unemployment continues to fall; the traditional economy of indigenous small-numbered peoples receives a decent amount of financial support; the transport infrastructure is gradually being improved; new hospitals, schools and sport centres are being built; and residents of the okrug are able to purchase ticket to Petropavlovsk-Kamchatsky at discounted prices.

In socioeconomic terms, the merger of the two regions thus had a mostly positive effect. The situation was only complicated by difficulties that had nothing to do with the reform itself.

In terms of management, as we mentioned earlier, the reform only made the lives of the people of the okrug more difficult – the new centre of Petropavlovsk-Kamchatsky is more difficult to get to due to the adverse weather conditions that often hit the region, as well as because of technical problems.

Two constituent entities of the Russian Federation in the remote, but extremely important Kamchatka peninsula, united to form a single Kamchatka Krai. As in other regions, a lively discussion broke out in the 2000s about the prospects of creating a new administrative and territorial unit, about the possible advantages and disadvantages. The federal authorities sought to create a single entity in which the economic, political and administrative situation would improve. The regional authorities of Kamchatka Oblast and Koryak Autonomous Okrug were more sceptical about the prospects of the new region developing successfully, with the leadership of Koryak Autonomous Okrug having more grounds to be displeased. The population of Kamchatka Oblast was concerned with its enlargement, while the population of Koryak Autonomous Okrug did not want their region to be eliminated, with the merger negatively affecting a low standard of living.

Nevertheless, the region, which was made up of two heavily subsidized constituent entities that were deep in debt and suffering numerous other problems, started, slowly but surely, to develop and gradually extricate itself from its problems. As for the region's economy, a number of industries continue to lag behind, the road network is in a primitive state, and the morbidity rate remains high. However, the reform gave a positive impetus to further socioeconomic development, which then turned into a negative trend due to unforeseen circumstances in 2014. In political and administrative terms, the federal centre got a more governable territory, something that the authorities in the okrug and their electorate were not expecting. The federal and regional authorities continue to experience great difficulties in this area: governability depends on geography, and it will be difficult to achieve the necessary level of governability as long as the region's transport infrastructure remains underdeveloped.

The Merger of Ust-Orda Buryat Autonomous Okrug and Irkutsk Oblast

Rostislav Shilovskiy

The project to unite Ust-Orda Buryat Autonomous Okrug and Irkutsk Oblast is one of the longest and most problematic compared to the other reforms. The process was launched at the initiative of the Presidential Plenipotentiary Envoy to the Siberian Federal District back in 2002, four years before the referendum. The federal government said that the new region would receive large economic and social benefits if the people supported merger: Irkutsk Oblast would become the industrial driver of the new region and promote the industrial development of Ust-Orda Buryat Autonomous Okrug, while Ust-Orda Buryat Autonomous Okrug would use its agro-industrial sector to stimulate agricultural development in the unified oblast (Latynina 2016).

The project to create a single region was met with fierce resistance from the authorities of both Ust-Orda Buryat Autonomous Okrug and Irkutsk Oblast. The Irkutsk Oblast budget was in deficit, and it was not prepared to welcome Ust-Orda, whose economy was suffering a depression, as it could negatively affect the socioeconomic situation (Vostochno-Sibirskaya Pravda 2002). However, the leadership of Irkutsk Oblast for the most part quickly changed its tune and agreed to the changes: in 2003, the acting chairman of the Legislative Assembly of Irkutsk Oblast talked to *Vostochno-Sibirskaya pravda* about the positive aspects of the initiative put forward by the federal authorities (Khamidullina 2016). Deputies who continued to view the results of the referendum in a negative light claimed that the arguments in favour of merger were unfounded, and that the project would both worsen the situation in the agro-industrial sector and destabilize the socio-political situation in the region due to the dissatisfaction of the vast majority of the population of the potential region with merger (Bezformata.ru 2019). In other words, there were conflicting assessments within the regional authorities regarding the consequences of the referendum in the socioeconomic sphere, which complicated the procedure for deciding on whether or not to hold a referendum at all.

The situation with Ust-Orda Buryat Autonomous Okrug was even more complicated. Given the fact that the okrug was once part of the united Buryat-Mongol Autonomous Soviet Socialist Republic, and that it had an impressive degree of autonomy after separation (including in the cultural sphere safeguarded by the local authorities), the Buryat people were never going to react kindly to being made part of a municipal district in a larger oblast, and it was not part of the plans of the Buryat elites. When the merger project was announced in 2002, a round table for the general public was held in the village of Ust-Ordynsky, where the decision was made for Ust-Orda Buryat Autonomous Okrug to maintain its status. In 2003, an extraordinary meeting of the IV All-Buryat Congress was convened, which was attended by cultural figures, deputies from other Buryat regions and many others. Some 300 delegates spoke out against the merger of Irkutsk Oblast and Ust-Orda Buryat Autonomous Okrug, arguing that it was important to "guarantee the right of the Buryat people to maintain the status of Ust-Orda Okrug" (Bezformata.ru 2019). In April 2004, eight deputies from the Ust-Orda Buryat Autonomous Okrug Duma once again opposed the redesignation of the Okrug as a municipal district. And it was only after discussion with representatives of the federal authorities, and after the legislative authorities of Ust-Orda Buryat Autonomous Okrug and Irkutsk Oblast had come to an agreement on the main principles of the special status of the okrug, that they turned to the president with a request for merger. This happened in October 2005.

In addition to preserving the national identity, representatives of Ust-Orda Buryat Autonomous Okrug were also concerned about the socioeconomic aspect of the changes, because 80% of the Duma's budget came from federal sources, meaning that the *okrug* enjoyed greater budget security than Irkutsk Oblast (Vostochno-Sibirskaya Pravda 2002). The standard of living in the okrug was in danger of falling sharply if the merger project was successful, and this prompted Buryats to resist the reform any way they could.

After the federal authorities got Irkutsk Oblast and Ust-Orda Buryat Autonomous Okrug to agree to hold a referendum, officials in the two regions started to make the necessary preparations. According to observers, the supporters of merger, who used such slogans as "Think in Siberian," "Strength in Unity" and "All for the Referendum," resorted to administrative pressure. People who turned up early at the polling stations were given gifts and tickets for special lotteries. Employees who came to vote received special ballot papers with the inscription "gratitude for active citizenship," which they had to give to their employers in order to be eligible for bonuses. The propaganda campaign made its way into education too, with students being offered extra days off for voting, and schoolteachers were required to go to their pupils' houses to talk their parents into voting (REGNUM. 2006a).

According to experts, the local authorities were afraid that the turnout for the referendum would be low – turnout had to be at least 50% for the results to count (the turnout for the Kamchatka referendum, which was held before the referendum in Irkutsk, barely exceeded the threshold and reached 55%, despite the fact that various methods of persuading people to vote were used there too) (Bezformata.ru 2019). Naturally, the carrot and stick approach did influence voter turnout and the number of votes "for" merger. However, this would suggest that the federal authorities did not achieve their goals, as they were clearly hoping for the people to vote "against" becoming a single region.

Opponents of the referendum failed to get their message across because their numerous initiatives in this direction were blocked. For example, the only citizens' initiative group that represented those who were against the referendum was twice denied registration during the preparations for the vote due to inconsistencies in their registration documents (REGNUM. 2006a). Despite the fact that Buryat public organizations in Ust-Orda Buryat Autonomous Okrug picketed against the referendum, its opponents could campaign (albeit with certain difficulties) only in the Republic of Buryatia: the *Erkhe* youth human rights movement did hand out propaganda materials, but ran into numerous problems with law enforcement, thus complicating their activities.

Representatives of the *Erkhe* association claimed that the local authorities saw their actions as either organized crime or terrorism (Baikal Media Consulting Information Agency 2006). However, they managed to continue their activities throughout the referendum campaign. This made sure that not only many residents of the *okrug*, but also Buryats from other regions were made aware of the disadvantages of merger – people who sought to maintain the standard of living of the population and preserve their national identity.

Thus, having agreed to hold a referendum on the merger of the two constituent entities of the Russian Federation, the residents and leadership of Ust-Orda Buryat Autonomous Okrug, as well as some representatives of the authorities of Irkutsk Oblast, were well aware of the shortcomings of the merger. While there were hopes in Irkutsk Oblast that the complementarity of the economies of the two regions could help raise living standards and speed up economic development – which is why it was agreed within a year to hold the referendum – the authorities in Ust-Orda Buryat Autonomous Okrug did not want to give up the subsidies, and this became the source of fierce debates between the Buryats and the federal authorities that raged for years. What is more, the question of the Buryats place within the new constituent entity was also a source of disagreement. The merger project thus only got moving as a result of concessions and the federal authorities leaning on the local administration.

The referendum was held in April 2006, with the majority of the population voting in favour of merger: 89.76% of voters in Irkutsk Oblast and 97.7% in Ust-Orda Buryat Autonomous Okrug. The unified Irkutsk Oblast was created in 2008. The city of Irkutsk was made the capital. Legislative power belongs to the Legislative Assembly of Irkutsk Region, and executive power is exercised by the governor and the government. The reform affected Ust-Orda Buryat Autonomous Okrug and Irkutsk Oblast in different ways, so it makes sense to look at the consequences for each separately.

The 2009 Charter of Irkutsk Oblast outlines the special status of Ust-Orda Buryat Okrug. According to the document, the creation of this administrative and territorial unit pursues three goals: to preserve the national identity of the local peoples; to harmonize the socioeconomic development of the regions; and to increase the effectiveness of the Irkutsk Oblast authorities (Zakon Irkutskoy oblasti No. 121-OZ 'Ob Ust'-Ordynskom Buryatskom okruge kak administrativno-territorial'noy edinitse Irkutskoy oblasti s osobym statusom 2010 (Irkutsk oblast)).

It is impossible to say with any certainty whether the first goal was achieved. Unlike the Agin-Buryat Okrug, which was merged with Chita Oblast in 2007, the special status of Ust-Orda Buryat Okrug does not include the establishment of a special authority in the power structures of Irkutsk Oblast in charge of ensuring and protecting the national identity of the Buryat people – these issues are dealt with exclusively by the legislative (the Legislative Assembly of Irkutsk Oblast) and executive (the governor and government of Irkutsk Oblast) branches. Initially, the interests of the Buryats in the Legislative Assembly were represented by just four deputies from the region (8% of all seats), but that number has since dwindled to two. The only independent body set up to deal with issues of the *okrug* was the Council for the Affairs of Ust-Orda Buryat Okrug, which, aside from having coordinating and advisory functions, does not have any real impact on processes related to the *okrug*'s special status.

At the *okrug* level, the administration is involved in the preservation of national culture, but it answers to the Irkutsk authorities: having limited powers, it is lower in status than ministries, services and agencies, and is only a body of special sectoral competence (Damdinov 2016). The administration of Ust-Orda Buryat Okrug is responsible for the preservation and development of national culture, language and sports. Two departments carry out this work: the Department for National Culture and the Department for National Languages and National Sports (the latter was created in 2016 following the merger of two separate departments, one responsible for languages and the other for sports).

To preserve the national identity of the local population living in the *okrug*, the administration coordinates the activities of seven subordinated institutions, including a museum, a library, a centre for folk arts and crafts, a state song and dance ensemble, a movie and concert hall, a folk art centre, and a newspaper for the *okrug*. The main advantage of having such a wide range of powers is that the administration continues to hold various national events, including events that take place as part of the two main national holidays in the region – *Sagaalgan* (the Buryat New Year according to the lunar calendar) and *Surkharban* (a cultural and sports festival) (Zakon Irkutskoy oblasti No. 121-OZ 'Ob Ust'-Ordynskom Buryatskom okruge kak administrativno-territorial'noy edinitse Irkutskoy oblasti s osobym statusom 2010 (Irkutsk oblast)). Moreover, many note that is has become easier to tour the *oblast* and hold cultural programmes in different parts of the region. But these positive aspects of the administration's work, which were visible before merger, are overshadowed by one big disadvantage of the reform – the lack of funding from within the administration itself. Its staff are forced to beg for money for such events from the Irkutsk authorities, which takes time and thus affects the number of events held and the content of their programmes.

Work to support for the national language is not running smoothly either. Judging by official figures, the merger of the two regions was unequivocally positive. For example, in 2012 (just four years after merger), the Irkutsk government launched a long-term target programme "On the Preservation and Further Development of the Buryat Language in Ust-Orda Buryat Okrug" for 2013–2016, which spelled out the goals and objectives of the programme, the amount of funding allocated to it and the measures being taken to ensure its implementation. A comparison of official statistics for 2012 and 2017 shows that certain indicators have improved (there was an increase in the number of students studying the Buryat language, for example), and some targets have been fully achieved (the number of Buryat language instructors who have completed training, and the provision of schools with computers and presentation equipment). But, judging by what the residents of the *okrug* have said, there has been no visible progress on this issue. Quite the contrary – there has been a noticeable decline in the language. For example, despite the growth in the number of schools that teach the Buryat language and the number of people who study it, and despite the improvement in the technical equipment used at educational institutions, problems persist in terms of the quality of education provided: class hours have been reduced and teachers speak in Russian more often than in Buryat. However, it was not merger that caused the language to lose its significance. Merger was merely a catalyst for its natural departure from the national and cultural life of the *okrug*, which has more to do with the declining interest in the language as a whole (Irkutskaya oblast'. Ofitsial'nyy portal 2018; Postanovlenie N 353-pp ob utverzhdenii dolgosrochnoy tselevoy programmy Irkutskoy oblasti 'O sokhranenii i dal'neishem razvitii buryatskogo yazyka v Ust'-Ordynskom Buryatskom okruge' na 2013-2016 gody 2012 (Irkutsk oblast)).

The development of national sports is the only area the local population has not complained about. The *okrug* administration is implementing a departmental target programme called "Development of National and Mass Sports on the Territory of Ust-Orda Buryat Okrug" for 2014–2020, which it adopted in 2013. Official figures show that the targets in terms of the number of people taking part in these events were not only achieved, but even exceeded in 2017 (Irkutskaya oblast'. Ofitsial'nyy portal 2018; Prikaz No. 25-pr 'Ob utverzhdenii vedomstvennoy tselevoy programmy "Razvitie natsional'nykh i massovykh vidov sporta na territorii Ust'-Ordynskogo Buryatskogo okruga" na 2014-2020 gody' 2013 (Ust-Orda Buryat Okrug)).

Local self-government bodies have almost no powers when it comes to national and cultural issues. According to Irkutsk laws, they "*may* [emphasis added] be endowed" with certain powers in the field of ethnocultural relations (Ustav Irkutskoy oblasti 2009 (Irkutsk Oblast)), which highlights the weakness of these structures.

It is difficult to assess the next goal of granting special status to Ust-Orda Buryat Okrug – socioeconomic development – due to the fact that merger took place at a time of socioeconomic crisis throughout the country. That said, certain socioeconomic trends in the years that followed were a direct result of the reform of the administrative and territorial units.

Positives of the merger of the two regions:

- Gaps in the social infrastructure of the *okrug* have been filled. Almost all of the 15 social facilities announced for construction in the Decree "On Measures to Ensure the Socioeconomic Development of Irkutsk Oblast and Ust-Orda Buryat Autonomous Okrug" were built, including a perinatal centre, a tuberculosis dispensary, an orphanage, central district hospitals, clinics and schools, all of which were opened in Ust-Orda and the surrounding districts. The only facility that was not completed was the House of Sports, and it is unclear when and if it will be finished (Ukaz Presidenta Rossiyskoy Federatsii 'O merakh po sotsial'no-ekonomicheskomu razvitiyu Irkutskoy oblasti i Ust'-Ordynskogo Buryatskogo avtonomnogo okruga' 2006 (Russia)).
- Improved healthcare. This was thanks, first of all, to the construction of new social facilities in the *okrug*. Second, it has become far easier for residents to receive treatment at Irkutsk Oblast hospitals, with bureaucratic issues being resolved.

Unfortunately, however, there were far more negatives:

- The administration of the *okrug* lacks financial resources and is forced to deal with fiscal issues at the *oblast* level. It had previously received subsidies from Moscow that it could use to deal with pressing problems. The law on the special status of Ust-Orda Buryat Okrug says nothing about the economic rights of the *okrug*'s administrative bodies, with the *oblast* authorities being responsible for this aspect.
- The construction of many social projects dragged on for many years and has only been completed recently. For example, one hospital only opened in 2018, and another will commence operations in June 2019.
- The most painful issue in the *okrug* following the administrative and territorial reform was unemployment. The liquidation of federal structures and law enforcement agencies in the *okrug* led to employees (highly educated and qualified workers) losing their jobs (Latynina 2016). The only options left to them were to find employment in

Irkutsk (meaning they would have to leave early in the morning and return late in the evening and cost a lot in travel) or by moving to a different region.
- This led to another problem – people leaving the *okrug*. According to official statistics, the population of Ust-Orda Buryat Okrug dropped by 11,000 people between 2006 and 2017.

Surveys show that the local population takes these problems very seriously. According to them, the socioeconomic situation in the *okrug* leaves much to be desired. And this is due to the fact that the government subsidies which largely financed the *okrug*'s development were cancelled, the standard of living of the population went down, and certain social projects were not implemented (people regard the reduction of red tape as the only positive change) (Lebedeva 2012).

The pursuit of another goal – improving the quality of work of the public authorities – also had its positive and negative sides. The only plus was that the system for distributing budgetary funds became more transparent, as the Irkutsk authorities are responsible for monitoring this aspect. In this respect, the level of corruption that existed before merger simply cannot exist now.

The administrative and territorial reform had a negative impact on the functioning of the state authorities in the *okrug*:

- The *okrug* lost its subjectivity, with numerous state structures being liquidated.
- The administration was reduced from more than 300 people to 26, and they have no real political power in the *okrug*, being entirely dependent on decisions made in Irkutsk (Latynina 2016).

Turning to the situation in the former territory of Irkutsk oblast, we can see that certain shifts have taken place there too. In national and cultural terms, the region discovered the rich cultural world of the Buryat people – *Sagaalgan* and *Surkharban*, as well as the *Yordyn* Games, are growing in popularity (Latynina 2016). In terms of socioeconomic development, social infrastructure facilities that were promised under the Decree "On Measures to Ensure the Socioeconomic Development of Irkutsk Oblast and Ust-Orda Buryat Autonomous Okrug" were built, including a bridge crossing over the Angara River in Irkutsk and an Irkutsk transport bypass with a bridge crossing over the Irkut River (Ukaz Presidenta Rossiyskoy Federatsii 'O merakh po sotsial'no-ekonomicheskomu razvitiyu Irkutskoy oblasti i Ust'-Ordynskogo Buryatskogo avtonomnogo okruga' 2006 (Russia)). Both were completed in the years immediately after merger. Irkutsk also gained financial control over Ust-Orda Buryat Okrug, overseeing the distribution of funds for its socioeconomic and national and cultural projects. In terms of governance, the system was streamlined throughout the region. However, this was not achieved as a result of vesting local structures with special powers on national issues. Rather, it was a consequence of the simplification of the governance system and the liquidation of intermediate bodies between Irkutsk authorities and the population of the *okrug*. At the *oblast* level, not a single body of state power is prepared to govern the *okrug*'s affairs. In addition, the Irkutsk authorities were able to keep the name of the *oblast* – even this shows that the Irkutsk state authorities were given full control of the *okrug*'s administration, and the new structures created there would be fully accountable to them.

The reform thus did not have any negative consequences for Irkutsk Oblast. A survey of its residents reflects this: merger, as far as they are concerned, is a natural process in bilateral relations between the *oblast* and the *okrug*. This shows their general ambivalence to the referendum as a whole (Badmaeva 2010).

So, what was the result of the reform? *First,* the administrative and territorial structure was simplified, and governance efficiency was improved as a result, as all power was concentrated in Irkutsk. Ust-Orda Buryat Okrug enjoys a special status in name only, since all the powers to enact political, national and economic rights of the people are in the hands of the Irkutsk authorities. *Second,* on the one hand, merger helped solve some serious socioeconomic problems. On the other hand, it created other problems that hit residents of Ust-Orda Buryat Okrug hard. The reform did not lead to significant changes in the *oblast*. *Third,* merger partly inspired the preservation and development of the national culture in the *okrug*. At the same time, however, it proved to be the main obstacle to the work of the *okrug*'s authorities in preserving the Buryat identity in the region. The cultural life of Irkutsk Oblast was enriched with the addition of the national and cultural features of Ust-Orda Buryat Autonomous Okrug.

The Merger of Agin-Buryat Autonomous Okrug and Chita Oblast

Rostislav Shilovskiy

As we mentioned earlier, the issue of unifying regions was on the agenda in the early 2000s. It was extensively discussed in all media, and scientific and practical conferences were held on the issue. Merger projects were subsequently launched in 2003. That said, the thought of merging Chita Oblast and Agin-Buryat Autonomous Okrug occurred to very few people.

These two constituent entities were next in line, nevertheless. The governor of Chita Oblast, Ravil Geniatulin, who actively supported the position of the authorities, stated *first and foremost* that the merger of the region would give impetus to the economic development of the new region, as it would open up new investment opportunities. *Second*, the governor's attitude towards merger was explained by "objective" factors, because the two constituent entities have long had close cultural ties (Popov 2006). A 2016 interview proved that the ex-governor was sincere in his intentions, as he claimed that the region had *de facto* been united several years before the referendum even took place, since Chita Oblast already dominated Agin-Buryat Autonomous Okrug both politically and financially, and that the process simply had to be completed. What is more, he talked of the need to continue the process of enlarging the regions and reducing the number of constituent entities of the Russian Federation (Zab.ru 2016). In other words, the main arguments in favour of the referendum were the shared history and culture of the two regions and their economic problems.

It all went down differently in Agin-Buryat Autonomous Okrug. Even though three referendums had successfully been held in other Russian regions, the *okrug*'s leadership did not agree to the merger. The head of the administration, Bair Zhamsuev, announced that he would resign his post if the decision on the merger of the two regions went through (Tikhomirov 2017). His position was based on the specific features of the Agin-Buryat Autonomous Okrug, which is unique in terms of its ethnic composition (61% Buryats), national culture and religious traditions (Buddhism). Moreover, he claimed that Agin Buryats have a special "mentality" that separates them from the Buryat diasporas in different regions. Another reason cited by Zhamsuev was that he enjoyed good relations with the head of Chita Oblast, and this helps increase the governability of the okrug by Chita (Tikhomirov 2017). Economic and socio-demographic indicators were also a factor: in 2005, Agin-Buryat Autonomous Okrug ranked second in the country in terms of economic growth in Russia, and it had restored much of its industry following the collapse of the Soviet Union (68% of the 1990 level). Meanwhile, Chita's industry was operating at just 34% of the 1990 level, with all its non-mining industries having fallen into decline. What is more, the population of Chita Oblast had declined as a result of natural factors and migration, whereas the opposite was observed in Agin-Buryat Autonomous Okrug (Verkhoturov 2007b). Poverty declined by three times, unemployment fell to the national average, and housing construction experienced a boom. B. Damdinov argues that Agin-Buryat Autonomous Okrug does not fit into the model of a "weak subject joining a stronger subject of the Federation": in this situation, a dynamically developing region would be absorbed by a depressed region, and that is not in Russia's national interests (Damdinov 2009). Thus, the head of the *okrug* could not allow a depressed region to absorb a successful and prosperous *okrug* with its own unique culture and successful governance structure.

This position could not persist forever. In light of the strengthening of the vertical power structure and creation of a single legal space in the 2000s, the central government could not allow the local authorities to deviate from the general plan for the development of the state. Bair Zhamsuev later said in an interview that he had talked to a number of politicians in the ten years since the referendum, including the plenipotentiary for the Siberian Federal District, who clarified the position of the federal government on the issue, insisting on the positives it was supposed to bring for the new constituent entity (such as the improvement of the investment climate). "I accepted that the process was irreversible," he said. The development of investment projects was thus one of the main arguments presented by the head of Agin-Buryat Autonomous Okrug in support of the referendum.

Preparations for the referendum were set in motion. A survey of the political and administrative elite and political analysts conducted by Natalya Anuchina revealed that 70% of respondents saw the use of administrative pressure on the part of the local authorities as one of the main difficulties in uniting the two constituent entities (Anuchina 2011a). This included intimidation and the creation of problems at work or university for those who did not vote in favour of merger (Anuchina 2011a). In addition, voters were given letters of thanks with a serial number on voting day that they had to deliver to their employers as proof that they had taken part in the referendum (Anuchina 2011b). Just like in the case of Irkutsk and Ust-Orda, this approach shows that the authorities were unsure about how many people would actually turn out to vote and whether or not they would vote in favour of merger.

Some media outlets reported that the 2007 referendum was held calmly and without incident, unlike the referendum on the merger of Irkutsk Oblast and Ust-Orda Buryat Autonomous Okrug, where the *Erkhe* movement was more active. However, this can be explained by the use of administrative pressure and the suppression of protest movements under various pretexts. For example, a picket in Chita was prohibited on the grounds that, according to the mayor, a criminal investigation had been launched "against persons suspected and accused of committing crimes" (Verkhoturov 2007c). The distribution of leaflets with anti-referendum slogans was similarly banned, the instigators had their registrations revoked and thus could not influence the results of the referendum.

The policy of the local authorities was criticized by those who opposed the creation of Zabaykalsky Krai. Despite all the obstacles put in their way, the opponents of merger were not discouraged in their attempts to enlist the support of the majority of the population. For example, they sent hundreds of letters to the residents of Agin-Buryat Autonomous Okrug, a move that shocked the local authorities and led to tighter controls on the post office and roads (Khamaganov 2017). The protest movement reached extreme levels when a Buryat climber carrying Buryat flags and a poster called for an end to the destruction of autonomous regions in Russia while scaling Mount Elbrus (Anuchina 2011b).

The authorities in Chita Oblast and Agin-Buryat Autonomous Okrug thus had fundamentally different positions on the merger of the constituent entities, based on economic and cultural considerations. The leaders of each region defended their respective positions: in Chita Oblast, they wanted to achieve economic growth, while in Agin-Buryat Autonomous Okrug, they sought to preserve the national heritage and the high pace of economic development. This explains why the authorities in the former supported the referendum, and why those in the latter did not. In the end, however, it was the influence of the federal authorities and the desires of Chita Oblast that prevailed, and the head of Agin-Buryat Autonomous Okrug agreed to hold a referendum.

Those who opposed merger did not achieve their goal. The referendum was held on March 11, 2007, with over 90% of voters in Chita Oblast and 94% of voters in Agin-Buryat Autonomous Okrug voting "for." Zabaykalsky Krai was officially formed on March 1, 2008. Its Charter was adopted the following year, setting out the provisions on the administration of the new *krai*: Chita would be its capital, the Legislative Assembly would have legislative power, and the governor and the government of the *krai* executive power.

The reform affected Agin-Buryat Autonomous Okrug more than it did Chita Oblast, and this was reflected in the political, administrative, socioeconomic, national and cultural spheres. In terms of governance, the following changes were implemented. The Charter of Zabaykalsky Krai states that Agin-Buryat Okrug is an administrative and territorial unit with a special status (Zakon Zabaykal'skogo kraya No. 125-33K 'Ustav Zabaykal'skogo kraya' (s izmeneniyami i dopolneniyami) 2009 (Zabaykalsky Krai)). At the *krai* level, this was reflected in the creation of a new consultative and advisory body – the Assembly of Representatives of Agin-

Buryat Okrug – which has the right to protect the interests, culture, language, etc., of the peoples living on its territory. This means that, in the course of the integration of regions and the elimination of unnecessary administrative and territorial elements, a new body had been created, although it did not play a significant role, being advisory in nature. What is more, the Agin-Buryat Okrug elites were able to gain fairly solid representation in the Legislative Assembly of Zabaykalsky Krai – five of the 50 available seats, or 10% of the total (of all the constituent entities subsumed into larger territories during the 2000s, only Koryak Okrug won more seats in the regional assembly, with 20%). In addition, representatives of Agin-Buryat Okrug were given positions in the executive authorities. This was initially perceived as a concession to the *okrug*, which had been developing successfully on its own in the years before merger. Finally, it was thanks to the negotiating efforts of the Agin-Buryat Okrug elites that the newly formed region was given a brand-new name – Zabaykalsky Krai.

At the *okrug* level, the Agin-Buryat administration was actually given greater powers, which was not the case with Ust-Orda Buryat Okrug. As such, it "acts as an intersectoral body for interaction and coordination with law enforcement." The administration's competencies stretch beyond the ethno-cultural sphere to include a wide range of economic issues – for example, it has a say on budget matters. Moreover, the Agreement "On the Special Status of an Administrative and Territorial Unit as Part of a New Constituent Entity of the Russian Federation Formed as a Result of the Merger of Agin-Buryat Autonomous Okrug and Chita Oblast" stresses that "the structure of the administration of the okrug is formed with due account for the sectoral structure of the economy and the social sphere" (Soglashenie 'Ob osobom statuse administrativno-territorial'noy edinitsy v sostave novogo sub'ekta Rossiyskoy Federatsii, obrazovannogo v rezul'tate ob'edineniya Aginskogo Buryatskogo avtonomnogo okruga i Chitinskoy oblasti' 2007 (Chita oblast, Agin-Buryat Autonomous Okrug)). This is why the administration includes such divisions as the Department for the Development of the Territories and the Department for Social Issues as part of its structure. The fact that there are so many functions devoted to the economic and social sphere within the administration makes the reform unique (Damdinov 2016) and distinguishes the Agin-Buryat Okrug administration from that of Ust-Orda Buryat Okrug, where far greater attention is paid to the national and cultural aspect. That said, such a variety of functions does not play a significant role given the fact that the administration does not have its own budget, as it is controlled by the Chita authorities.

The latter circumstance played a fatal role in terms of the *okrug*'s continuing socioeconomic development. Before merger, Aginsky Offshore – a territory with special economic incentives for entrepreneurs and home to several dozen companies – was in operation (Makhschkeev 2014). All tax and non-tax revenues from their activities went into the construction of the transport and social infrastructure, equipping schools and hospitals with the necessary technology, and the implementation of various social programmes. As a result, the *okrug* came along in leaps and bounds in terms of its socioeconomic development and had one of the fastest growing economies in the entire country. The most telling proof of this was the size of subsidies it received from the government – 80% in 1997, compared to just 6.6% in 2006 (Dobchinov 2017). However, the offshore ceased to exist following merger, and the budget was transferred to Chita. This led to a decline in several indicators after the reform, primarily in terms of payments to the population under social programmes and the construction of infrastructure facilities. The impoverished Chita, which received substantial subsidies, could not offer anything in return. There was a noticeable exodus of people from the region as a result, with most heading to the Republic of Buryatia. And it was not just young people who had become disillusioned with the prospects in the *okrug*, but also small and medium-sized enterprises, which stopped investing in infrastructure development following the dissolution of the offshore zone and the loss of financial benefits.

These trends were reflected in the moods of both the elites and the residents of the *okrug*. Realizing that they would lose their financial opportunities, representatives of the okrug's elite started to spend everything before merger that was left in the region's budget, investing in all kinds of projects and programmes (even in those that did not need money). That is, the elites understood that the underdeveloped Chita Oblast would bring the *okrug* nothing but financial losses and additional issues, and plunge the okrug's economy into a stagnant state.

The *okrug*'s residents were similarly unimpressed with the merger, with the majority stating that the situation had deteriorated significantly on all grounds, with the exception of ethnic conflicts. The areas in which the population was most dissatisfied were the availability of jobs (74.4%) and the outflow of people from the region (65.6%) (Vasilyeva and Anuchina 2012).

Similar resentment could be detected in the assessments of experts. The survey of Natalya Anuchina revealed that most experts (46%) believe that the formation of the *krai* brought a number of negative consequences: the mass outflow of people, lower wages, the suspension of some social programmes, and a decrease in the budgetary security of Agin-Buryat Okrug (87% of respondents cited this problem) (Anuchina 2011a).

In terms of support for national culture, two points should be noted. *First*, the Buryat language was made official alongside Russian, and it can be used in all media. *Second*, the Charter of Zabaykalsky Krai talks about the creation of additional cultural and educational institutions to protect the diversity of local languages and cultures (Damdinov 2016). The consolidation of these aspects at the legislative level suggests that certain efforts have been made to develop the special status of the former autonomous *okrug*, and this is what makes the reform project different from those that came before.

Unlike Agin-Buryat Autonomous Okrug, the former Chita Oblast did not undergo any major changes following merger. In terms of the political and administrative aspects, Agin-Buryat Autonomous Okrug and its budget were transferred into the hands of the Chita authorities. Although the two constituent entities were closely connected before the merger politically (the people of Agin-Buryat Autonomous Okrug were allowed to vote in the Chita Oblast gubernatorial elections), they now form a single entity headed by Chita. In the terms of socioeconomics, the problems that existed before have still not been resolved, and in some cases (such as the budget and the standard of living of the population), the situation has even worsened. And as for the preservation of national culture, things look much like they do in the case of the merger of Ust-Orda Buryat Okrug and Irkutsk Oblast, as there is a growing interest throughout the krai in the culture, traditions, customs and religion of Buryats living in the *okrug*.

Given that the state of affairs did not change in Chita Oblast, a survey of its residents conducted in 2012 did not reveal any differences in their perception of the socioeconomic situation in the *krai* (in terms of healthcare, employment, etc.) (Vasilyeva and Anuchina 2012).

So, how successful was the merger of Chita Oblast and Agin-Buryat Autonomous Okrug? On the one hand, the *okrug* received significant bonuses in terms of politics, administration and the preservation of the national culture (compared to other administrative and territorial reforms), including a significant number of seats in the legislative body at the *krai* level, a diverse range of powers at the *okrug* level, and institutional consolidation of the specifics of Buryat culture. On the other hand, the *okrug* experienced a sharp decline in social and economic development, which affected the state of its infrastructure and the standard of living of the population. The situation in the *oblast* remained almost exactly the same. The only changes were the geographical scope of the activities of the Chita authorities and the cultural enrichment of the new region thanks to the addition of Agin-Buryat Autonomous Okrug.

The Attempt to Merge Nenets Autonomous Okrug and Arkhangelsk Oblast

Petr Oskolkov

The prospects for further mergers were widely discussed in Russia after 2008, but fell by the wayside following pushback from the local elites in the remaining okrugs. However, in May 2020, the newly appointed interim head of Arkhangelsk Oblast and the head of Nenets Autonomous Okrug signed a memorandum demonstrating their intention to create a new region by merging the two.

Nenets Autonomous Okrug is one of the indigenous autonomies still listed in the Constitution of the Russian Federation. The Nenets (or, previously, the Samoyedic) people are the most numerous of all the legally recognized Nordic small-numbered indigenous peoples of Russia, totaling 44,640 people in 2010 (Bogoyavlenski 2012). However, they do not constitute a majority in the okrug and make up only 17.83 per cent of the 44,000-strong population (Rosstat 2010). Some researchers note that "for twenty-five years, the Nenets people have maintained the dominant ethnopolitical position in the Russian Arctic internationally and federally" (Perevalova 2019, 243). The Nenets people are separated into two groups: the Tundra Nenets and Forest Nenets. The main traditional occupations are reindeer herding, fishing, and hunting. However, many people of Nenets origin have become involved in a variety of modern professions in the 20th century. According to 2002 Census data, nineteen per cent of the Nenets people were living in urban areas, while the remaining Nenets population living in the countryside. As of 2010, a total of twenty-four per cent of the Nenets population in Nenets Autonomous Okrug were urban dwellers. 2002 Census data indicated that only 25.7 per cent on Nenets people were engaged in "traditional" occupations (unfortunately, more recent disaggregated data is unavailable) (Sokolovsky 2007, 43-45).

The Statute (Ustav) of Nenets Autonomous Okrug states in its Preamble that "the Okrug was founded [...] based on the will of the Nenets people." A specialized organization –*Yasavey* Association established in Naryan-Mar in 1989 – works in the Okrug to protect the rights of the Nenets people (the word *yasavey* means "guide" in Nenets). The organization is even explicitly referred to in the Statute: "The okrug's state institutions, while considering issues of socioeconomic and cultural development of the Nenets people, cooperates with the Yasavey Association of the Nenets people."[1] *Yasavey*'s goals are quite typical for an ethnocultural civil society organization: "to promote national consciousness and preserve the language, culture and traditional way of life of the Nenets people."

The protests in Nenets Autonomous Okrug that took place 22th–23th May 2020 demonstrated that the okrug was not going to easily give up the idea of the rights as a federal entity. At 7pm on both days in question, people gathered in the central square of the okrug's administrative center, Naryan-Mar, to sing its anthem. 23th May, thirty-one indigenous kin communities of the okrug signed a collective open letter to Yuri Bezdudny, the interim head of the region: "Our okrug was created as a manifestation of the will of the Nenets people, but this fact is ignored to demonstrate disrespect towards the will and the interests of the Nenets and other ethnic groups living in the okrug" (Melnikova 2020). The very fact that such a letter came into existence at least partly confirms the importance of the ethnic political status of indigenous communities.

The (partly) ethnic component of the protest against the merger was also explicitly manifested in the official position of the above-mentioned Yasavey association that functions as an official representative of the Nenets people in the okrug. Irina Khanzerova, the organization's vice-president, said: "Our people are very much afraid of losing their identity (…). We already have enough

---

1   Chapter 4, Article 16 of the Statute is devoted entirely to the Nenets ethnic group (Ustav Nenetskogo avtonomnogo okruga 1995 (Nenets Autonomous Okrug)).

problems with the preservation of our culture and language, and if we are merged with Arkhangelsk oblast... (...) This is a one-sided decision" (Interfax 2020).

The protest was supported by local members of the ruling United Russia political party. Eleven of the nineteen seats in the Assembly of Deputies of the Nenets Autonomous Okrug are occupied by United Russia, with nine representatives publicly refusing to vote for the reform (Vinokurov, Litvinova, and Kadik 2020). As a result, the parliamentary discussion in Arkhangelsk and Naryan-Mar of a possible merger was postponed indefinitely. 27th May, Secretary of the General Council of United Russia Andrey Turchak officially stated that the "referendum issue" was "temporarily closed" following meetings with the heads of Arkhangelsk Oblast and Nenets Autonomous Okrug, as well as with the Yasavey elders, that also explicitly demonstrates the significance of the ethnic component in the process (Mukhametshina 2020). The decision was likely taken because of the negative response among the population and the discontent with the merger plans in the local branch of United Russia.

Interestingly, a constitutional referendum was held in Russia 1st July 2020. The proposed changes would further consolidate presidential powers, and a massive state-funded campaign was rolled out in the run-up to the vote. Nenets Autonomous Okrug was the only Russian region to vote against the constitutional amendments ("only" 43.78 per cent voted "for"). Yuri Bezdudny linked this to the failed reform plans: "They did not vote against the amendments, but rather it was a reaction to the merger plans of Nenets Autonomous Okrug and Arkhangelsk oblast" (Antonova and Kalyukov 2020).

PART II

Assessing the Consequences of Merging Regions of the Russian Federation

The Institutional Aspect

Petr Oskolkov

Article 66, Part 4 of the Constitution of the Russian Federation reads: "Relations among autonomous okrugs within krais and oblasts may be regulated by federal law or by a treaty between State government bodies of the autonomous okrug and, accordingly, State government bodies of the krai or oblast." This is the only attempt to regulate officially at the highest level possible the relationship between the *matryoshka* constituent entities of the Russian Federations (that is, constituent entities that contain other constituent entities as part of). There were a number of such entities in the country before the series of constitutional reforms in 2003-2008, but now the only *matryoshkas* that remain are Tyumen and Arkhangelsk oblasts. At the same time, Article 65 of the Constitution, which lists the constituent entities of the Russian Federation, says nothing about this specific phenomenon: from a formal point of view, all constituent entities are equal, and the issue of delimitation of powers between them is extremely complicated.

The enlargement of the regions of the Russian Federation pursued several goals: to solve the abovementioned governance problems; to achieve greater symmetry in the administrative and territorial division of the country; and to reduce the number of constituent entities and thus strengthen the power vertical. In each individual case, these goals were achieved in different ways, since, *first*, the process took place in several stages, leaving room for improvements to be made, and *second*, the initiators of the reform had to deal with the socioeconomic and political obstacles unique in each case. As a result, various mechanisms of interaction between the former autonomous regions, on the one hand, and the authorities of the newly formed constituent entity and the federal centre, on the other, were formed.

In all cases of enlargement, constituent entities that had been formed according to "national" (de facto, ethnic) and territorial principles lost their status as constituent entities, becoming administrative and territorial units with special status. Thus, following the model, the national and territorial constituent entities of the Russian Federation that existed alongside republics and autonomous regions were not dissolved, but were "merely" stripped of their status and rights as full-fledged constituent entities of the Russian Federation. If the goal of the reform was to simplify the administrative and territorial division of the country, then it was not achieved: the administrative and territorial units with a special status that replaced the *matryoshka* constituent entities are not mentioned in the Constitution; their position within the country's administrative structure is unclear and does not lend itself to merger. Researchers into the issue note that the relevant federal constitutional laws do not say anything about what "special status" actually means, which means that the issue is the subject of bargaining on the part of the authorities of different parts of the *matryoshka* (Kynev 2010a). This is why the resulting constituent entities each have a different status. What unites them is the fact that they are no longer mentioned in the Constitution's list of constituent entities, meaning they have lost their "subjective" rights. And while in the past the autonomous regions had the right to appeal directly to the federal centre, now the highest authority they can turn to is that of the *oblast* or *krai* in which they are located. The "administrative and territorial units with a special status" are mostly responsible for ethnopolitical and cultural issues, with their respective powers varying greatly in other areas.

There are several options for how the new administrative and territorial entities should eventually look like. At the same time, the most obvious difference lies in the fates of the Taymyr Dolgano-Nenets and Evenk autonomous okrugs, which were "inside" Krasnoyarsk Krai, on the one hand, and the other former autonomous regions on the other: while the last four retained the word "okrug" in their names, Taymyr and Evenk were "downgraded" to *"raions"* (literally "districts" or "areas"; an administrative and territorial unit with a special status from the point of view of the administrative and territorial division of the country, or a municipal district from the point of view of the municipal structure). That said, it is debatable whether or not it was actually a "downgrade": on the one hand, *raions* obviously have fewer rights than larger entities, and most departments in the respective *okrugs* (such as the military commissariat and the State Labour Commission) were moved to Norilsk (Artobolevsky and Gontmakher 2010, 60), which, having previously been part of the Taymyr Dolgano-Nenets Autonomous Okrug, was officially subordinated to Krasnoyarsk. On the other hand, the rights of municipal districts (which Taymyr Dolgano-Nenets Region and Evenk Region are from the point of view of the municipal structure), albeit small, are formalized (and guaranteed under Article 15 of the Federal Law "On the General Principles of Organizing Local Self-Government in the Russian Federation"), while the rights of the *okrug*, which does not have regulatory status in the modern system of local government can, as we mentioned earlier, be interpreted arbitrarily.

In 2008, a separate executive body – the Ministry for the Affairs of Koryak Okrug – was created as part of the Kamchatka government. In 2011, it was reorganized into the Ministry for the Affairs of Koryak Okrug and the Territories of Traditional Residence of the Indigenous Peoples of the North. And in 2013, the Koryak Okrug administration was established as a ministerial body. In addition to the Koryak Okrug administration (made up of 14 people, including the head of the *okrug* and two departments – one to ensure the *okrug*'s special status and another for the development of reindeer farming), executive power in the *okrug* can be exercised exclusively by the regional territorial bodies (Article 30, parts 2 and 3 of the Charter of Kamchatka Krai). Just like with Komi-Permyak Okrug and Ust-Orda, Koryak Okrug's powers mostly included social and cultural issues. At the same time, the "sectoral" divisions of the executive bodies were transferred to the direct subordination of the administration of the respective regions that have been merged (Artobolevsky and Gontmakher 2010, 6). In the city of Palana, for example, the district court, the prosecutor's office, the Department of Internal Affairs and other structures were all abolished (Kynev 2010a). At first glance, it would seem that, in terms of representation at the *krai* level, the achievements of Koryak Okrug are the most impressive, with its representatives being guaranteed 10 of the 50 available seats in the Legislative Assembly of Kamchatka Krai. However, this guarantee was only good for the transition period and the first legislative term of the Legislative Assembly following the merger. Just two representatives of Koryak Okrug currently have seats there.

Ust-Orda Buryat Autonomous Okrug is governed in a similar fashion. The structure of the *okrug*'s administration includes departments for ethnic culture, languages and sports, finance and economy, legal affairs, and labour and organizational work. However, Article 7 of the *okrug*'s Charter only delegates issues of national and cultural identity to the purview of its administration. Ust-Orda Buryat Autonomous Okrug representatives have just four of the 50 seats in the Irkutsk Legislative Assembly.

Agin-Buryat Autonomous Okrug – another *okrug* with a large Buryat population – was also given its own administration, which, similar to that of Ust-Orda Buryat Autonomous Okrug, is headed by a deputy prime minister of the *matryoshka* region. The administration, however, has more real powers, running a department for the development of the territory with sub-departments involved in the development of infrastructure and the agro-industrial complex. What is more, Agin-Buryat Autonomous Okrug is unique among the "consolidated" regions in that it has both an executive and a legislative body (more precisely, a consultative and advisory body in the *krai*'s Legislative Assembly) called the Assembly of Representatives of Agin-Buryat Autonomous Okrug. The Assembly is made up of 15 people and has the authority to formulate proposals on protecting the interests of the peoples of the *okrug*, draw up relevant draft laws, take part in the development of target programmes in the *krai*, and monitor compliance with the *krai*'s laws within the *okrug*. It has established commissions on economic, social and cultural issues, as well as on issues of regional importance and self-government.

A. Kynev notes that Agin-Buryat Autonomous Okrug retained most of its rights (Kynev 2010a), the local authorities kept the majority of their powers, and the former administrative division and the local government system remained intact. What is more, local administration structures were preserved as territorial bodies of departments at the *krai* level (Kynev 2010b). According to a preliminary agreement on the special status of Agin-Buryat Autonomous Okrug as part of Zabaykalsky Krai, the constituency was supposed to receive one-third of the seats in the *krai*'s Legislative Assembly (although this promise was never fulfilled, and the constituency has to make it with five of the 50 available seats) (Artobolevsky and Gontmakher 2010, 77).

We can assume that this is connected with the large-scale public and administrative protests that took place in the region: Buryat public organizations, as well as the leadership of the *okrug* itself and the neighbouring Republic of Buryatia actively opposed the merger. The agreement on the special status of Agin-Buryat Autonomous Okrug within Zabaykalsky Krai was signed even before the referendum took place (on February 15, 2007), and the approval of the reform was seen as a mere formality. Nevertheless, despite the fact that it has more powers, the law on the special status of the Agin-Buryat Okrug has not yet been adopted by the regional Legislative Assembly. At the same time, it is the Ministry of Territorial Development of Zabaykalsky Krai that is in charge of the development of the *okrug* (Shibaeva 2011, 67).

The legal scholar B. Damdinov offered an interesting comparison in 2016, noting about the administration of Ust-Orda Buryat Autonomous Okrug, "the extremely narrow purview of the *okrug* administration, which has essentially been reduced to dealing with certain ethno-cultural issues, confirms that, in terms of status, the *okrug* is in fact near the very bottom of the hierarchy of regional executive authorities" (2016, 29). Meanwhile, Damdinov describes the Agin-Buryat administration thus: "The competencies of the administration extend to a very wide range of issues, among which questions of an ethno-cultural nature occupy a small place in comparison with issues relating to the socio-economic development of the *okrug*" (2016, 29). This comparison is yet further evidence of the dissimilarity of the institutional design of the new administrative and territorial units.

Only one executive body of the Komi-Permyak Autonomous Okrug remained in the new configuration, and that is the Ministry for the Affairs of the Komi-Permyak Autonomous Okrug in the structure of the Government of Perm Oblast. Granted, it has more powers and employs more people than, say, the respective ministries in Koryak Okrug and Ust-Orda Buryat Okrug, with departments of socio-economic development, finance, ethno-cultural development, legal, personnel and document work, and work with territories. The Ministry is responsible for approving the *okrug* development projects. It also remains in charge of ethno-cultural issues and has "limited opportunities in the planning and regulating of the economy" (Artobolevsky and Gontmakher 2010, 46). However, the Charter of Perm Krai points out that "the state power of Perm Krai over the territory of Komi-Permyak Okrug is exercised by the state authorities of Perm Krai" (Article 37, part 2). The Ministry is led by the head of the *okrug*, who is appointed by the Governor of Perm Krai at the request of the Chairman of the Government of Perm Krai. Thus, the Komi-Permyak Okrug authorities have no say on who will lead it for five years and represent it in its relations with the authorities of Perm Krai, the territorial structures of the federal authorities and the local self-government bodies.

Since Komi-Permyak Autonomous Okrug served as a "pilot" region for the project of merging constituent entities of the Russian Federation, the concept of "special status" caused quite an uproar there. The idea of transforming the Autonomous Okrug into an association of municipal districts or a single municipality was put forward (Milchakov n.d.). Prior to the merger, Komi-Permyak Autonomous Okrug was led by a representative body of 15 people, with the constituency being represented by two deputies in the Legislative Assembly of Perm Oblast (of 40 total seats). In the run-up to the referendum, the movement "For the Future of the Okrug" demanded greater representation in the Legislative Assembly, between six and eight deputies (Milchakov n.d.). The agreement between Perm Oblast and Komi-Permyak Autonomous Okrug on the legal status of Komi-Permyak Okrug of Perm Krai that was signed before the merger provided for the creation of an independent *duma* in Komi-Permyak Okrug consisting of 20 deputies (Milchakov 2007, 37). Federal Constitutional Law No. 1 of 2006 offered a different solution: the number of seats in the

Legislative Assembly of Perm Krai was increased to 60, with two deputies elected from single-member constituencies in Komi-Permyak Okrug, 28 from single-member constituencies in the rest of the *krai* territory, and another 30 from the entire Krai constituency.

The structure of the authorities of the newly formed (municipal) *raions* (districts) in Krasnoyarsk Krai is much better developed. In addition to the head of the municipal district, both Taymyr Dolgano-Nenets Raion and Evenkia Raion have a district council of deputies (20 deputies in Taymyr and 24 in Evenkia), an administration and a control and accounting commission, while the *raion* council elects the head of the *raion*. Both administrations contain several departments whose activities cover almost all areas of the functioning of the municipal *raion*. The *raion* councils have permanent commissions on legal, financial, economic, and social issues, as well as on the affairs of the indigenous peoples of the North, agriculture, environmental management and ecology, housing and communal services, construction, transport and communications, the development of local self-governing bodies and intermunicipal and regional policy (in Taymyr Dolgano-Nenets Raion). The exclusive competencies of the *raion* councils include, among other things, approving the *raion* budget, setting local tax rates, determining the procedure for the *raion*'s participation in intermunicipal cooperation, and deciding on whether or not to dismiss the head of the *raion*. However, this status also has some significant disadvantages: with Taymyr Dolgano-Nenets Region and Evenk Region becoming municipal districts, internal zoning was abolished, and Dudinka, previously an urban district, became a municipal settlement (this was not possible in the case of Kudymkar, the capital of Komi-Permyak Okrug) (Kynev 2010b). Both *raions* were allotted just two of the 52 available seats in the Krasnoyarsk Krai Legislative Assembly.

What these consolidation scenarios have in common is the fact that former autonomous *okrug*s became administrative and territorial units with a special status. However, there was no indication whatsoever of what this status actually meant, and in each case, the matter was resolved differently, following the political bargaining of the various parts of the *matryoshka*. All the *okrugs/raions* that have been merged are represented in the legislative assemblies of their surrounding *oblasts/krais*, although the level of their representation in these bodies was determined extremely unevenly – from as high as 20% in Koryak Okrug (during the transition period) to just 3.3% in Komi-Permyak Okrug.

Three models can be observed:

1. The transformation of autonomous *okrugs* into *raions* (districts), in which the new territorial entity is given an elected head, a district council and an administration (as in the case of Taymyr Dolgano-Nenets Region and Evenk Region).
2. The transformation of autonomous *okrugs* into *okrugs*, where the leadership of the new territorial entity is transferred to the executive power of the *krai* by including the ministry for the affairs of the *okrug* in question in the structure of executive power (as in the case of Komi-Permyak Okrug), or by giving the administration of the *okrug* the status of a ministry (as in case of Agin-Buryat Okrug), with the *okrug* retaining significant powers, including in the socio-economic sphere (in addition to an administration created in just this manner, Agin-Buryat Okrug also has a consultative and advisory body in the Legislative Assembly of Zabaykalsky Krai – the Assembly of Representatives of Agin-Buryat Okrug).

3. The transformation of autonomous *okrug*s into *okrug*s, in which the leadership of the new territorial entity is transferred to the executive power of the *krai/oblast* by including the administration of the *okrug* that has been granted the status of a ministry (as in the case of Ust-Orda Buryat Autonomous Okrug and Koryak Autonomous Okrug) in the structure of executive power, with the district retaining limited powers in the ethno-cultural sphere. At the same time, ethnic and cultural issues are still the main purview of these ministries/administrations, and their head is appointed by the governor (Komi-Permyak Okrug, Koryak Okrug), or is appointed *ex officio* as a deputy chair of the *krai* government (Agin-Buryat Okrug, Ust-Orda Buryat Autonomous Okrug).

The authorities of the "merged" regions are as follows (Table 1).

Table 1: Authorities of "Merged" Regions

Region	Executive authority	Body of (quasi-) legislative power	Head of administrative-territorial unit
Taymyr Dolgano-Nenets Raion	Raion administration	Raion council of deputies	Elected
Evenk Raion	Raion administration	Raion council of deputies	Elected
Komi-Permyak Okrug	Ministry of Affairs of Komi-Permyak Okrug (part of the Government of Perm Krai)	None	Corresponding minister appointed by the governor
Koryak Okrug	Okrug administration with ministerial status as part of the Government of Kamchatka Krai	None	Appointed by the governor
Agin-Buryat Okrug	*Okrug* administration with ministerial status as part of the Government of Zabaykalsky Krai	Caucus of representatives of the *okrug* at the Legislative Assembly of Zabaykalsky Krai	*Ex officio*, as deputy chair of the Government of Zabaykalsky Krai
Ust-Orda Buryat Okrug	*Okrug* administration with ministerial status as part of the Government of Irkutsk Oblast	None	*Ex officio*, as deputy chair of the Government of Irkutsk Oblast

The Electoral Aspect

Emma Bibina

This chapter analyses the change in voting behaviour of residents of the *okrug*s that were merged into larger constituent entities of the Russian Federation. This is done by comparing the turnout rates for elections at the federal and regional levels in the periods before and after the merger, as well as by identifying potential changes in party preferences. The point of the research here is to show the degree to which federal reform influences electoral processes in *okrug*s we are looking at.

We will be looking at presidential elections, elections to the State Duma, gubernatorial elections, and elections to regional parliaments. The exact timeframe for each kind of election differs, since our analyses run from the last regional or federal election before the merger to the most recent federal elections, held in 2018. This gives us a period of 2000 to 2018. An analysis of the dynamics of voter turnout in the presidential elections and elections to the State Duma is provided at the end of each section.

The majority of the data in this section is taken from the official website of the Central Election Commission of the Russian Federation.

Komi-Permyak Autonomous Okrug and Perm Oblast

Elections to the State Duma of the Federal Assembly of the Russian Federation of the third legislative term were held on December 19, 1999 (Table 2). Single-Seat Electoral District No. 216 in Komi-Permyak Autonomous Okrug saw a voter turnout of 62.36%, compared to 61.85% in Russia as a whole.

Table 2: 1999 State Duma Elections, 5 of votes

Party	Russia, %	Perm Oblast, %	Komi-Permyak Autonomous Okrug, %

Communist Party of the Russian Federation	24.29	14.57	17.02
Unity	23.32	19.80	26.75
Fatherland – All Russia	13.33	9.41	8.1
Union of Right Forces	8.52	14.24	7.24
Bloc of Zhirinovsky	5.98	7.48	11.52
Yabloko	5.93	7.04	2.05

Presidential elections were held in the Russian Federation on March 26, 2000. Turnout was 68.70% nationwide, and 69.9% in Komi-Permyak Autonomous Okrug (Table 3).

Table 3: 2000 Russian Presidential Elections, % of votes

Candidates	Russia, %	Perm Oblast, %	Komi-Permyak Autonomous Okrug, %
Vladimir Putin	51.95	60.79	70.12
Gennady Zyuganov	29.48	19.98	17.92
Grigory Yavlinsky	5.80	7.30	1.89
Vladimir Zhirinovsky	2.70	3.40	4.02

On December 9, 2001, elections were held to the Legislative Assembly of Komi-Permyak Autonomous Okrug of the third legislative term. Voter turnout was 48.37%. Elections to the State Duma of the fourth legislative term were held on December 7, 2003, along with the referendum on the merger of Komi-Permyak Autonomous Okrug and Perm Oblast (Table 4). Turnout for the State Duma elections was 55.67% nationwide, compared to 62.4% in Perm Oblast and 65.64% in Komi-Permyak Autonomous Okrug.

Table 4: 2003 State Duma Elections, % of votes

Party	Russia	Perm Oblast	Komi-Permyak Autonomous Okrug
United Russia	37.56	30.7	46.3
Communist Party of the Russian Federation	12.61	7.6	7,.5
Liberal Democratic Party of Russia	4.54	12.9	8.5
Rodina	9.02	5.8	3.1

Tables 5–7 constitute an analysis of the elections to the State Duma following the merger (2007–2016).

Table 5: State Duma Elections 2007–2016, % of votes

Party	Russia	Perm Oblast	Komi-Permyak Autonomous Okrug
2007			
United Russia	64.3	62.06	61.24
Communist Party of the Russian Federation	11.57	8.94	8.7
Liberal Democratic Party of Russia	8.14	12.46	12.09
A Just Russia	7.74	6.25	6.53
2011			
United Russia	49.32	36.28	44.83
Communist Party of the Russian Federation	19.19	21.02	14.29
Liberal Democratic Party of Russia	11.67	17.89	15.9
A Just Russia	13.24	16.41	18.95
2016			
United Russia	54.2	42.7	44.3
Communist Party of the Russian Federation	13.34	14.24	15.5

| Liberal Democratic Party of Russia | 13.14 | 15.76 | 16.15 |
| A Just Russia | 6.22 | 9.02 | 8.09 |

Table 6: Voter Turnout for State Duma Elections in 1999–2016, %

Year	Russia	Perm Krai	Komi-Permyak Okrug
1999	61.85	–	62.36
2003	55.67	62.4	65.64
2007	63.71	54.83	57.86
2011	60.21	48.05	48.72
2016	47.88	35.17	32.27

Table 7: 2004 Russian Presidential Elections, % of votes

Candidates	Russia	Perm Oblast	Komi-Permyak Autonomous Okrug
Vladimir Putin	71.31	72.74	80.55
Nikolay Kharitonov	13.69	10.1	10.44
Sergey Glazyev	4.1	3.75	1.58
Irina Khakamada	3.84	5.18	2.2
Oleg Malyshkin	2.02	2.64	1.82
Sergey Mironov	0.75	1.02	1.11

Table 8 constitutes an analysis of the Russian presidential elections in 2008–2018.

Table 8: Russian Presidential Elections 2008–2018, % of votes

Candidates	Russia	Perm Oblast	Komi-Permyak Autonomous Okrug
2008			
Dmitry Medvedev	70.28	67.3	71.45
Gennady Zyuganov	17.72	16.7	14.34
Vladimir Zhirinovsky	9.35	13.23	12.17
2012			

Vladimir Putin	63.6	62.94	69.96
Gennady Zyuganov	17.18	15.78	12.93
Vladimir Zhirinovsky	6.22	4.6	5.06
Sergey Mironov	3.85	4.4	4.0
Mikhail Prokhorov	7.98	10.86	6.83
2018			
Vladimir Putin	76.69	75.35	77.02
Pavel Grudinin	11.77	10.55	10.38
Vladimir Zhirinovsky	5.65	6.84	9.1
Ksenia Sobchak	1.68	2.2	–
Grigory Yavlinsky	1.05	1.28	0.48
Boris Titov	0.76	0.9	–

Table 9: Voter Turnout for Russian Presidential Elections in 1999–2016, %

Year	Russia	Perm Oblast/Krai	Komi-Permyak Autonomous Okrug / Komi-Permyak Okrug
2000	68.7	–	69.9
2004	64.38	62	63.66
2008	69.81	55.75	59.77
2012	65.34	55.11	53.24
2018	67.54	66.51	70.0

Elections for deputies to the Legislative Assembly of Perm Krai of the first legislative term on December 3, 2006 (Table 10). Voter turnout in Kudymkar Single-Seat Electoral District No. 29 was 45.46%, with Andrey Agishev (self-nominated) being elected as deputy for the constituency. The election was held using proportional representation. The results for Perm Krai were as follows: United Russia (34.56% of votes), Union of Right Forces (16.35%), Liberal Democratic Party of Russia (13.81%), Russian Party of Pensioners (11.65%), Communist Party of the Russian Federation (8.59%). The results for the Kudymkar Electoral District were the same, albeit with different shares of votes: United Russia (32.59%), Union of Right Forces (19.8%), Liberal Democratic Party of Russia (10.61%), Russian Party of Pensioners (10.49%), Communist Party of the Russian Federation (7.57%).

Elections to the Legislative Assembly of Perm Krai of the second legislative term were held on December 4, 2011, simultaneously with the elections to the State Duma of the Russian Federation. Voter turnout in Perm Krai was 48.01%. Turnout in Kudymkar Single-Seat Electoral District No. 29 was 47.43%. The election was won by Aleksey Petrov. A proportional representation system was used, with the following results being recorded: United Russia (37.89% of votes), Communist Party of the Russian Federation (20.14%), Liberal Democratic Party of Russia (17.63%), A Just Russia (15.24%). The data for the Kudymkar Electoral District was markedly different: United Russia (44.76%), A Just Russia (18.29%), Liberal Democratic Party of Russia (16.55%), Communist Party of the Russian Federation (14.25%).

Elections to the Legislative Assembly of Perm Krai of the third legislative term were held on September 18, 2016 (see Table 10) on a single voting day, simultaneously with the elections to the State Duma of the Russian Federation. Voter turnout in the *krai* was 35.03% (Table 11). The following results were recorded: United Russia (43.75%), Communist Party of the Russian Federation (17.77%), Liberal Democratic Party of Russia (16.34%), A Just Russia – For Truth (11.29%). The results for the Kudymkar Electoral District were as follows: United Russia (46.19%), A Just Russia (11.17%), Liberal Democratic Party of Russia (18.49%), Communist Party of the Russian Federation (17.03%). Turnout was 47.80%.

Table 10: Elections to the Legislative Assembly of Perm Krai 2006–2016, % of votes

Party	2006		2011		2016	
	Perm Krai	Komi-Permyak Okrug	Perm Krai	Komi-Permyak Okrug	Perm Krai	Komi-Permyak Okrug
United Russia	34.56	32.59	37.89	44.76	43.75	46.19
Liberal Democratic	13.81	10.61	17.63	16.55	16.34	18.49

Party of Russia						
Communist Party of the Russian Federation	8.59	7.57	20.14	14.25	17.77	17.03
A Just Russia	–	–	15.24	18.29	11.29	11.17

Table 11: Voter Turnout for the Elections to the Legislative Assembly of Perm Krai in 2006–2016, %

2006		2011		2016	
Perm Krai	Komi-Permyak Okrug	Perm Krai	Komi-Permyak Okrug	Perm Krai	Komi-Permyak Okrug
–	45.46	48.01	47.43	35.03	47.8

Direct gubernatorial elections were held in Perm Krai on September 10, 2017. Maxim Reshetnikov was elected governor by an absolute majority of votes (over 80%), both in the region as a whole and in Komi-Permyak Okrug. Voter turnout in Perm Krai was 42.53%, compared to 36.87% for Komi-Permyak Okrug.

An analysis of the voting behaviour of residents of the former Komi-Permyak Autonomous Okrug shows that the level of turnout before and after the merger into Perm Krai was consistent with the national average for federal elections, comparable to the *oblast* average for regional elections, and then to the average for the *krai*. According to the data on elections to the State Duma, the party preferences of residents of the *okrug* before and after the merger differed somewhat from the rest of the country and were almost exactly the same as the average for *oblasts/krais*. In particular, Perm residents showed an increased affinity for the Liberal Democratic Party of Russia and A Just Russia, while the level of support for the Communist Party of the Russian Federation turned out to be lower than in the region and throughout the country. The data on the voter turnout for the elections to the Legislative Assembly of Komi-Permyak Autonomous Okrug of the third legislative term and the Perm Krai Legislative Assembly would suggest that Komi residents show roughly the same amount of interest in the work of the new united Perm Krai parliament as they did in the previous parliament of Komi-Permyak Autonomous Okrug. We can thus conclude that the merger with Perm Oblast did not affect the voting behaviour of Komi residents in any significant way.

Taymyr Dolgano-Nenets Autonomous Okrug, Evenk Autonomous Okrug and Krasnoyarsk Krai

Given the more significant political and economic role that Taymyr plays for Krasnoyarsk Krai, as well as the fact that it has a bigger population than Evenk Autonomous Okrug, the statistical data on these two municipal districts contrasts significantly. This state of affairs is the reason why the voting behaviour of the residents of the former Taymyr Dolgano-Nenets Autonomous Okrug is emphasized.

One of the key features of Taymyr Dolgano-Nenets Autonomous Okrug is the trust that the people have in candidates whose professional activities are directly related to Norilsk Nickel, which plays a central role in the development of the former autonomous *okrug* (now a municipal district). Elections for the post of Governor of Taymyr Dolgano-Nenets Autonomous Okrug were held on January 28, 2001. Three self-nominated candidates ran for the position: Gennady Nedelin, who was looking to win a second term as Governor of the *okrug*; Mikhail Steklov, Director of Logistics and Transportation of the Polar Branch of Norilsk Mining Company; and Alexander Khloponin, Chairman of the Board of Norilsk Nickel. Khloponin was elected Governor of Taymyr Dolgano-Nenets Autonomous Okrug, winning 62.80% of the votes, with a 63.94% turnout.

Elections for governor of Evenk Autonomous Okrug were held on April 8, 2001. Voter turnout was 68.28%, with 51.08% of whom voting for eventual winner Boris Zolotaryov.

Early elections for the post of Governor of Krasnoyarsk Krai were held on September 8, 2002, following the tragic death of incumbent Alexander Lebedev, who had served as head of the territory since 1998. Voter turnout was 47.20%. Since none of the candidates received more than 50% of the votes, the decision was taken to hold a second round of elections for the two nominees who had received the most votes: Alexander Uss (27.62% of the votes); and Alexander Khloponin (25.25%). The second round of voting would largely be decided on the sentiments of voters in Norilsk and Taymyr, where turnout had traditionally been very high compared to the rest of the region.

The second round took place on September 22, 2002, with 46.80% of voters turning out. Khloponin was elected governor after receiving 48.07% of the votes. Voter turnout in Taymyr was 54%, approximately 10% higher than the average for the region, and 51% in Krasnoyarsk.

With Alexander Khloponin being elected Governor of Krasnoyarsk Krai, elections for his former post of Governor of Taymyr Dolgano-Nenets Autonomous Okrug were held on January 26, 2003. Voter turnout was 49.82%. Mayor of Norilsk Oleg Budargin was victorious, receiving 68.69% of the votes.

Elections for the State Duma of the Federal Assembly of the Russian Federation of the fourth legislative term were held on December 7, 2003 (Table 12). A total of 50.66% of registered voters in Evenk Autonomous Okrug took part.

Table 12: 2003 State Duma Elections, % of votes

Party	Russia	Krasnoyarsk Krai	Taymyr	Evenk Autonomous Okrug
United Russia	37.56	30	48	52.26
Communist Party of the Russian Federation	12.61	13.5	4.63	4.8
Liberal Democratic Party of Russia	4.54	13	14.73	10.48
Rodina	9.02	17	6.48	8.1

Russian presidential elections were held on March 14, 2004. Voter turnout in Evenk Autonomous Okrug was 63.74%.

Table 13: 2004 Russian Presidential Elections, % of votes

Candidates	Russia	Krasnoyarsk Krai	Taymyr	Evenk Autonomous Okrug
Vladimir Putin	71.31	60.31	79.05	81.09
Nikolay Kharitonov	13.69	11.09	3.9	4.34
Sergey Glazyev	4.1	17.23	4.3	4.56
Irina Khakamada	3.84	4.03	5.58	4.43
Oleg Malyshkin	2.02	2.08	2.23	1.39
Sergey Mironov	0.75	0.65	0.84	0.71

Following the April 17, 2005 referendum on the merger of Taymyr Dolgano-Nenets Autonomous Okrug, Evenk Autonomous Okrug and Krasnoyarsk Krai and the creation of a new constituent entity of the Russian Federation as of January 1, 2007, elections to the Legislative Assembly of Krasnoyarsk Krai of the first legislative term were held on April 15, 2007. Average voter turnout was 34.38%, with the highest turnout being among voters in Evenk Municipal District (over 52%). The Legislative Assembly is made up of 52 deputies, 26 of which are decided by proportional representation, and 26 are elected by majority. Under the proportional representation system, United Russia representatives won 42.52% of the votes, followed by representatives of the Communist Party of the Russian Federation (20.32%), A Just Russia (12.4%), and the Liberal Democratic Party of Russia (11.75%). The preferences of Dudinka residents with regard to the three runners-up were different, with the Liberal Democratic Party receiving 16.27% of the votes, the Communist Party 12.97%, and A Just Russia 7.62%. Under the majoritarian system, two United Russia candidates won seats in Taymyr Dolgano-Nenets Autonomous Okrug – Nikolai Fokin (30.11% of the votes) and Vasily Nechaev (16.54%). The same success was observed in Evenk Autonomous Okrug, with United Russia candidates Anatoly Amosov (34.51%)

and Alexei Nechepurenko (42.51%) being voted to the Legislative Assembly.

The lack of free access to much of the data on elections to the councils of deputies of the Taymyr and Evenk municipal districts meant that we were unable to analyse all legislative terms. Elections to the first legislative term of the Evenk District Council were held in September 2005. Twenty-four deputies from each rural settlement in the district were elected. Deputies were elected for the second legislative term in September 2007. Elections to the Evenk District Council of Deputies of the third legislative term were held on March 13, 2011. The turnout for these elections was 45.37%. Under the proportional system, six United Russia candidates, four Just Russia – For Truth candidates, and one Liberal Democratic Party of Russia won seats in the Council.

Elections to the State Duma of the fifth legislative term were held on December 2, 2007 (Table 14).

Table 14: 2007 State Duma Elections, % of votes

Party	Russia	Krasnoyarsk Krai	Taymyr	Evenk Autonomous Okrug
United Russia	64.3	60.68	71.11	75.02
Communist Party of the Russian Federation	11.57	12.72	5.86	5.62
Liberal Democratic Party of Russia	8.14	10.57	11.2	8.04
A Just Russia	7.74	7.91	5.96	5.85

Russian presidential elections took place on March 2, 2008 (Table 15).

Table 15: 2008 Russian Presidential Elections, % of votes

Candidates	Russia	Krasnoyarsk Krai	Taymyr Region	Evenk Region
Dmitry Medvedev	70.28	62.47	73.59	74.92

| Gennady Zyuganov | 17.72 | 20.62 | 12.01 | 11.65 |
| Vladimir Zhirinovsky | 9.35 | 14.07 | 12.95 | 10.83 |

Elections to the State Duma of the sixth legislative term were held on December 4, 2011 (Table 16).

Table 16: 2011 State Duma Elections, % of votes

Party	Russia	Krasnoyarsk Krai	Taymyr Region	Evenk Region
United Russia	49.32	36.37	54.89	49.23
Communist Party of the Russian Federation	19.19	23,6	12.94	11.31
Liberal Democratic Party of Russia	11.67	17	15,59	13.82
A Just Russia	13.24	15.9	–	20.27

Elections to the Legislative Assembly of Krasnoyarsk Krai of the second legislative term were held that same day. Turnout in the *krai* was 49.4%, with over 50% of Taymyr Dolgano-Nenets Region residents exercising their right to vote (Table 17).

Table 17: Elections to the Legislative Assembly of Krasnoyarsk Krai of the Second Legislative term, % of votes

Party	Krasnoyarsk Krai	Taymyr Dolgano-Nenets Region
United Russia	36.86	54.27
Liberal Democratic Party of Russia	17.48	16.13
Communist Party of the Russian Federation	23.66	13.45
A Just Russia	17.93	–

Russian presidential elections were held on March 4, 2012 (Table 18).

Elections to the Legislative Assembly of Krasnoyarsk Krai of the third legislative term were held on the same day as the presidential elections. Turnout was 36.67% in the *krai* and 40.02% in Taymyr. Of the 52 seats available, 26 were elected by party, and 26 by single-member constituencies. The following parties met the 5% threshold: United Russia (38.5%), Liberal Democratic Party of Russia (20.2%), Communist Party of the Russian Federation (14.7%), Patriots of Russia (6.5%), and A Just Russia (5.4%). United Russia candidates Valery Vengo and Nikolai Fokin were elected to represent the interests of the people of Taymyr Dolgano-Nenets Region, and Valery Farukshin and Anatoly Amosov were elected to do the same for the people of Evenk Region.

Elections to the Evenk District Council of the fourth legislative term were held on September 18, 2016. Voter turnout was 50.84%. United Russia received 59.28% of the votes, followed by the Liberal Democratic Party of Russia (13.57%), the Communist Party of the Russian Federation (9.14%), and A Just Russia (7.65%).

Russian presidential elections took place on March 18, 2018 (Table 20).

Table 20: 2018 Russian Presidential Elections, % of votes

Candidates	Russia	Krasnoyarsk Krai	Taymyr Region	Evenk Region
Vladimir Putin	76.69	74.28	81.1	81.8
Pavel Grudinin	11.77	12.78	7.42	5.83
Vladimir Zhirinovsky	5.65	7.39	7.1	8.23
Ksenia Sobchak	1.68	1.61	1.24	1.25
Grigory Yavlinsky	1.05	0.89	0.44	0.35
Boris Titov	0.76	0.67	0.4	0.41

Table 21: Voter Turnout for Elections to the State Duma in 2003–2016, %

Year	Russia	Krasnoyarsk Krai	Taymyr Region	Evenk Region
2003	55.67	42.8	51.8	50.66
2007	63.71	59.54	57.09	62.7
2011	60.21	49.4	50	53.12
2016	47.88	36.67	40.02	52.66

Table 22: Voter Turnout for Presidential Elections in 2004–2018, %

Year	Russia	Krasnoyarsk Krai	Taymyr Region	Evenk Region
2004	64.38	51.12	64.7	63.74
2008	69.81	61.27	60.26	64.81
2012	65.34	59.53	62.44	55.38
2018	67.54	60.34	63.03	66.24

We analysed the results of the presidential elections in 2004–2018, the State Duma elections in 2003–2016, and elections to *krai*, *okrug* and district parliaments. The Liberal Democratic Party of Russia has proven to be popular throughout Krasnoyarsk Krai, and in Taymyr in particular. This trend is observed in elections at all levels, and it is especially remarkable in comparison with the figures for Russia as a whole. At the same time, support for the Communist Party in Taymyr and Evenk is weak, although in Krasnoyarsk Krai it is more or less in line with the average for Russia, occasionally even slightly higher. As for voter behaviour following the 2005 merger, we can see that little changed in Taymyr Dolgano-Nenets Region and Evenk Region. The growth in support for the Liberal Democratic Party in these regions, for example, reflected the general trend in Russia. The jump is voter turnout for the 2007 State Duma elections and its subsequent gradual decline were also in line with the general trend across the country. We cannot thus state that the merger of the reasons was the main reason for the decline in voter turnout in the *krai* or its new regions (indicators for these regions were among the highest in the *krai*, but slightly lower than the national average). In any case, both before and after the merger, Taymyr Dolgano-Nenets Autonomous Okrug/Region and Evenk Autonomous Okrug/Region demonstrate an exceedingly high level of support for the ruling party and the incumbent president compared to the average for Krasnoyarsk Krai, and for Russia as a whole.

Koryak Autonomous Okrug and Kamchatka Oblast

Some background information about Koryak Autonomous Okrug before we can proceed to our analysis of this case. As A. Kynev noted in his article entitled "The December 19, 2004 Elections to the Koryak Okrug Duma: Electoral Experiments Against the Backdrop of the Collapse of Housing and Communal Services": "The situation in Koryak Autonomous Okrug is so hopeless and depressing that the majority of the population really has 'nothing to lose,' meaning that the authorities can't use pressure or bribery to line everyone up in some kind of vertical. The result is that local political life is remarkably active, and we see constant conflicts between the Governor and the Duma, the district and local authorities, disputes, disagreements, litigation. Elections in Koryak Autonomous Okrug never fail to fascinate thanks to their plurality and unpredictability, and this small okrug is surprisingly rich in all sorts of electoral experiments" (Kynev n.d.).

Gubernatorial elections were held in Koryak Autonomous Okrug on December 3, 2000. Five candidates were running for the post:

1. Valentina Bronevich – Governor of Koryak Autonomous Okrug;
2. Sergei Leushkin – Trade Advisor at the Embassy of the Russian Federation in North Korea;
3. Vladimir Loginov – CEO of Koryakgeoldobycha construction company;
4. Yevgeny Mel – CEO of LESh;
5. Mikhail Popov – Chief Administrator of Palana urban locality.

Voter turnout for the election was 63.38%. Vladimir Loginov was appointed Governor of Koryak Autonomous Okrug, having received 50.68% of the votes.

Elections to the Koryak Autonomous Okrug Duma of the third legislative term were held on the same day, where 12 seats were contested – 8 by majoritarian system in two-member constituencies, and four in the general constituency. A total of 63.31% of eligible residents turned out to vote, with nine of the twelve seats being filled.

Table 23: 2003 State Duma Elections, % of votes

Party	Russia	Kamchatka Oblast	Koryak Autonomous Okrug
United Russia	37.56	35	47.35
Communist Party of the Russian Federation	12.61	8.6	8.53
Liberal Democratic Party of Russia	4.54	16.8	12.98
Rodina	9.02	8.2	5.91

Russian presidential elections were held on March 14, 2004 (Table 24).

Table 24: 2004 Russian Presidential Election, % of votes

Candidates	Russia	Kamchatka Oblast	Koryak Autonomous Okrug
Vladimir Putin	71.31	71.83	84.34
Nikolay Kharitonov	13.69	9.25	4.89
Sergey Glazyev	4.1	5.58	2.37
Irina Khakamada	3.84	5.05	3.27
Oleg Malyshkin	2.02	2.59	1.66
Sergey Mironov	0.75	0.89	0.79

Elections for Governor of Koryak Autonomous Okrug were held on the same day as the Russian presidential elections. Turnout was

71.88%. Ten candidates ran for office, all self-nominated, with incumbent Governor Vladimir Loginov (37.43%) and the *okrug*'s prosecutor-general B. Chuev (17.92%) receiving the most votes. A second round of voting was held on April 4, 2004 for the people decide between these two candidates. Turnout for this round was 66.1%. As a result, Vladimir Loginov was re-elected Governor of Koryak Autonomous Okrug after securing 50.88% of the votes. The share of votes against all candidates was 7.16%.

Elections to the Koryak Autonomous Okrug Duma of the fourth legislative term were held on December 19, 2004, with 38.59% of voters turning out to cast their vote. The opposition scored a huge victory in the elections, with the Communist Party of the Russian Federation receiving 35.13% of the votes (three seats), followed by United Russia with 22.68% of the votes (two seats; United Russia candidates had received 48% of the votes in December 2003, thus losing more than half of their voter base). The Russian Party of Pensioners and the Liberal Democratic Party of Russia, both of which positioned themselves as opposition parties but were in fact supporters of the governor, received 11.38% and 9.89% of the votes, respectively. A total of 12.65% of the votes were cast against all candidates.

All three candidates from the Communist Party of the Russian Federation were elected in the single five-member constituency: Chair of the Koryak Autonomous Okrug Duma N. Solodyakova (41.29%), Federation Council member A. Suvorov (31.62%), and former head of Karaginsky District V. Atyashkin (20.14%). The other two successful candidates were also supported by the Communists: former prosecutor-general of Koryak Autonomous Okrug B. Chuev (26.25%), who had run against Vladimir Loginov in the gubernatorial elections, and former vice-governor V. Myshlyaev (16.14%), a wealthy businessman by local standards who had had a falling out with Loginov in early 2004 and had gubernatorial ambitions of his own. Some 12.56% of voters in the five-mandate constituency voted against all candidates. All of the United Russia candidates in the five-mandate constituency received fewer than 12.56% of the votes. The opposition thus won 8 of the 12 seats in the Duma, or a two-thirds majority, which would make life difficult for the governor moving forward. This represents the biggest success of opposition forces in elections to regional assemblies in the "Putin era," and United Russia's biggest failure to date.

On October 23, 2005, a referendum was held on the merger of Koryak Autonomous Okrug and Kamchatka Oblast. The new constituent entity of the Russian Federation was duly established on July 1, 2007.

Elections to the State Duma of the Federal Assembly of the fifth legislative term were held on December 2, 2007 (Table 25).

Table 25: 2007 State Duma Elections, % of votes

Party	Russia	Kamchatka Krai	Koryak Okrug
United Russia	64.3	68.35	71
Communist Party of the Russian Federation	11.57	6.93	7.26
Liberal Democratic Party of Russia	8.14	9.99	9.03
A Just Russia	7.74	5.28	4.14

That very same day, elections to the Legislative Assembly of Kamchatka Krai of the first legislative term were held. Turnout in Kamchatka Krai as a whole was 56.43%, compared to 56.87% in Koryak Okrug (Table 26).

Table 26: Election Results for Kamchatka Krai and Koryak Okrug, %

Party	Kamchatka Krai	Koryak Okrug
United Russia	62.89	64.88
Communist Party of the Russian Federation	11.38	13.6
Liberal Democratic Party of Russia	12.86	8.78
Patriots of Russia	7.38	4.46

Russian presidential elections took place on March 2, 2008 (Table 27).

Table 27: 2008 Russian Presidential Elections, % of votes

Candidates	Russia	Kamchatka Krai	Koryak Okrug
Dmitry Medvedev	70.28	69.39	74.47
Gennady Zyuganov	17.72	14.83	11.72
Vladimir Zhirinovsky	9.35	12.92	11.51

Two sets of elections were held concurrently on December 4, 2011 – elections to the State Duma of the Federal Assembly of the sixth legislative term (Table 28), and elections to the Legislative Assembly of Kamchatka Krai of the second legislative term (Table 29).

Table 28: 2011 State Duma Elections, % of votes

Party	Russia	Kamchatka Krai	Koryak Okrug
United Russia	49.32	45.25	60.76
Communist Party of the Russian Federation	19.19	17.08	8.5
Liberal Democratic Party of Russia	11.67	18.61	14.36
A Just Russia	13.24	10.06	11.06

Table 29: Results of Elections to the Legislative Assembly of Kamchatka Krai (Turnout: Kamchatka Krai – 53.47%; Koryak Okrug – 60.87%)

Party	Kamchatka Krai, %	Koryak Okrug, %
United Russia	44.83	61.29
Communist Party of the Russian Federation	17.63	8.09
Liberal Democratic Party of Russia	19.77	14.97
A Just Russia	10.77	11.65

Presidential elections were held in Russia on March 4, 2012 (Table 30).

Table 30: 2012 Russian Presidential Elections, % of votes

Candidates	Russia	Kamchatka Krai	Koryak Okrug
Vladimir Putin	63.6	59.84	74.19
Gennady Zyuganov	17.18	15.97	9.14
Vladimir Zhirinovsky	6.22	10.54	7.85
Sergey Mironov	3.85	3.47	2.68
Mikhail Prokhorov	7.98	8.95	5.24

Snap gubernatorial elections were held in Kamchatka Krai on September 13, 2015.

Voter turnout was 31.86% in Kamchatka Krai, and 48.92% in Koryak Okrug.

Five candidates ran for the post of Governor, with United Russia representative Vladimir Ilyukhin winning with an absolute majority (75.4% in Kamchatka Krai, and 71.73% in Koryak Okrug).

Elections to the State Duma of the Federal Assembly of the seventh legislative term were held on September 18, 2016 (Table 31). Elections to the third legislative term of the Legislative Assembly of Kamchatka Krai were held concurrently (Table 32).

Table 31: 2016 State Duma Elections, % of votes

Party	Russia	Kamchatka Krai	Koryak Okrug
United Russia	54.2	46.7	56.23
Communist Party of the Russian Federation	13.34	12.59	8.26
Liberal Democratic Party of Russia	13.14	21.31	20.06
A Just Russia	6.22	4.42	2.59

Table 32: Results of Elections to the Legislative Assembly of Kamchatka Krai (Turnout: Kamchatka Krai – 38.35%; Koryak Okrug – 49.7%)

Party	Kamchatka Krai, %	Koryak Okrug, %
United Russia	48.31	58.07
Communist Party of the Russian Federation	15.15	9.81

Table 18: 2012 Russian Presidential Elections, % of votes

Candidates	Russia	Krasnoyarsk Krai	Taymyr Region	Evenk Region
Vladimir Putin	63.6	6.16	73.52	68.32
Gennady Zyuganov	17.18	18.03	9.3	10.76
Vladimir Zhirinovsky	6.22	8.61	7.75	6.74
Sergey Mironov	3.85	3.54	2.69	3.54
Mikhail Prokhorov	7.98	8.42	5.68	9.37

Elections to the Taymyr Dolgano-Nenets District Council of Deputies of the third legislative term were held on September 8, 2013, with a turnout of 35%. Twenty seats were contested: ten in single-member constituency and ten in the okrug-wide constituency. United Russia candidates won eight of the seats in the single-member constituencies, with two self-nominees taking the remaining spots. Seven of the seats in the okrug-wide constituency were also taken by United Russia candidates, two were won by Liberal Democratic candidates, and one by a candidate for A Just Russia.

Elections to the State Duma of the Federal Assembly of the seventh legislative term took place on September 18, 2016 (Table 19).

Table 19: 2016 State Duma Elections, % of votes

Party	Russia	Krasnoyarsk Krai	Taymyr Region	Evenk Region
United Russia	54.2	40.45	54.19	56.66
Communist Party of the Russian Federation	13.34	14.41	7.43	8.07
Liberal Democratic Party of Russia	13.14	20.26	20.72	17.03
A Just Russia	6.22	4.86	3.79	5.71

| Liberal Democratic Party of Russia | 22.98 | 21.16 |
| A Just Russia | 7.01 | 4.85 |

Russian presidential elections were held on March 18, 2018 (Table 33).

Table 33: 2018 Russian Presidential Elections, % of votes

Candidates	Russia	Kamchatka Krai	Koryak Okrug
Vladimir Putin	76.69	69.44	79.92
Pavel Grudinin	11.77	16.95	6.73
Vladimir Zhirinovsky	5.65	8.48	9.46
Ksenia Sobchak	1.68	1.37	0.93

The dynamics of voter turnout for elections to the State Duma in 2003–2016 and the presidential elections in 2004–2018 are presented in Table 34 and Table 35, respectively.

Table 34: Voter Turnout for Elections to the State Duma in 2003–2016, %

Year	Russia	Kamchatka Oblast/Krai	Koryak Autonomous Okrug/Koryak Okrug
2003	55.67	51	62.17
2007	63.71	61.45	59.98
2011	60.21	53.47	60.87
2016	47.88	39.55	54.48

Table 35: Voter Turnout for Presidential Elections in 2004–2018, %

Year	Russia	Kamchatka Oblast/Krai	Koryak Autonomous Okrug/Koryak Okrug
2004	64.38	57.84	71.88
2008	69.81	59	71.28
2012	65.34	61.09	72.43
2018	67.54	67.74	83.86

Based on the data on federal and regional elections, it can be argued that the merger of Koryak Autonomous Okrug into Kamchatka Oblast did not affect the traditionally high turnout among the residents of Koryak Autonomous Okrug, given that the average turnout showed a downward trend both nationally and across Kamchatka Krai. What is more, Koryak Okrug residents have demonstrated a consistently high level of support for the ruling party and the incumbent president compared to the national average and the average for Kamchatka Krai – both before and after the merger. As for elections to the Legislative Assembly of Kamchatka Krai, Koryak Okrug are again more active in the political process than the people in the *krai* as a whole. The party preferences of people in Koryak Okrug and Kamchatka Krai also differ: there is greater support for United Russia in Koryak Okrug than in Kamchatka Krai, coupled with a lower level of support for the ideology of the Communist Party of the Russian Federation (a similar shift in the distribution of votes for the Liberal Democratic Party of Russia and A Just Russia in the federal elections is also observed).

Ust-Orda Buryat Autonomous Okrug and Irkutsk Oblast

Elections to the Ust-Orda Buryat Autonomous Okrug Duma of the third legislative term were held on November 19, 2000, with a turnout of 54.04%. Fifteen deputies were elected (one from each constituency).

Elections to the State Duma of the Federal Assembly of the fourth legislative term took place on December 7, 2003 (Table 36).

Table 36: 2003 State Duma Elections, % of votes

Party	Russia	Irkutsk Oblast	Ust-Orda Buryat Autonomous Okrug
United Russia	37.56	32.8	46.37
Communist Party of the Russian Federation	12.61	16.3	10.2

| Liberal Democratic Party of Russia | 5.54 | 16.4 | 7.45 |
| Rodina | 9.02 | 7.3 | 2.25 |

Presidential elections were held in the Russian Federation on March 14, 2004 (Table 37).

Table 37: 2004 Russian Presidential Elections, % of votes

Candidates	Russia	Irkutsk Oblast	Ust-Orda Buryat Autonomous Okrug
Vladimir Putin	71.31	61.92	72.76
Nikolay Kharitonov	13.69	16.78	14.34
Sergey Glazyev	4.1	5.75	2.13
Irina Khakamada	3.84	5.57	4.83
Oleg Malyshkin	2.02	3.99	2.25
Sergey Mironov	0.75	1	0.94

The referendum on the merger of Irkutsk Oblast and Ust-Orda Buryat Autonomous Okrug took place in Irkutsk Oblast on April 16, 2006.

The new constituent entity of the Russian Federation was created on January 1, 2008.

Elections to the State Duma of the fifth legislative term were held on December 2, 2007 (Table 38).

Table 38: 2007 State Duma Elections, % of votes

Party	Russia	Irkutsk Oblast	Ust-Orda Buryat Autonomous Okrug
United Russia	64.3	58.69	71.73
Communist Party of the Russian Federation	11.57	10.89	5.74
Liberal Democratic Party of Russia	8.14	11.46	4.65
A Just Russia	7.74	9.06	4.98

Russian presidential elections were held on March 2, 2008 (Table 39).

Table 39: 2008 Russian Presidential Elections, % of votes

Candidates	Russia	Irkutsk Oblast	Ust-Orda Buryat Autonomous Okrug
Dmitry Medvedev	70.28	61.24	74.09
Gennady Zyuganov	17.72	21.82	16.31
Vladimir Zhirinovsky	9.35	14.05	7.83

Elections to the Legislative Assembly of Irkutsk Oblast of the first legislative term were held on October 12, 2008 (Table 40). The Legislative Assembly was elected for a term of five years and was made up of 50 deputies, including:

- 21 deputies elected from single-member constituencies created as a result of the establishment of the new constituent entity of the Russian Federation, with the exception of the administrative and territorial unit that had been granted special status (Ust-Orda Buryat Autonomous Okrug);
- 4 deputies elected from a multi-member constituency created on the administrative and territorial unit that had been granted special status (Ust-Orda Buryat Autonomous Okrug)
- 25 deputies elected from a single constituency proportionally to the number of votes cast for regional lists of candidates for members of parliament nominated by political parties that had met the threshold of 7% of the votes in the elections (United Russia – 15 deputies; Liberal Democratic Party of Russia – 4 deputies; Communist Party of the Russian Federation 4 deputies; A Just Russia: Rodina/Pensioners/Life – 2 deputies).

The Agrarian Party of Russia received the highest share of votes in Ust-Orda Buryat Autonomous Okrug (20.5%), although it failed to reach the threshold of 7% in Irkutsk Oblast to receive a seat in parliament.

Table 40: Results of Elections to the Legislative Assembly of Irkutsk Oblast of the First Legislative term (Turnout: Irkutsk Oblast – 38.49%; Ust-Orda Buryat Autonomous Okrug – 64.5%), %

Party	Irkutsk Oblast	Ust-Orda Buryat Autonomous Okrug
United Russia	49.45	52.18
Liberal Democratic Party of Russia	15.07	8.59
Communist Party of the Russian Federation	13.25	8.46
A Just Russia: Rodina/Pensioners/Life	8.11	5.55

Elections to the State Duma of the Federal Assembly of the Russian Federation of the sixth legislative term were held on December 4, 2011 (Table 41).

Table 41: 2011 State Duma Elections, % of votes

Party	Russia	Irkutsk Oblast	Ust-Orda Buryat Autonomous Okrug
United Russia	49.32	34.93	56.78
Communist Party of the Russian Federation	19.19	27.79	21.44
Liberal Democratic Party of Russia	11.67	17.34	9.34
A Just Russia	13.24	13.36	8.74

Presidential elections were held in the Russian Federation on March 4, 2012 (Table 42).

Table 42: 2012 Russian Presidential Elections, % of votes

Candidates	Russia	Irkutsk Oblast	Ust-Orda Buryat Autonomous Okrug
Vladimir Putin	63.6	55.45	67.96
Gennady Zyuganov	17.18	22.57	19.03
Vladimir Zhirinovsky	6.22	8.24	5.02
Sergey Mironov	3.85	3.84	2.52
Mikhail Prokhorov	7.98	8.76	4.71

Elections to the Legislative Assembly of Irkutsk Oblast took place on September 8, 2013 (Table 43).

Under the Charter of Irkutsk Oblast, Legislative Assembly was elected for a term of five years and was made up of 45 deputies, including 23 from party lists and 22 from single-member districts (Ust-Orda Buryat Autonomous Okrug would be a single-member constituency from this moment forth). Four parties gained seats in the Legislative Assembly: United Russia» (32 seats), the Communist Party of the Russian Federation (6 seats), the Liberal Democratic Party of Russia (4 seats), and Civic Platform (2 seats).

Table 43: Results of Elections to the Legislative Assembly of Irkutsk Oblast of the Second Legislative term (Turnout: Irkutsk Oblast – 25.29%; Ust-Orda Buryat Autonomous Okrug – 55.07%), %

Party	Irkutsk Oblast	Ust-Orda Buryat Autonomous Okrug
United Russia	42.36	59.68
Liberal Democratic Party of Russia	11.28	8.08
Communist Party of the Russian Federation	18.87	12.05
Civic Platform	8.51	4.6

The powers of then Governor of Irkutsk Oblast Sergei Yeroshchenko were set to expire in May 2017, but he ended up resigning in May 2015 and asked President Vladimir Putin for permission to run again in order to "rally the support of the people of the region for his plans" (TASS 2015).

Two rounds of snap elections were subsequently held in Irkutsk Oblast (Table 44). The first took place on September 13, 2015, with Sergei Yeroshchenko and Communist Party candidate Sergei Levchenko receiving the most votes. The second round of voting was held two weeks later, on September 27, 2015, resulting in a victory for the Communist Party candidate. Voter turnout in Irkutsk Oblast was 29.19% (for the first round) and 37.22% (for the second round), and 35.12% (for the first round) and 41.97% (for the second round) in Ust-Orda Buryat Autonomous Okrug.

Table 44: Irkutsk Oblast Gubernatorial Elections, %

Candidate	Irkutsk Oblast	Ust-Orda Buryat Autonomous Okrug	Irkutsk Oblast	Ust-Orda Buryat Autonomous Okrug
	Round 1		Round 2	
Sergei Yeroshchenko	49.6	58.62	41.46	49.04
Sergei Levchenko	36.6	33.61	56.39	49.45

Elections to the State Duma of the Federal Assembly of the seventh legislative term took place on September 18, 2016 (Table 45).

Russian presidential elections were held on March 18, 2018 (Table 46).

ELECTORAL ASPECT 115

Table 45: 2016 State Duma Elections, % of votes

Party	Russia	Irkutsk Oblast	Ust-Orda Buryat Autonomous Okrug
United Russia	54.2	39.8	52.43
Communist Party of the Russian Federation	13.34	24.05	24.82
Liberal Democratic Party of Russia	13.14	17.02	10.64
A Just Russia	6.22	5.18	2.42

Table 46: 2018 Russian Presidential Elections, % of votes

Candidates	Russia	Irkutsk Oblast	Ust-Orda Buryat Autonomous Okrug
Vladimir Putin	76.69	73.06	79.69
Pavel Grudinin	11.77	15.92	12.95
Vladimir Zhirinovsky	5.65	6.44	4.38
Ksenia Sobchak	1.68	1.21	0.91
Grigory Yavlinsky	1.05	0.72	0.3
Boris Titov	0.76	0.5	0.25

Elections to the Legislative Assembly of Irkutsk Oblast of the third legislative term were held on September 9, 2018 (Table 47).

Table 47: Results of Elections to the Legislative Assembly of Irkutsk Oblast of the Third Legislative term (Turnout: Irkutsk Oblast – 26.33%; Ust-Orda Buryat Autonomous Okrug – 47.42%), %

Party	Irkutsk Oblast	Ust-Orda Buryat Autonomous Okrug
United Russia	27.83	36.37
Liberal Democratic Party of Russia	15.8	11.19
Communist Party of the Russian Federation	33.94	34.21
A Just Russia	7.04	5.76

The United Russia candidate was elected in Ust-Orda Buryat Autonomous Okrug

Table 48: Voter Turnout for Elections to the State Duma in 2003–2016, %

Year	Russia	Irkutsk Oblast	Ust-Orda Buryat Autonomous Okrug
2003	55.67	45.6	68.8
2007	63.71	58.8	75.4
2011	60.21	47.15	59.71
2016	47.88	32.92	47.17

Table 49: Voter Turnout for Presidential Elections in 2004–2018, %

Year	Russia	Irkutsk Oblast	Ust-Orda Buryat Autonomous Okrug
2004	64.38	52.44	68.87
2008	69.81	65	85.15
2012	65.34	56.03	61.5
2018	67.54	55.68	58.66

An analysis of the voting behaviour of Ust-Orda residents in federal and regional elections before and after the merger with Irkutsk Oblast demonstrates a generally high turnout, with overwhelming pro-government sentiments. While data on voter turnout for the State Duma elections indicates an overall decline in political participation in the *okrug* since 2007, this reflects the general trend observed in the region throughout the country, which makes it less likely that the merger had a negative effect on voting behaviour. At the same time, Ust-Orda residents typically demonstrate significantly greater activity in regional elections (elections to the Legislative Assembly and gubernatorial elections) than residents in Irkutsk Oblast as a whole. The most likely explanation for this is the widespread use of administrative pressure to ensure a high voter turnover and a cultural tradition that does not welcome protest sentiments and opposition. As for the party preferences of the residents of Ust-Orda Buryat Autonomous Okrug, United Russia consistently receives the most votes regardless of the type of election, and affects the number of votes for the Communist Party of the Russian Federation and the Liberal Democratic Party of Russia considerably (both perform significantly worse than in Irkutsk Region, and in the country as a whole). That notwithstanding, the Communist Party typically receives greater support than the Liberal Democratic Party in Ust-Orda Buryat Autonomous Okrug.

Agin-Buryat Autonomous Okrug and Chita Oblast

Elections to the State Duma of the fourth legislative term were held on December 7, 2003 (Table 50).

Presidential elections took place in the Russian Federation on March 14, 2004 (Table 51).

Elections to the Agin-Buryat Autonomous Okrug Duma of the fourth legislative term were held on October 30, 2005.

Voter turnout was 66.31%, with United Russia receiving 66.64% of the votes, the Communist Party of the Russian Federation 15.07%, and the Liberal Democratic Party of Russia 9.45%.

Table 50: 2003 State Duma Elections, % of votes

Party	Russia	Chita Oblast	Agin-Buryat Autonomous Okrug
United Russia	37.56	58.1	58.08
Communist Party of the Russian Federation	12.61	7,.2	7.19
Liberal Democratic Party of Russia	4.54	6.5	6.5
Rodina	9.02	3	3.04

Table 51: 2004 Russian Presidential Elections, % of votes

Candidates	Russia	Chita Oblast	Agin-Buryat Autonomous Okrug
Vladimir Putin	71.31	72.49	84.25
Nikolay Kharitonov	13.69	14.78	7.82
Sergey Glazyev	4.1	3.11	1.66
Irina Khakamada	3.84	2.57	3.24
Oleg Malyshkin	2.02	2.86	1.19
Sergey Mironov	0.75	0.93	0.6

The referendum on the merger of Agin-Buryat Autonomous Okrug and Chita Oblast into a new constituent entity of the Russian Federation – Zabaykalsky Krai – was held in Agin-Buryat Autonomous Okrug on March 11, 2007.

Elections to the State Duma of the fifth legislative term were held on December 2, 2007 (Table 52).

Table 52: 2007 State Duma Elections, % of votes

Party	Russia	Chita Oblast	Agin-Buryat Autonomous Okrug
United Russia	64.3	62.75	83.24
Communist Party of the Russian Federation	11.57	8.74	4.5
Liberal Democratic Party of Russia	8.14	15.03	6.07
A Just Russia	7.74	7.04	2.37

Presidential elections were held in the Russian Federation on March 2, 2008 (Table 53).

Elections to the Legislative Assembly of Zabaykalsky Krai took place on October 12, 2008 (Table 54). Fifty deputies were elected to the assembly, including: 25 from single-member constituencies (Agin-Buryat Autonomous Okrug made up multi-member constituency No. 13); 25 from the single regional constituency – regional branches of political parties (14 from United

Russia, 4 from the Communist Party of the Russian Federation, 3 from the Liberal Democratic Party of Russia, 2 from A Just Russia, and 2 from the Agrarian Party of Russia).

Voter turnout in was 45.14%Zabaykalsky Krai, and 73.06% in Agin-Buryat Okrug.

Table 53: 2008 Russian Presidential Elections, % of votes

Candidates	Russia	Zabaykalsky Krai	Agin-Buryat Okrug
Dmitry Medvedev	70.28	65.81	81.55
Gennady Zyuganov	17.72	17.35	9.73
Vladimir Zhirinovsky	9.35	14.75	7.5

Table 54: Results of Elections to the Legislative Assembly of Zabaykalsky Krai of the First Legislative term, %

Party	Zabaykalsky Krai	Agin-Buryat Okrug
United Russia	54.81	74.99
Communist Party of the Russian Federation	13.41	7.5
Liberal Democratic Party of Russia	10.81	7.02
A Just Russia	9.3	4.18
Agrarian Party of Russia	6.9	4.7

Elections to the State Duma of the sixth legislative term were held on December 4, 2011 (Table 55).

Table 55: 2011 State Duma Elections, % of votes

Party	Russia	Zabaykalsky Krai	Agin-Buryat Okrug
United Russia	49.32	43.28	62.48
Communist Party of the Russian Federation	19.19	18.64	14.35
Liberal Democratic Party of Russia	11.67	19.18	7.63
A Just Russia	13.24	14.1	12.08

Russian presidential elections were held on March 4, 2012 (Table 56).

Table 56: 2012 Russian Presidential Elections, % of votes

Candidates	Russia	Zabaykalsky Krai	Agin-Buryat Okrug
Vladimir Putin	63.6	65.69	74.55
Gennady Zyuganov	17.18	14.37	11.38
Vladimir Zhirinovsky	6.22	9.95	3.98
Sergey Mironov	3.85	3.01	2.8
Mikhail Prokhorov	7.98	5.91	6.67

Gubernatorial elections took place in Zabaykalsky Krai on September 8, 2013. Turnout in was 33.24% in the *krai*, and 56.63% in Agin-Buryat Okrug. Acting Governor Konstantin Ilkovsky representing A Just Russia was elected new Governor of Zabaykalsky Krai with 71.63% of the votes (85.52% in Agin-Buryat Okrug).

Elections to the Zabaykalsky Krai Duma of the second legislative term were held on the same day as the gubernatorial elections (Table 57). Fifty seats were contested, of which 25 were from single-member constituencies, and 25 were from the regional electoral list.

The distribution of seats according to the results of the voting were as follows: United Russia (36 seats); Communist Party of the Russian Federation (4 seats); Liberal Democratic Party of Russia (4 seats); A Just Russia (4 seats); independents (2 seats).

Table 57: Results of Elections to the Legislative Assembly of Zabaykalsky Krai of the Second Legislative term, %

Party	Zabaykalsky Krai	Agin-Buryat Okrug
United Russia	43.09	63.22
Communist Party of the Russian Federation	14.15	8.08
Liberal Democratic Party of Russia	13.38	5.19
A Just Russia	10.45	12.1

Elections to the State Duma of the Federal Assembly of the seventh legislative term took place on September 18, 2016 (Table 58).

A snap election for the post of Governor of Zabaykalsky Krai was held that same day following the resignation of Konstantin Ilkovsky, with Acting Governor Natalya Zhdanova, who had previously held the post of Chair of the Legislative Assembly of Zabaykalsky Krai, emerging victorious after winning 54.39% of the votes in the *krai*, and 71.76% of the votes in Agin-Buryat Okrug.

Table 58: 2016 State Duma Elections, % of votes

Party	Russia	Zabaykalsky Krai	Agin-Buryat Okrug
United Russia	54.2	39.87	56.99
Communist Party of the Russian Federation	13.34	15.93	12.99
Liberal Democratic Party of Russia	13.14	26.4	13.34
A Just Russia	6.22	4.17	5.44

Russian presidential elections were held on March 18, 2018 (Table 59).

Table 59: 2018 Russian Presidential Elections, % of votes

Candidates	Russia	Zabaykalsky Krai	Agin-Buryat Okrug
Vladimir Putin	76.69	72.03	72.29
Pavel Grudinin	11.77	13.62	18.14
Vladimir Zhirinovsky	5.65	10	5.43
Ksenia Sobchak	1.68	1.04	1.61
Grigory Yavlinsky	1.05	0.46	0.35
Boris Titov	0.76	0.46	0.44

Elections to the Legislative Assembly of Zabaykalsky Krai of the third legislative term were held on September 9, 2018 (Table 60). A mixed electoral system was used: of the 50 seats available, 25 were elected from party lists in a single constituency (by proportional system), and 25 were elected from single-member constituencies (by majoritarian system). The threshold for getting into the regional parliament under the proportional system was 5%, with candidates in the *okrug*s having to secure a relative majority of votes. Turnout was 22.04% in Zabaykalsky Krai, and 46.86% in Agin-Buryat Okrug.

The data on the results of the federal and regional elections shows a high level of political involvement among the inhabitants of Agin-Buryat Okrug, together with a preponderance of pro-government sentiments, regardless of the period of consideration – i.e., both before and after the merger with Chita Oblast. Voter turnout is consistently higher in Agin-Buryat Okrug than in Russia as a whole, as well as in Chita Oblast/Zabaykalsky Krai.

Table 60: Results of Elections to the Legislative Assembly of Zabaykalsky Krai of the Third Legislative term, %

Party	Zabaykalsky Krai	Agin-Buryat Okrug
United Russia	28.3	49.71
Communist Party of the Russian Federation	24.59	20.47
Liberal Democratic Party of Russia	24.6	10.17
A Just Russia	8.97	11.97
Russian Party of Pensioners	6.04	3.97

Table 61: Voter Turnout for Elections to the State Duma in 2003–2016, %

Year	Russia	Chita Oblast/Zabaykalsky Krai	Agin-Buryat (Autonomous) Okrug
2003	55.67	50.6	68.9
2007	63.71	66.29	86.42
2011	60.21	53.58	69.54
2016	47.88	36.46	53.25

Table 62: Voter Turnout for Presidential Elections in 2004–2018, %

Year	Russia	Chita Oblast/Zabaykalsky Krai	Agin-Buryat (Autonomous) Okrug
2004	64.38	54.76	73.82
2008	69.81	70	88.2
2012	65.34	59.97	72.56
2018	67.54	52.38	67.54

The trend towards lower turnouts for elections to the State Duma that was observed across the country is also evident in Agin-Buryat Okrug, but to a far lesser degree. What is more, political participation among Agin-Buryat residents spiked during the 2008 presidential elections, shortly after the merger of the two constituent entities. As for party preferences, the people of Agin-Buryat Okrug are more likely to vote (after United Russia) for Communist Party of the Russian Federation than for the Liberal Democratic Party, although the difference is negligible. A Just Russia appears to have gained popularity in recent years.

Judging by the results of the federal and regional elections in all five cases, we can say that the mergers did not directly affect the voting behaviour of the people in the former autonomous *okrugs*. No sharp downturns or upturns in electoral activity were observed, neither were there any major changes in party preferences. Voter turnout in all of the *okrugs* that have been merged into larger constituent entities of the Russian Federation remains high, which can be explained by the widespread use of administrative pressure (as confirmed by the data obtained during in-depth interviews), as well as the influence of local traditions and ways of thinking that do not welcome oppositionist sentiments.

The drop-off in voter turnout for the State Duma elections after 2007 is reflective of a nationwide phenomenon, which means that federal reform cannot be posited as the main reason for the lower political activity of the people in the territories that had been merged into larger constituent entities. United Russia has been the most popular party in all of the former autonomous okrugs throughout the period we are looking at, receiving more support than the national average, and the average for the krais/oblasts to which they belong. There are differences when it comes to the second-most popular party, however. For example, the Liberal Democratic Party of Russia enjoys extensive support in Parma, Taymyr, Evenk Region and Koryak Okrug, while the Communist Party of the Russian Federation traditionally wins more votes in the Buryat regions. In the first case, this can be explained by the presence of opposition sentiments, while nostalgia for the communist past appears to be the reason in the second case. With all that said, this study found no evidence that party preferences are based on the attitude of the parties towards federal reform.

The Socio-Economic Aspect

Maria Tislenko

Our three-year study of the consequences of the Russian regions' enlargement in the 2000s allowed us to collect enough evidence to suggest that the mergers were aimed primarily at increasing governability and strengthening the "power vertical". Nevertheless, in terms of public policy, the process of merging constituent entities was aimed at the development of the territories at the level of discourse to legitimize the changes. Most of the negative consequences were obvious not only for the local elites, but also for the people living in the regions that were to be merged into larger entities – from reduced economic powers because of the fiscal autonomy loss to the disappearance of previously autonomous territories from the federal agenda. The enlargement of the regions was at odds with the interests of the merged territories, although the comprehension of this fact should not have had a negative impact on the course of the reforms, and especially on the results of the referendums, where the populations of both constituent entities were intended to be allowed to decide on whether a merger was what they actually wanted. In this respect, the federal authorities and regional officials who were responsible for implementing t the reform used various strategies to convince the people why merging territories is a good thing.

Two main strategies can be identified here. The first was the leitmotif of "We have always been together, so becoming one will only strengthen the way things already are." The rationale behind this thinking was that the Soviet authorities had often approached the issue administrative and territorial division in a rather arbitrary fashion, as well as the fact that the centrifugal forces that were set in motion after the collapse of the USSR had allowed Koryak Autonomous Okrug, Komi-Permyak Autonomous Okrug, Agin-Buryat Autonomous Okrug and other *matryoshka* regions to be given special status. Economic ties between the relevant pairs of constituent entities of the Russian Federation were indeed strong:

Ust-Orda Buryat Autonomous Okrug and Agin-Buryat Autonomous Okrug agricultural produce was sold on the markets of Irkutsk and Chita Oblasts, respectively; Komi-Permyak timber was delivered, among other places, to woodworking plants in Perm Oblast, and so on. This provided a compelling argument for the "marriage" of the respective regions, although opponents were quick to point out that the nuptials were unequal and inequitable (Dmitriev 2007).

The second strategy was to convince the people that merger would foster the socioeconomic development of the respective regions. The logic went like this: if we combine a large, rich constituent entity with a small and poor one, then, having been allocated the budget of the small *matryoshka* region by the federal centre (even in a reduced form), the larger entity will spend the funds of the former constituent entity more efficiently, while also "adding" its own money and being involved in the development of the newly acquired region. The problem was that in three of the six cases, the logic of an affluent big brother and a struggling little brother did not work – precisely, for Kamchatka Oblast–Koryak Autonomous Okrug, Irkutsk Oblast–Ust-Orda Buryat Autonomous Okrug, and Chita Oblast–Agin-Buryat Autonomous Okrug – as the larger constituent entities were themselves not economically stable. What is more, the federal centre promised to help the new constituent entities through the system of presidential decrees that were essentially "gifts" to the regions for being "obedient" and going through with the mergers, aimed at boosting socioeconomic development of territories that were lagging behind and "sweetening the pill" of the merger, as hardly anyone expected things to get better immediately.

The socioeconomic situation in the regions slated for merger before the reforms

Let us look at this from the point of view of the dynamics of such metrics as gross regional product per capita (which illustrates the gap between the relevant constituent entities and whether it was even feasible for one of them to "drag" the other along), and the number (proportion) of officials in the state authorities and local self-government bodies among the population of the constituent entity being absorbed (which allows us to answer the question of whether the national autonomies were truly "bureaucratic" regions). This is by no means a comprehensive analysis, as the researchers were unable to reliably track the dynamics of these indicators in the municipal districts of the former constituent entities of the Russian Federation and thus quantitatively assess the development of these territories. It is for this reason that we moved away from quantitative criteria to qualitative criteria – specifically, the degree to (and speed with) which the relevant presidential decrees were implemented.

Gross regional product per capita (in current base prices, in rubles, without accounting for inflation) (Rosstat n.d.). The timeframe we are looking at covers the period from 1998 to 2013, since two factors intervene following 2013 – the economic crisis and changes in the methodology used by the Federal State Statistics Service of Russia to calculate gross regional product (GRP).

A stable trend is observed in that the GRP per capita of the autonomous *okrug*s was on average two times lower than that of the constituent entities into which they were merged. Koryak Autonomous Okrug is an exception here, but one that can be explained not so much by a growth in the production of goods and provision of services, but rather by the denominator effect caused by the outflow of people from the territory. This also explains why Evenk Autonomous Okrug demonstrated GRP per capita that was comparable to that of Krasnoyarsk Krai. In addition, Agin-Buryat Autonomous Okrug's GRP was only close to that of Chita Oblast in the final year of its existence as an autonomous region thanks to a special tax regime that did nothing to affect production levels but provided sufficient tax revenues for the regional authorities to better carry out their social responcibility to the population. Overall, except for Chita Oblast, the GRP per capita of the enlarged constituent entities was in line with the national level. Even so, the years in which the mergers took place did not constitute a point of bifurcation for the new territories, since the trend lines in all five regions remained the same. Looking at it this way, if we regard GRP per capita as the main aggregate indicator, then the reforms did not provide a major impetus to the regions as separate unified constituent entities of the Russian Federation.

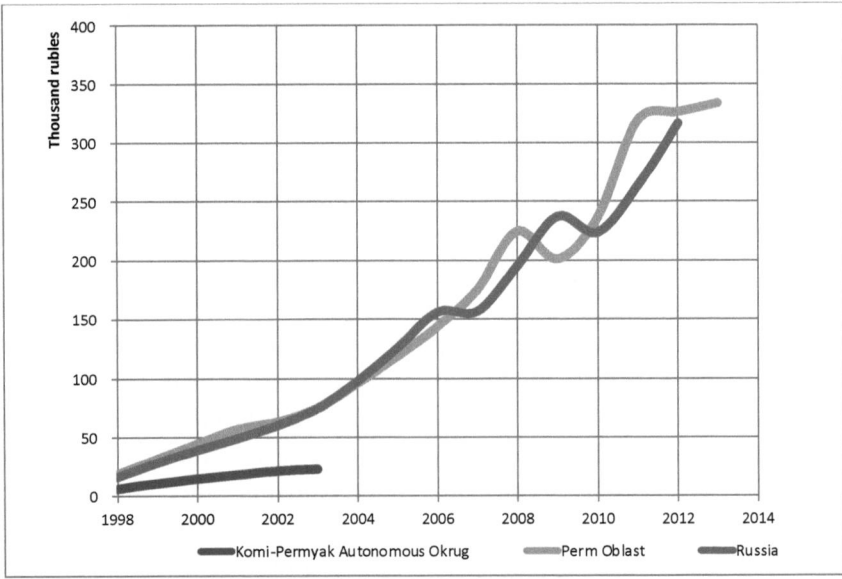

Fig. 1. GRP Dynamics in Perm Oblast and Komi-Permyak Autonomous Okrug

SOCIO-ECONOMIC ASPECT   129

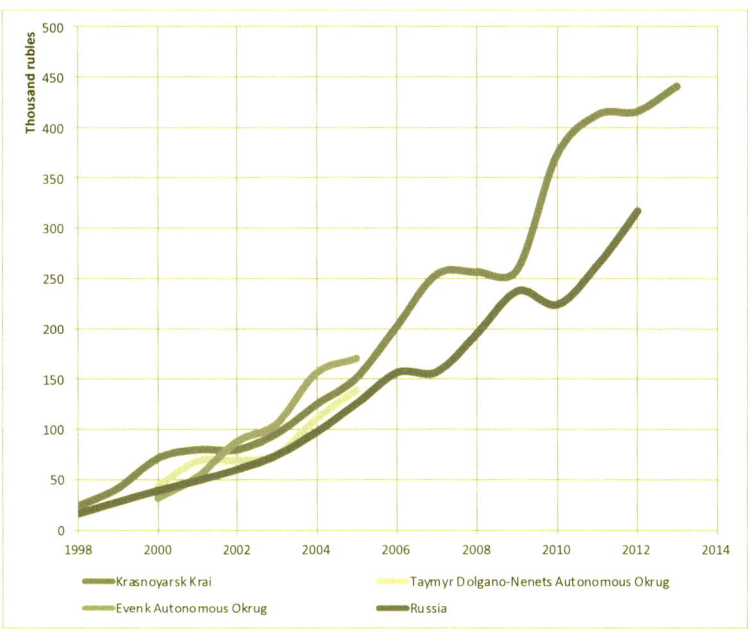

Fig 2. GRP Dynamics in Krasnoyarsk Krai, Taymyr Dolgano-Nenets Autonomous Okrug, and Evenk Autonomous Okrug

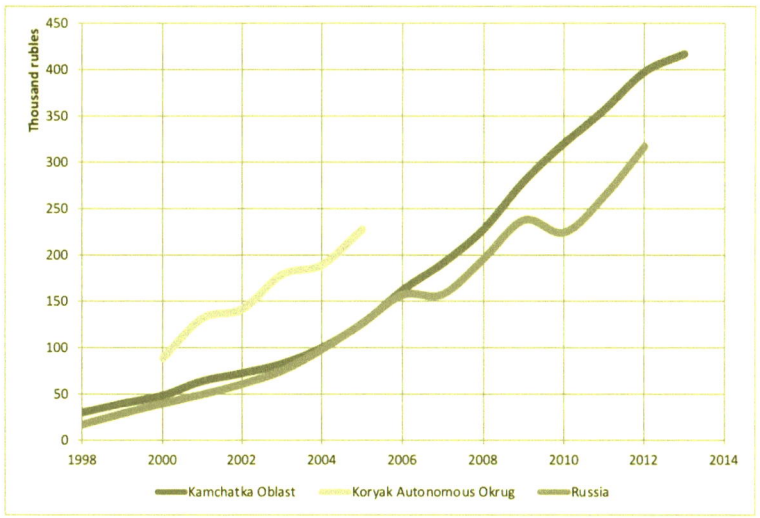

Fig 3. GRP Dynamics in Kamchatka Oblast and Koryak Autonomous Okrug

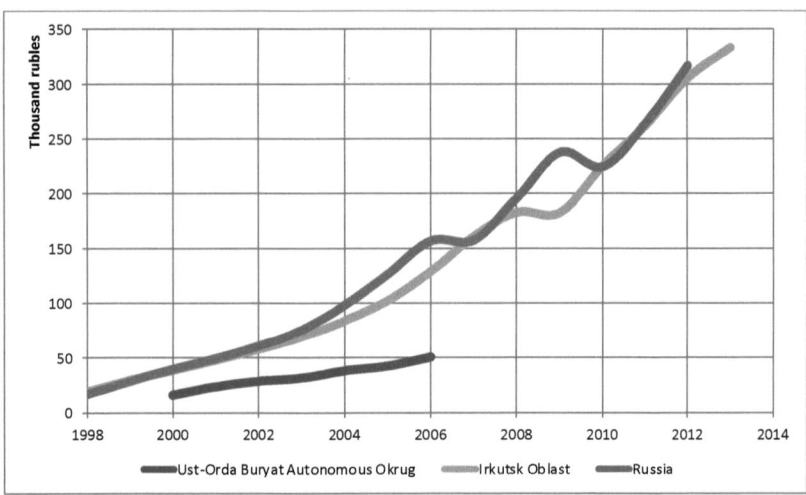

Fig 4. GRP Dynamics in Irkutsk Oblast and Ust-Orda Buryat Autonomous Okrug

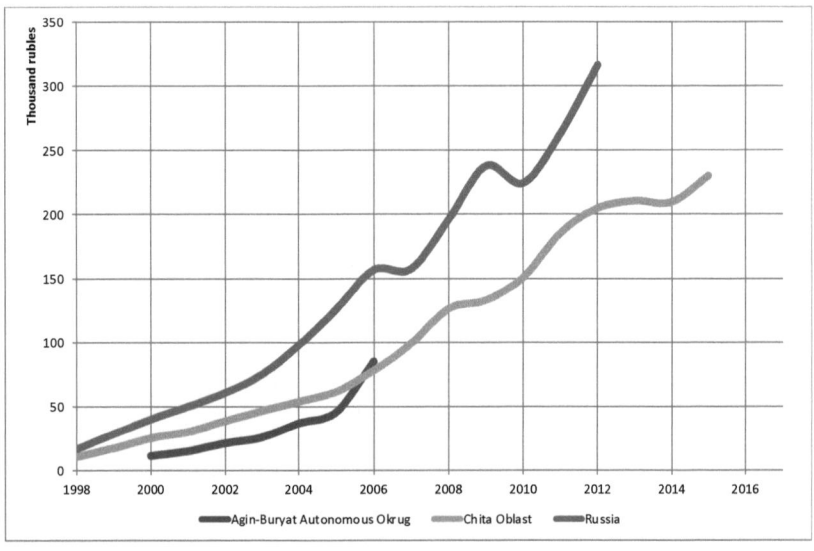

Fig 5. GRP Dynamics in Chita Oblast and Agin-Buryat Autonomous Okrug

Proportion of officials among the population. The charts (figures) show the number of officials per 1 000 population (Rosstat n.d.). This indicator allows us to estimate how many people are employed in public services, a non-production sector of the economy. In all the cases, the number of officials per 1000 population in the autonomous regions is higher than in the regions with which they were merged. Koryak Autonomous Okrug and Agin-Buryat Autonomous Okrug stand out in this regard, with more than 55 and 30 officials per 1000 population, respectively. Does this speak to an excessive number of officials in these former constituent entities of the Russian Federation? Or are we still talking about the denominator effect? If we look at the totals, then in 2005, for example, there were 1300 officials in Koryak Autonomous Okrug, whose population was approximately 23,000 people; and in Kamchatka Oblast, there were 7500 officials among the population of 350,000 people. That is, there were 15 times more people and 5.7 times more officials in the *oblast* than in the autonomous *okrug*. We can thus conclude that there were significant disproportions in the government offices of the two regions, and that the reform should have aimed to reduce the gap. What we actually found was the phenomenon of "elite transfer," when the top officials from the former autonomous regions moved to the centre of the enlarged constituent entity of the Russian Federation. The charts, however, do not show these upsurges because we are talking primarily about a thin layer of officials.

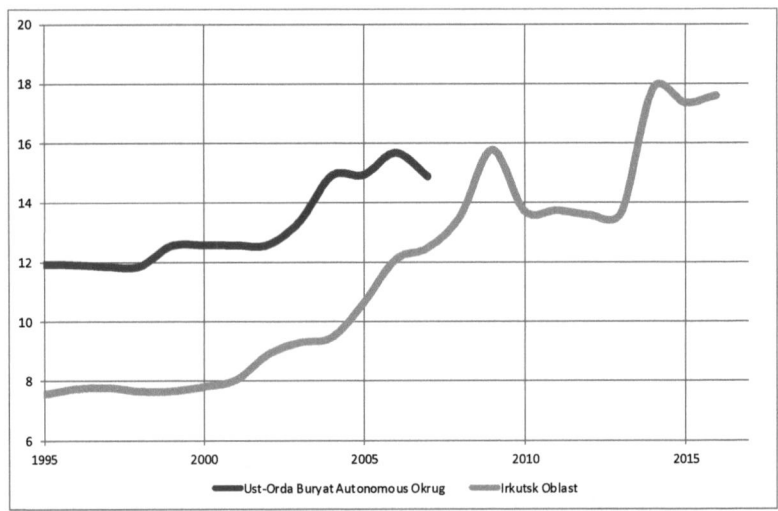

Fig. 6. Dynamics of the number of officials (per 1 000 people) in Irkutsk Oblast and Ust-Orda Buryat Autonomous Okrug

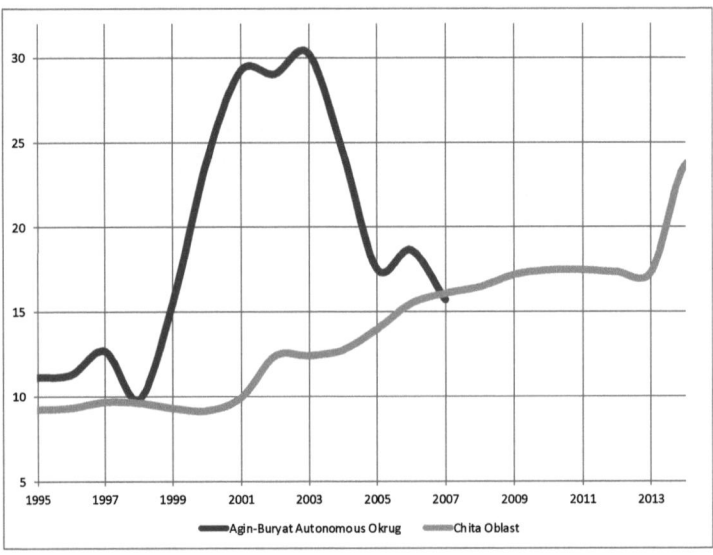

Fig. 7. Dynamics of the number of officials (per 1 000 people) in Chita Oblast and Agin-Buryat Autonomous Okrug

SOCIO-ECONOMIC ASPECT 133

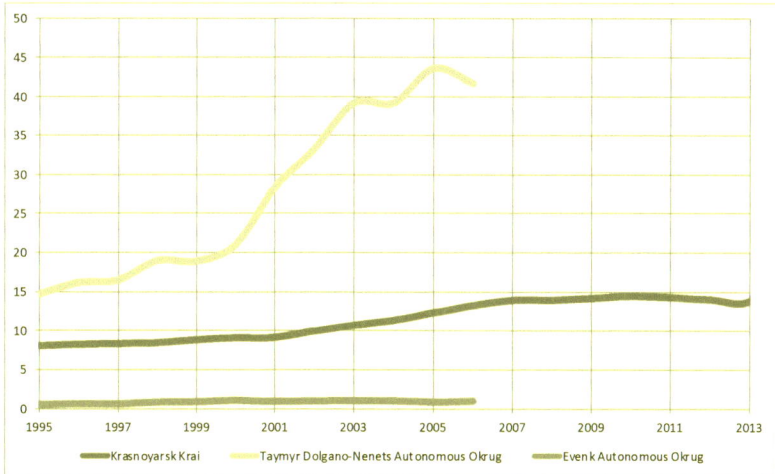

Fig. 8. Dynamics of the number of officials (per 1 000 people) in Krasnoyarsk Krai, Taymyr Dolgano-Nenets Autonomous Okrug, and Evenk Autonomous Okrug

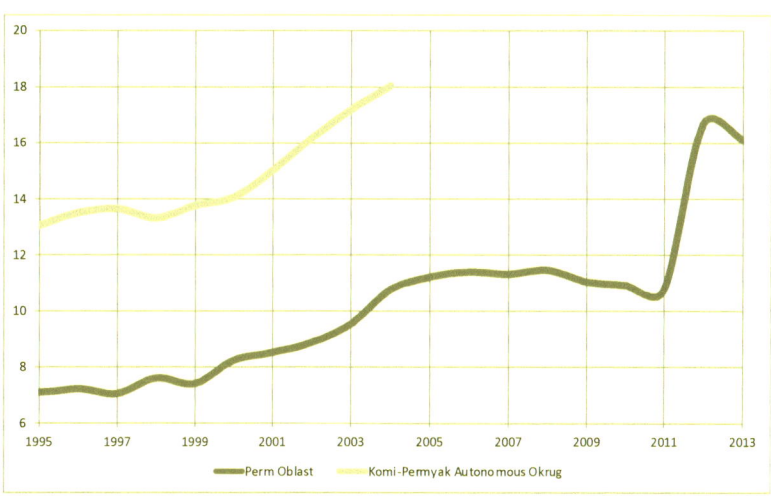

Fig. 9. Dynamics of the number of officials (per 1 000 people) in Perm Oblast and Komi-Permyak Autonomous Okrug

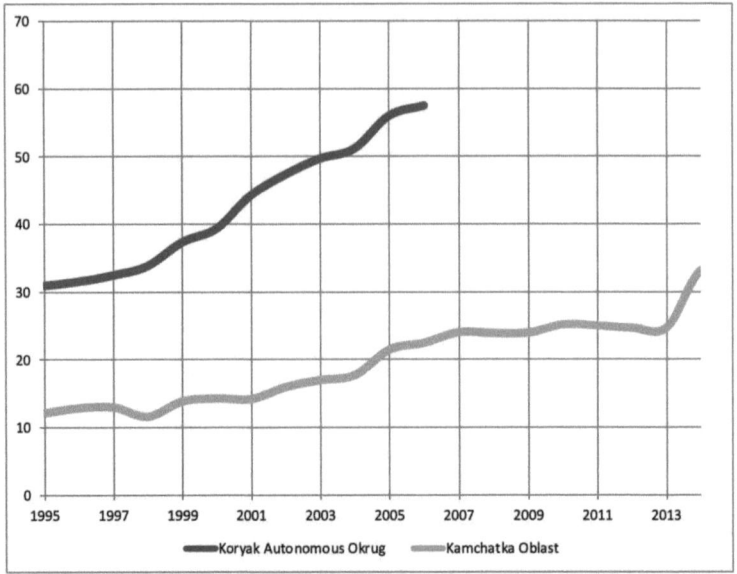

Fig. 10. Dynamics of the number of officials (per 1 000 people) in Kamchatka Oblast and Koryak Autonomous Okrug

In the next section, we will take a closer look at the degree to which the promises made as part of presidential decrees and during the election campaigns in the autonomous regions were kept.

Komi-Permyak Autonomous Okrug and Perm Oblast

In the period up until 2006, the following construction was planned in the region (Ukaz Presidenta Rossiyskoy Federatsii No. 1283 'O merakh po sotsial'no-ekonomicheskomu razvitiyu Komi-Permyatskogo avtonomnogo okruga i Permskoy oblasti' 2003 (Russia)):

- The Ochyor–Kudymkar–Kupros gas pipeline, scheduled for commissioning in 2006.
- Public highways and attendant structures along the Kudymkar– Syktyvkar route (to the border with the Komi Republic), as well as the first stage of a bridge over the Kama River near Perm.

The first complex of the gas pipeline was put into operation in 2005, with construction being completed in 2008. However, the regional authorities later included it in the privatization plan, although it took a long time for potential buyers to appear. According to *Kommersant*, the project cost a total of 970 million rubles (Kommersant 2015), and in late 2013, the authorities of the Perm krai signed an agreement with Gazprom under which the state-owned company would receive a property tax exemption. Gazprom was expected to purchase the Ochyor–Kudymkar pipeline for 227.9 million rubles. Not a single bid was received at the tender, and when a repeat tender was announced in 2014, the starting price had been dropped by almost 100 million rubles, which still failed to attract buyers. A public offering was equally unsuccessful. The Perm krai authorities eventually sold the pipeline to Gazprom subsidiary Gazprom Transgaz Tchaikovsky LLC for 3.4 million rubles, 285 times less than the costs incurred by the state during the construction (ProPerm 2015).

The situation with the road construction was objectively more successful, although the project did hit some delays along the way: the first stage of the Krasavinsky Bridge across the Kama River was put into operation in October 2005. The second stage was opened in 2008, along with the Southern bypass of Perm. By 2014, sections of the Kudymkar–Syktyvkar, Kama–Shmeiny, and Kosa–Solikamsk highways had been built, and the condition of the Yukseyevo–Kosa highway had been brought in line.

While the construction of the Syktyvkar–Kudymkar railway and the modernization of Kudymkar Airport were not included in the presidential decree, they nevertheless served as incentives for the development of infrastructure in the territories. The railway was planned as part of the wider-reaching Belkomur project connecting the Urals and the White Sea. The project was partly implemented, with the Chinese company China Poly Group Corporation joining as a partner and co-investor in 2015 (RIA Novosti 2015). As of right now, the project remains on paper, and there are no trains running between Kudymkar and Syktyvkar. A similar situation has arisen with Kudymkar Airport: restoration work has yet to be carried out, the complex is slowly sinking under water and is currently unsuitable for aviation.

Another victim of the protracted merger was the Kudymkar Drama Theatre, where reconstruction lasted until 2014, with the original cost estimate doubling during this time and criminal proceedings being launched (Suvorova 2014).

Thus, the ambitious projects that were supposed to accelerate the development of the territory were only partially implemented and did not produce the desired effect.

Koryak Autonomous Okrug and Kamchatka Oblast

This case does not really fit the model of a "rich region towing a poorer region." According to the typology of Russian regions by socioeconomic development level, Kamchatka Oblast belonged to the poorly developed "middling" regions. Its GRP per capita adjusted for cost of living in 2006 was 62% of the national average. In Koryak Autonomous Okrug, GRP per capita technically exceeded the national average, although this can be put down to the denominator effect we talked about – with its small population, Koryak Autonomous Okrug was one of the least developed and most subsidized regions of the country (Proyekt 'Sotsial'nyi atlas rossiyskich regionov' n.d.). In addition, the case of Koryak Autonomous Okrug was further complicated by the socioeconomic and natural disasters that struck the region in the 2000s. Specifically, we are talking about the energy crisis in the winter of 2004/2005, when the *okrug* was left without heat and electricity for several months and the heating and water supply systems were completely frozen. The damage caused to the housing and communal services in the *okrug* was estimated at several hundred million rubles (Radio Svoboda 2005). The second disaster was the 6.0-magnitude earthquake that hit Olyutorsky District in Koryak Autonomous Okrug. While there were no fatalities, diesel power plants, boiler houses, social and transport infrastructure facilities in the villages of Korf, Tilichiki and Khailino were damaged. Thus, the merger was never going to be smooth from the point of view of the economies of the two remote and depressed areas. What did the authorities do to make the transition easier?

Pursuant to Decree No. 1227 of the President of the Russian Federation "On Measures to Ensure the Socioeconomic Development of Kamchatka Oblast and Koryak Autonomous Okrug" dated October 21, 2005, a set of measures to develop the energy, transport and social infrastructure of Kamchatka Oblast and Koryak Autonomous Okrug was to be carried out in 2006–2008, including:

- The provision of state support for the construction of low-capacity heat and power plants in the villages of Tilichiki and Palana (to be commissioned in 2006), and Manily, Tigil and Ossora (to be commissioned in 2008), as well as the infrastructure creation for the delivery of locally produced power-generation coal.
- The provision of state support to carry out urgent work to restore power supply networks in the villages and settlements of Koryak Autonomous Okrug.
- The construction of the Milkovo – Klyuchi – Ust-Kamchatsk highway (completed in 2008, although the key bridge over the Kamchatka River was only finished in 2012).
- The construction of an airport and a runway in Palana (opened in 2014).
- The completion of the reconstruction of the sea terminal in Petropavlovsk-Kamchatskiy (started in 2009 and completed in 2014).
- Providing Federal State Unitary Enterprise Koryak Air Enterprise with aircraft for the development of air passenger transportation in remote and hard-to-reach areas via local airlines (three L-410 UVP-E20 Turbolets were purchased in 2010–2011).
- The provision of state support in the acquisition of off-road vehicles for the development of land passenger routes between the villages and settlements in the region (completed).
- The seismic retrofitting of social facilities in Kamchatka Oblast (completed).

- The resettlement of residents from dilapidated and condemned buildings (not completed as of 2011).
- The preparation of proposals for speeding up the construction of a gas pipeline from Sobolevsky District to Petropavlovsk-Kamchatskiy, including by attracting financing from non-budgetary sources (Ukaz Presidenta Rossiyskoy Federatsii No. 1227 'O merakh po sotsial'no-ekonomicheskomu razvitiyu Kamchatskoy oblasti i Koryakskogo avtonomnogo okruga' 2005 (Russia)).

This is the most extensive list of socioeconomic development projects among the merging regions, although their implementation dragged on for many years. A perfect example of this was the construction of a mini-plant of combined heat and power (mini-CHP). The acceptance certificate for the construction of the plant was signed in December 2009, albeit with an overestimation of the cost – for work that had not even been carried out. It turned out that more than 38.5 million rubles had simply been stolen (Trud. 2012). The fate of other mini-CHPs in the region is not less intriguing: the Palana mini-CHP, for example, has yet to commence operations, even though it has had a ceremonial launch. More than 700 million rubles were earmarked for the construction of four mini-CHPs as part of the Federal Target Programme "Economic and Social Development of the Far East and Transbaikalia for the Period up to 2013," even though the projects were flawed due to the fact that engineering networks had not been provided for them. In 2008, a working group made up of representatives of energy companies and research centres determined that further construction would not be economically viable, and construction of all four facilities was "frozen" (Kamchatka-Inform 2014).

Two audits were carried out to assess the implementation of the items contained in the presidential decree, neither of which was glowing: the 2008 audit carried out by the Presidential Control Directorate revealed that, as of September 2008, only preparatory work had been carried out to implement the decree, despite the persisting difficulties in the socioeconomic sphere and the fact that the Government of the Russian Federation had allocated 5 billion rubles to reduce energy prices (RIA Deita 2008). On September 30, 2010, the Accounts Chamber of the Russian Federation published the results of its audit of the implementation of the presidential decree in Kamchatka Krai, which stated that only half of the ten points contained in the degree had been fulfilled (Pravitel'stvo Kamchatskogo Kraya 2011).

Taymyr Dolgano-Nenets Autonomous Okrug, Evenk Autonomous Okrug and Krasnoyarsk Krai

Both *matryoshka* regions were rich in resource potential. However, the natural resources of Taymyr Dolgano-Nenets Autonomous Okrug were gradually developed by Norilsk Nickel, a Russian nickel and palladium mining and smelting company, while Evenk Autonomous Okrug lagged behind due to its isolation and the difficulty of developing deposits with poorer raw materials. Decree No. 41233 of the President of the Russian Federation was issued on April 12, 2005, to jump-start the socioeconomic development of the enlarged Krasnoyarsk Krai, which included Taymyr and Evenk autonomous okrugs (Ukaz Presidenta Rossiyskoy Federatsii No. 412 'O merakh po sotsial'no-ekonomicheskomu razvitiyu Krasnoyarskogo Kraya, Taymyrskogo (Dolgano-Nenetskogo) avtonomnogo okruga i Evenkiyskogo avtonomnogo okruga' 2005 (Russia)). The first paragraph of the decree refers to assistance in the implementation of the investment project for the development of Vankor Oil and Gas Field in 2005–2009, which was completed in full. Initial attempts to drill oil in 2008 were unsuccessful, but this setback was soon overcome, and commercial operation of Vankor Field commenced on August 21, 2009. The second project was government support to make sure that Boguchanskaya hydro-based power plant (HPP) was launched by 2010, and that the flood zone in the territory be dealt with. Construction of the hydro-based power plant started back in the 1970s, but was marred by constant interruptions, and the state used the merger of Evenk Autonomous Okrug and Krasnoyarsk Krai to push the project through to completion. Even with this support, Boguchanskaya HPP was put into operation in 2013, four years late. What is more, experts have been critical of the hydroelectric power plant and its effect on the environment, claiming that it has changed the ecosystem in the south of Evenk Autonomous Okrug, because of the floods in the region (Plotina.Net n.d.). Flooding has also had an effect on the population, forcing the resettlement of people from 29 villages in the flood zone (four of which were located in Irkutsk Oblast) – a total of 1977 flats were allocated to 5137 people displaced because of the floods (NIA Krasnoyarsk 2013).

The next item in the decree concerned the reconstruction of the runways at Yemelyanovo (Krasnoyarsk) Airport, which was to be completed in 2006 (this target was met), and Khatanga Airport to be commissioned in 2007 (work was completed in 2009 since it took a long time to find an investor). Another infrastructure project set out in the document was the construction of the first stage of the transport bypass of Krasnoyarsk, with a bridge crossing over the Yenisei River, slated for commissioning in 2009 (this target was met).

The fifth measure of the decree was the construction of the first stage of the Kansk–Aban–Boguchany highway on the 208–220km section of the road, to be commissioned in 2006. This project was completed within the set timeframe in Krasnoyarsk Krai (within the former administrative boundaries). As for the implementation of the final point in the decree – the resettlement in 2005–2010 of residents of the regions in the Russian Far North and the equivalent in Taymyr Dolgano-Nenets Autonomous Okrug, Evenk Autonomous Okrug and Krasnoyarsk Krai who receive housing subsidies as a priority – it is difficult to assess its effectiveness objectively, since the resettlement programme from the regions of the Far North is ongoing and affects the entire country. What is more, reliable data on this issue could not be found.

In general, the Krasnoyarsk Krai merger can be considered more successful than the one in Perm Krai. However, there is a tendency to implement Krasnoyarsk Krai projects on time and in full, while those of Taymyr Dolgano-Nenets Autonomous Okrug and Evenk Autonomous Okrug often run beyond the deadlines, have trouble finding investors, and the projects themselves often have shaky foundations in terms of their environmental risks.

Ust-Orda Buryat Autonomous Okrug and Irkutsk Oblast

What makes this case stand our is the fact that, according to the description, it appears to fit the logic of the "strong helping the weak," since Ust-Orda Buryat Autonomous Okrug is a poor agricultural region with a predominantly rural population that receives 80% of its budgetary funds in the form of subsidies from the central government. As for Irkutsk Oblast, not everyone was excited about the prospect of merging with Ust-Orda Buryat Autonomous Okrug – after all, it was not exactly affluent enough to take on the burden of a developing backward agrarian region.

The wording of Decree No. 323 of the President of the Russian Federation dated April 6, 2006, differs from that of the previous decrees – it is softer and more streamlined, thus allowing greater room for interpretation (Ukaz Presidenta o prinyatii mer po sotsial'no-ekonomicheskomu razvitiyu Ust'-Ordynskogo AO i Irkutskoy oblasti 2006 (Russia)). For example, the key wording is "to implement a set of measures in 2006–2007 for the development of the social infrastructure of Irkutsk Oblast and Ust-Orda Buryat Autonomous Okrug that provided for state support in the construction of […] facilities." Note the absence of deadlines for the construction of specific facilities, only that the state would provide support for their construction. Thus, the focus had shifted away from carrying out projects within specific deadlines, something that the other entities had trouble doing.

Let us take a look at the projects that were set out in the decree and the degree to which the decree itself was implemented. Initially, the plan was to build:

- an orphanage, perinatal centre, anti-tuberculosis dispensary, and sports centre in the settlement of Ust-Ordynsky;

- regional hospitals in the villages of Bayandai (Bayandaevsky District), Bokhan (Bokhansky District), and Kutulik (Alarsky District);
- health clinics in the settlements of Novonukutskii (Nukutsky District) and Osa (Osinksy District);
- schools in the settlements of Kamenka and Khokhorsk (Bokhansky District), Russkiye Yanguty (Osinksy District), Tyrgetui (Alarsky District), Khogot (Bayandaevsky District), and the village of Kharanut (in Aluzhinsky, Ekhirit-Bulagatsky District);
- a bridge over the Angara River in Irkutsk;
- a transport bypass in Irkutsk with a bridge over the Irkut River.

The only financial mechanism prescribed in the decree is subsidies to the Irkutsk Oblast region for the provision of financial assistance to the Ust-Orda Buryat Autonomous Okrug budget in an amount not lower than the 2006 level, with adjustments for inflation for 2007–2009.

All the facilities planned for construction in the former Ust-Orda Buryat Autonomous Okrug are geared towards the social sphere, while the two in Irkutsk Oblast are geared towards transport and infrastructure. That is, not a single item in the decree concerns the kind of economic development we observed with regard to Perm and Krasnoyarsk Krais, namely, industrial development. This is likely due to the specific features of the economy of Ust-Orda Buryat Autonomous Okrug and the natural resource potential of Irkutsk Oblast.

All the facilities were completed, although construction dragged on for ten years. According to a report submitted by Minister of Road Construction of Irkutsk Oblast Svetlana Svirkina at the September 2016 session of the Irkutsk Oblast Legislative Assembly, four facilities had still not been completed (the central hospitals in Kutulik and Bokhan, and the sports centre and orphanage in Ust-Ordynsky) (Baikal Info 2016), as funds had not been allocated for their construction. By 2018, the facilities had been completed, and the decision was made to convert the orphanage in

Ust-Ordynsky into a 400-place school, since the children who were going to live at the orphanage were placed with families during the construction, and the orphanage was not needed by the time it was finished (Teleinform 2016).

If we use indicators other than the completeness and speed of the implementation of the decree to measure its success, then more positive aspects do reveal themselves. For example, it became easier for residents of Ust-Orda Buryat Autonomous Okrug to access medical services in Irkutsk Oblast, something that was very important for the *okrug* given the poor quality of services provided there. Before the merger, Ust-Orda residents could receive treatment at Irkutsk Regional Hospital, but with certain restriction. While some of these restrictions remain, residents of the former autonomous *okrug* admit that improvements have been made, and social benefits have been increased to the level received in the *oblast*s. In addition, more agricultural products from Ust-Orda are now available in the markets of Irkutsk, something that has benefitted both Irkutsk residents and Ust-Orda farmers.

Agin-Buryat Autonomous Okrug and Chita Oblast

This merger is noteworthy for the economic conditions that both constituent entities were in at the time. Chita Oblast was suffering because of the downturn in its mining industry. Agin-Buryat Autonomous Okrug, on the other hand, was turning a profit for a while thanks to its status as a zone with a special tax regime, a fact that convinced a number of companies to register a legal entity in the *okrug*. In this regard, the standard of living in the relatively small Agin-Buryat Autonomous Okrug was higher than in other villages in Zabaykalsky Krai.

This was the last merger of constituent entities to take place, and the corresponding Decree No. 260 of the President of the Russian Federation dated March 1, 2007, is noticeably short on details (Ukaz Presidenta Rossiyskoy Federatsii No. 260 'O merakh po sotsial'no-ekonomicheskomu razvitiyu Chitinskoy oblasti i Aginskogo Buryatskogo avtonomnogo okruga' 2007 (Russia)). It contained the followed measures:

- to include a provision in the draft federal law on the federal budget for 2008–2010 on subsidies in the amount of 2.5 billion rubles to be provided to the budgets of Chita Oblast and Agin-Buryat Autonomous Okrug in order to implement a set of measures to develop the transport and social infrastructure for the period 2008–2009, as well as funds provided from the federal budget in the form of aid to equalize the budgets of Chita Oblast, Agin-Buryat Autonomous Okrug and the newly formed constituent entity of the Russian Federation in an amount not lower than the amount allotted for the equalization of the budget security of the constituent entities of the Russian Federation in 2007, with due account of the increased inflation rates in 2008 and 2009;
- to assist in the preparations for the geological study of subsoil in order to develop mineral deposits in Chita Oblast and Agin-Buryat Autonomous Okrug;
- to assist in the implementation of investment projects for the construction and reconstruction of motorways located in Chita Oblast and Agin-Buryat Autonomous Okrug.

This decree is similar to the decree on the merger of Irkutsk Oblast and Ust-Orda Buryat Autonomous Okrug in that the measures outlined in it are somewhat vague: assistance is prescribed, but no specific projects in the form of roads, social institutions and industrial facilities are mentioned.

Where this decree differs is that it sets out the amount of money to subsidize transport and social infrastructure in the amount of 2.5 billion rubles. The decree was supplemented by Law No. 799-ZAO of the Agin-Buryat Autonomous Okrug dated November 28, 2007, which provided for the construction of 10 facilities (Zakon Aginskoy Buryatskoy okruzhnoy Dumy Aginskogo Buryatskogo avtonomnogo okruga No. 799-ZAO 2007 (Agin-Buryat Autonomous Okrug)): a school with 500 places and a kindergarten with 90 places in the village of Duldurga; a school and a children's art centre in the village of Aginsky; schools in the villages of Ortui, Alkhanai, and Uzon; engineering networks and an elementary school in the village of Mogoitui; and Boiler House

No. 3 in Aginsky. All the facilities were completed by 2013, and a total of 956.5 million rubles were allocated for the implementation of the law, primarily from the federal budget, with a part coming from the regional budget and a small amount from the municipalities. However, no specific measures for the socioeconomic development of the rest of Zabaykalsky Krai were outlined.

The results of the merger would suggest that Agin-Buryat Autonomous Okrug came out worse. Its special tax status could not prop it up forever, although the funds accumulated during that time allowed it to maintain an above-average level of socioeconomic development for Zabaykalsky Krai for some time. This particular merger happened during the global financial crisis, and many of those whom we interviewed during out research trip to Zabaykalsky Krai blamed the crisis for stalling the process, and the funds earmarked and programmes created did not produce the desired results.

The declared goal of the socioeconomic development of these territories was not implemented in full: GRP per capita dynamics were barely impacted statistically, and the measures carried out as part of the presidential decrees were done so with massive delays, which stripped the process of merging constituent entities of any real meaning, especially for those regions that lost their autonomy, as they revealed significant problems with the implementation of the projects. In this sense, the mergers only partially influenced the socioeconomic development of the regions.

The Ethnic Aspect

Petr Oskolkov

In recent decades, the term "ethnicity" has increasingly become a part of the ethno-political discourse in Russia, encroaching on the space previously occupied exclusively by the words "ethnos" and "nationality." It would seem that, at least in relation to the interaction between and reciprocal influence of ethnic parameters and political/institutional status, it really makes more sense to talk about ethnicity (as a dynamic characteristic or state) than about ethnos, nationality or nation (as a static object). One of the most prominent Russian ethnopolitical scientists of the constructivist school, Valery Tishkov, notes that ethnicity is a category that denotes "the existence of culturally distinctive (ethnic) groups and forms of identity" (2001, 229). The Soviet and Russian ethnologist Sergey A. Arutyunov believes that the "basis for the emergence of and self-maintenance of ethnic groups are clots of communicational and informational links" (1995, 7). In other words, ethnicity is a product of informational interaction. In this sense, it might be worth recalling Hans Kohn, who called nationalism – the most common form of the politicization of ethnicity – a state of mind (1965, 9). The characteristics that allow us to classify a community as an ethnic community conventionally include shared ideas about a common history and territory, a common language (albeit often with regional differences), and a sense of distinctiveness (which also gives rise to various forms of solidarity). However, we think we might even reduce this set of characteristics to just distinctive cultural traits combined with the idea of hereditary membership in a community (Rothschild 1981, 9; Chandra 2012, 10; Oskolkov 2022, 156). In our opinion, statehood is not of fundamental importance for ethnicity: whether an ethnic group is organized politically or is content with one form or another of cultural autonomy naturally affects how intensely ethnic characteristics manifest themselves, but not their presence or absence.

Ethnicity is one of those characteristics that are most vulnerable to emotional and psychological influence. As such, attempts to politicize ethnicity are inevitable, and they often work (as a rule, ethnic identity has a cognitive component and an affective/emotional-evaluative component (Stefanenko 2000, 211), which are ostensibly of equal importance). We should not assume that it is always members of the political elite – "ethnic entrepreneurs" – who engage in this kind of politicization. In the vast majority of cases, this is an objective process that is conditioned on the achievement of a certain stage of self-awareness by a given ethnic group. What is more, ethnic identity is more salient for minorities (non-dominant groups) and people living in a multi-ethnic environment than it is for people who live in an ethnically homogenous environment and where nothing threatens their dominance (Drobizheva 2017, 419). According to a 2015 study by the Institute of Sociology of the Russian Academy of Sciences, 77% of Russians and 87% of the Russian citizens of non-Russian ethnicity "never forget about their ethnicity" (Gorshkov and Petukhov 2015, 191).

In this context, the hypotheses put forward by Yuri Shabaev that "a significant part of the [Komi-Permyak] ethnic group [...] attaches greater importance to civil, rather than ethnic identity and views themselves as Russians first and foremost" is open to criticism (2006, 66). While civic identity is undoubtedly an important component of the multi-level *matryoshka* of identities (local–regional–ethnic–national/civic–supranational/civilizational), ethnic identity has no less emotional and political charge, and it is unlikely to lose its significance in the coming decades. After all, if one of the *matryoshkas* is removed from the overall construction, the "largest" doll will be incomplete. What we see here is a comprehensive underestimation of the ethnic factor compared to the economic factor, which is exactly what Walker Connor (1994) warned against, as he saw economic differences as only indirectly influencing ethnic parameters. This kind of underestimation is rather dangerous, at least for the fact that the former Komi-Permyak Autonomous Okrug, Agin-Buryat Autonomous Okrug and Koryak Autonomous Okrug were among the few ethnoterritorial constituent entities of the Russian Federation where the population of the eponymous ethnic group dominated.

The politicization of ethnicity can be done by singling out its various aspects: primordial-biological, territorial, historical, linguistic, cultural, and religious. For everyday ethnic nationalism, "education in a particular language, having a TV channel in one's own language or the protection of ancient sacred sites" are usually sufficient to serve as symbolic goals (Özkırımlı 2010, 144). In the case of the former autonomous *okrug*s of the Russian Federation, we can talk about the cultural "modality" of ethnicity (in all subjects affected by a series of reforms), while the linguistic aspect is relevant primarily for the Komi-Permyak and Buryat people. The territorial factor plays a special role in the case of Ust-Orda Buryat Autonomous Okrug and Agin-Buryat Autonomous Okrug, whose elites were involved in the 1990s – even more so than the elites of the Republic of Buryatia – in the discourse on "divided ethos" (citing the fact that Agin, Ust-Orda, Olkhonsky and Ulan-Ononsky regions left the Buryat Autonomous Soviet Socialist Republic in 1937, and using the term "ethnic Buryatia" extensively) (Khamutaev 2005, 155).

The Russian Federation is built on both the territorial and ethnic principles of the spatial organization. Even the very first versions of the administrative division of the Russian Soviet Federative Socialist Republic contained an ethno-national component. Since "an ethnofederal state is a federal state in which at least one constituent territorial governance unit is intentionally associated with a specific ethnic category" (Hale 2004, 167), the Russian administrative system may be regarded as an example of partial ethnofederalism. All republics (except for Dagestan), autonomous okrugs and a single autonomous oblast (the Jewish Autonomous Oblast) have a "titular" (eponymous) ethnic group (or two groups) that have given their name to the region.

According to the 2010 Russian Census, Russia is populated by more than 190 ethnic groups. Ethnicity became strongly politicized during the initial stages of Bolshevik nation-building in the 1920s and 1930s as a way to consolidate the newborn federal entities and help them form a strong identity, even though the "titular group" did not constitute a numerical majority in many regions (in modern Russia, eponymous ethnic groups comprise eighty per cent or more of the population in just three ethnic regions – the republics of Chechnya, Ingushetia and Tuva) (Panov and Filippova 2015, 37). This process reached its peak with the officially proclaimed policy of indigenization (*korenizatsiya*). This was a means "for the power preservation of communist leaders of titular ethnic groups, for the control over the electoral space and clientelistic elite selection, and for the control over natural resources" (Heinemann-Grüder 2007, 20). However, later on, and especially after the collapse of the communist regime, this ethnicization of politics faded away, making way for ethnopolitical mobilization that was enforced by a combination of grievances and unexpected political opportunities in the changing state circumstances. The ethnicity of the ethnic regions became politicized not only administratively (as had been the case in the Russian Soviet Federative Socialist Republic), but also discursively. Indeed, "identification as an ethnic minority becomes a highly valued social resource to resist authoritarianism" (Yusupova 2018, 643).

As we see it, at the core of any ethnofederal system (imposed from above, which is the case in the USSR and in Russia) lie two underpinning rationales: 1) the wish to jettison communal differences and govern complex societies efficiently that pushes for maximal, though often formal, autonomy of ethnic components; and 2) the fear of the break-up of a multinational polity that forces the authorities to seek mechanisms of keeping the territories together. Both these rationales were taken into account while constructing a Soviet federal system. Notably, the Bolsheviks "created a state that was federal in form, but unitary in substance," granting "the appearance of sovereignty without the substance of sovereignty as an underlying organizational principle of the state" (Beissinger 2015, 481).

Though Jack Snyder (2000, 327) famously attributed the collapse of the USSR (together with the former Yugoslavia and Czechoslovakia) to the federal system that created statehood institutions,[1] Walker Connor (1984) easily made his argument invalid: in his assumption, communist federalism was de facto anti-federal in nature, and it was this false federalism that led to the break-up of the state, not federalism itself. Indeed, the Soviet (and Yugoslav) authorities widely employed tactics that cannot be ascribed to a normal federal system, such as the administrative "gerrymandering" of ethnic boundaries, deportations and other kinds of forced demographic transfers. The "indigenous" regions have not been lucky exceptions: the "native" boundaries were drawn in such a manner that the indigenous peoples constituted only a slight minority in the respective regions. Moreover, indigenous ethnic groups were not consolidated in "their" regions (which could indeed lead to the formation of strong statehood institutions and a strong national identity), but were rather dispersed, as the Nenets people in Yamalo-Nenets, Nenets and Taimyr Dolgano-Nenets okrugs, the Khanty and Mansi people in Khanty-Mansi and Yamalo-Nenets okrugs, the Evenks in Evenk Autonomous Okrug and Yakutia (in Yakutia, the Evenk population is approximately seven times greater than in Evenk Autonomous Okrug itself).

In Soviet ethnic theory, class determinism and hierarchy dominated (Filippov 2010). The former meant that ethnicity was a priori secondary compared to economic structure. The latter formed a hierarchic ladder of ethnic groups. Ethnic groups that were considered "nations" were given autonomous republics (known simply as "republics" since 1991); and smaller and less "developed" (in terms of "political consciousness" and "achievements in the construction of socialism") peoples (*narodnosti*) were granted autonomous oblasts. Some ethnic groups, including the indigenous peoples of the North, were entitled to "national okrugs" (known as autonomous okrugs from 1977) that were parts of the surrounding oblasts. In contemporary literature, it is assumed that this federal system provided "legal grounds for ethnic stratification" (Zisserman-Brodsky 2003, 24).

---

1 For a discussion of ethnofederalism being able to both silence and stimulate separatist discourses, see O'Driscoll, Costantini et al. 2020.

The overall trend in the 1990s was for the ethnic regions to acquire a higher status in the regional hierarchy. Though de jure all federal units enjoyed equal rights (which is explicitly stipulated in Article 5 of the Constitution of the Russian Federation), de facto republics were considered "more equal than others" (Drobizheva 2013, 31). So, all autonomous oblasts (Gorno-Altai, Khakas, Adyghe, Karachay-Cherkessia), previously being parts of krais (which actually made a unit eligible for the status of a krai), except for the Jewish Autonomous Oblast, unilaterally promoted themselves to republics. This was not the case with the autonomous okrugs: only Chukotka promoted itself to a fully self-governing region, no longer being a part of Magadan Oblast.[2]

It is difficult to dovetail the *matryoshka*-like nature[3] of the ethno-territorial constituent entities with their declared equality in relations with Moscow. And while the series of reforms we are looking at in this monograph may have made it possible to partly remove the problem of constitutional equality for autonomous okrugs from the agenda, it did not – and could not – eliminate the need for a carefully considered ethnic policy, which is dictated by the complex ethnic and demographic composition of the respective administrative and territorial units.

Let us look at this in terms of figures. The "titular" people of Ust-Orda and Agin-Buryat *okrug*s are Buryats who speak the Buryat language (formerly known as Buryat-Mongolian) belonging to the Mongolic subdivision of the Altaic language family alongside Mongolian, Kalmyk and a number of other languages with a small number of speakers. Buryats made up 62.5% of the population in Agin-Buryat Okrug in 2014 (according to the Agin-Buryat Okrug administration), and 39.6% of the population of the Ust-Orda Buryat Autonomous Okrug (according to the All-Russia Population Census of 2002; data from the 2010 data cannot be used here, as Ust-Orda Buryat Autonomous Okrug had ceased to be a constituent entity of the Russian Federation by that time and the

---

2   In 1990, Chukotka and Koryak Okrug even tried to claim the status of republics; however, they were not entitled for this by the Federative Law of 1992.

3   For more on this term, see: Drobizheva 2013, 30; Sidorenko 2009, 103.

ethnic composition of the population was thus not calculated there).

The "titular" ethnic group of Komi-Permyak Okrug are the Komi, who speak Komi-Permyak, a Finno-Permic language of the Finno-Ugric branch of the Uralic language family (the languages of the Komi-Zyryan, Komi-Yazva and Udmurt people are also spoken in the *okrug*). As of 2010, Komi-Permyaks made up 54.2% of the population in Komi-Permyak Okrug (Komi-Permyatskiy okrug n.d.). The Evenk Region was named after the Evenki (formerly Tungusic) people. Their native language is Evenki, which belongs to the Tungus-Manchurian group of the Altaic language family that also includes the languages of the Evens, Nanais and several other peoples. According to the 2002 census (like with Ust-Orda Buryat Autonomous Okrug, this is the last census containing data specifically for Evenk region), Evenks made up 21.5% of the population in Evenkia. Significant numbers of Evenks also live in the north of China, Yakutia, and another former autonomous *okrug* – Taymyr Dolgano-Nenets Region. Taymyr Dolgano-Nenets Autonomous Okrug was one of the constituent entities of the Russian Federation where there are several "titular" peoples, namely Dolgans, Nenets, Evenks, Enets and Nganasans. Dolgans are a relatively young Turkic people whose language is the closest relative of Yakut, which demonstrates influence from Evenki. As of 2002, they made up 13.8% of the population in Taymyr Dolgano-Nenets Autonomous Okrug. The Nenets, Enets and Nganasans speak Samoyedic languages, which belong to the Uralic family. The Nenets (also known as Samoyeds) are the most numerous of the three, accounting for 7.6% of the population of Taymyr Dolgano-Nenets Autonomous Okrug in 2002. Finally, the titular people of Koryak Okrug are the Koryaks, who speak the Koryak language, the closest "relative" of Chukchi, both of which belong to the Chukotko-Kamchatkan language family. In 2002, the Koryaks made up 65% of the population in Koryak Autonomous Okrug.

When talking about the ethnic composition of the population, we should also take the internal heterogeneity of the titular peoples into account. For instance, the Buryats of Zabaykalsky Krai and Irkutsk oblast speak different dialects of the Buryat language, and religious affiliations differ among these people (the Buryats of Agin-Buryat Okrug and Buryatia proper mostly profess Buddhism, while shamanism is prevalent in Ust-Orda). Koryaks are subdivided into sedentary (the coastal Nymylan) and nomadic (the tundral Chavchuven). These groups also have different dialects. This division is of great importance when it comes to socioeconomic policy and assessing the consequences of the reform, which is what we are doing in this book. Naturally, reindeer farming and its regulation are of paramount importance for the Chavchuven. The transfer of the governing bodies of *Kamchatolenprom* (the main reindeer farming company in the region) to the regional capital, which is located far from the deer hunting areas, was not well received.

The majority of respondents noted that the merger of the regions did not have a noticeable impact on inter-ethnic relations – such interactions never reached the point of conflict anywhere. However, it cannot be denied that downgrading the status of the national *okrug*s led to a certain growth in the salience of ethnic identity of the "titular" ethnic groups. Shabaev notes that when the merger of Komi-Permyak Autonomous Okrug and Perm Oblast was taking place in 2003–2004, a number of articles appeared in newspapers and magazines about the plight of the Komi people. Respondents from Koryak Okrug said the same.

The Buryat *okrug*s are somewhat different: the prospect of merging with "non-national" regions aroused not only ethnic-regional sentiments, but also pan-Buryat pride. The congresses of the All-Buryat Association for the Development of Culture and the Congress of the Buryat People that took place during the merger period discussed the need to maintain the symbolic unity of the three Buryat regions. An alternative project was put forward to unite Ust-Orda Buryat Autonomous Okrug, Agin-Buryat Autonomous Okrug and the Republic of Buryatia and thus partially restore the borders of the Buryat-Mongol Autonomous Soviet Socialist Republic, the fragmentation of which was considered by a section of the Buryat intelligentsia as an act of repression against the Buryat people. In Ulan-Ude and Aginskoye, the nationalist *Erkhe* ("Right") movement protested against the merger, and in

March 2006, Buryat shamans (mostly representing the *Böö Mürgel* spiritual centre) even held a *tailagan* (prayer service) against the administrative reform (Krug 2006). The Buryat-Mongolian activists Vladimir Khamutaev, Rajana Dugarova and the leader of the *Erkhe* movement, Dorzho Dugarov, as well as the chairman of the *Buryaad Soyol* public organization Bulat Shagzhin, were forced to emigrate due to their attempts to bring a radical nationalist project to life. However, this version of the politicization of ethnicity had a very short-term effect and has been almost completely forgotten in the newly formed regions.

Returning to the thesis we put forward at the beginning of this chapter about the "cultural–linguistic" modality of ethnicity that dominates in the dissolved *okrug*s, we can state, citing the answers we obtained from the people who took part in our surveys, that the mergers have not had a negative impact on this aspect. The events of June 18, 2013, when the words "Russians, get out of Parma," and "Parma for Komi" (in Russian) had been scrawled across the walls of buildings in the centre of Kudymkar, were a rare moment of aggressive political ethno-nationalism, particularly among the Komi-Permyaks. But, like we said, this was very much an isolated incident.

In the case of Komi-Permyak Autonomous Okrug and the Buryat *okrug*s, we are also dealing with the so-called pan-national myths – pan-Mongolian and pan-Finno–Ugric nationalism, respectively. Those who subscribe to pan-nationalist ideologies see Komi-Permyaks and Buryats as organic elements of larger cultural and linguistic areas. Inclusion in the relevant pan-national projects is an additional incentive for people to show a renewed interest in their ethnic identity: congresses of Finno-Ugric people are held; and the pan-Mongolian movement is regarded as a possible basis for the national revival of Kalmyks, Buryats and even Tuvans (linguistically a Turkic people who belong, culturally and religiously, to the Mongolian geographical area). The problem of merging regions was brought up at the 4th World Congress of Finno-Ugric Peoples in Tallinn, Estonia in 2004, where concerns were expressed about the possible assimilation of the Komi-Permyaks as a result of losing their status as the titular ethnic group of a constituent entity of the Russian Federation (Kolmogorova 2010).

The dominant ethnicities in the former Taymyr Dolgano-Nenets Autonomous Okrug (Dolgans, Nenets, Evenks, Enets and Nganasans) belong to the group of so-called "Indigenous Peoples of the North," as do the Koryaks and Itelmens living in Kamchatka. There were no significant manifestations of nationalism on the part of the Indigenous Peoples of the North in connection with the merger of regions (with the exception of the Itelmen activist Dmitry Berezhkov, who was forced to emigrate to Norway). However, some respondents noted that the situation was ripe for such protest sentiments due to the difficulty accessing crucial natural resources. In the case of Koryak Okrug and Kamchatka Krai, there is also the problem of tribal communities as legal entities that are delegated fishing and other resource quotas by the government. Respondents mention "asphalt Koryaks" – Koryak families living in the region's capital that effectively trade in quotas received under the status of Indigenous Peoples of the North.[4]

Thus, the series of reforms of the administrative and territorial division of the Russian Federation did not significantly affect the ethno-political tensions in the regions, even though the ethnic identity of the titular ethnic groups was temporarily politicized and brought to the forefront. The loss of this symbolic resource, which was only partially compensated for by the rather ambiguous "special status" of administrative and territorial units, did not lead to a surge in ethno-nationalism. This may be due to the cultural and linguistic "focus" of ethnicity in the "enlarged" regions that was not affected by administrative changes, as well as to the low potential for political activity. The latter point was frequently mentioned by respondents and can be attributed to the subject political culture (a term coined by G. Almond and S. Verba), which speaks to a general lack of political initiative.

---

4 See, for example: Vakhrin 2014.

Analysis of Media Messages

Maria Tislenko

One of the most effective methods for studying spatial and regional identity is discourse analysis, which allows the researcher to approach the text in a critical manner in order to answer a number of questions: what the author said; what the author wanted to say; and what the author wanted to exclude.

We assumed that in our evaluation of the reform, the main difficulties would be of an economic, managerial, and, to a lesser extent, cultural and national nature; none of us took the spatial and identity aspects of unification into account – aspects which played a role in the failure of the reforms. The reason the mergers failed was not because the promises of economic assistance, support for indigenous peoples, or equitable political representation were not kept, but because the spaces created as a result of the reforms were not conducive to giving the inhabitants of the united regions a sense of belonging to the new entity.

To test this hypothesis, we collected a corpus of 55 texts from federal and regional media, interviews with / statements from officials (governors, vice governors, authorized representatives of the President of the Russian Federation in the federal districts, and federal and regional ministers), public figures, representatives of NGOs, and ordinary residents of the constituent entities of the Russian Federation we are looking at. The reason we collected such a diverse range of texts was to ensure that our sample reflected the widest range of opinions and was not limited to one or two social groups. The media messages were selected on the basis of the size of the audience; texts by officials and public figures were chosen based on functional criteria; and texts that did not belong to either category were selected at random. The texts were classified according to the following criteria:

- the time they were written (before or after the reform);
- whether or not the person responsible for the words in the text works for the public authorities;

- whether the text has a positive/negative attitude towards the reform.

Our discourse analysis involved searching for answers in the texts to the following group of questions:

1. *Did the text mention the economic, managerial and historical aspects of the reforms?*

When looking for relevant texts, we came to realize that the rhetoric about unification can be divided into three areas of discourse: 1) the discourse surrounding economic expediency, where close economic ties between the regions mean that unification is both logical and profitable, or where they are *matryoshka* regions with one region "feeding" the other; 2) the discourse surrounding managerial expediency, which involves the optimization of bureaucracy, as such small territories do not need, for instance, their own courts, prosecutors, and representation in the Federation Council of the Russian Federation. This also includes the idea of establishing a stronger vertical of power, which was the main goal of the central government with the reform; and 3) the discourse surrounding historical expediency, according to which these territories are considered to have always been single entities, and they were only split up as a result of an historical accident or mistake (committed, for example, by the Bolsheviks, or through the spontaneous declaration of sovereignty). These areas of discourse can be cited as conformation not only of the need for reform, but also of its impracticability. The argument in the latter case was that a rich autonomous *okrug* should not be merged with a poor and economically depressed constituent entity, which was precisely what happened with the merger of Agin-Buryat Autonomous Okrug and Chita Oblast.

2. *Does the writer/speaker criticize or speak positively about the representatives of the authorities of the merged territories?*

This is an indicator of several categories at once: what is the attitude of the speaker towards the administration that carried out the reform? What is their attitude towards the previous and subsequent administrations? What are relations between the administrations of the merged entities? Who is to blame for the failures?

3. *Does the writer/speaker criticize or speak positively about the representatives of the federal authorities? And do they talk about any help the region may have received from the central government following the merger?*

These two criteria demonstrate attitude towards the initiator of the reforms, the federal government, and provide an insight into how the government's role in the reforms was perceived: does the writer/speaker blame the central government for the reform? Do they see voluntarism in their actions? Do they feel support from Moscow? Or do they feel abandoned to deal with the consequences of the merger by themselves?

4. *Is the special cultural/national status of the constituent entity affected?*

This point is important for us because this status is directly related to issues of various types of identity, including national and – indirectly – spatial. The discourse surrounding national autonomy appears to be important in the context of reform, since different parties saw this special status in connection with the administrative and territorial transformations in different ways (their arguments are presented in Table 63).

The next step was to rank the criteria, giving them different weights, and derive the coefficient of attitudes towards the reforms in the regions based on an analysis of the texts. The results are presented below.

Table 63: The Attitude of the Parties to the National Issue in the Framework of the Reform

Attitude to the reform	Centre	Representatives of the Indigenous Peoples of the merged territories	Representatives of the constituent entities that "absorbed" the autonomous *okrug*s
Supporters of reform	The topic of indigenous peoples is a "card" played by opponents of the reforms and bureaucrats who will lose funding after the merger	Loss of status will not lead to the decay of national culture. Rather, it will enrich it through the dialogue of cultures	Economic and social ties between constituent entities are historically strong, and the merger will consolidate the order that already exists, and will therefore not deal a blow to the indigenous peoples
Opponents of reform	The course towards centralization will lead to the loss of cultural diversity in the Russian Federation	Loss of status leads to underfunding and, accordingly, the decay of national culture.	As part of the new constituent entity, the indigenous lobby will push its interests through the creation of an image of itself as a victim of the reform

Komi-Permyak Autonomous Okrug in Perm Oblast

There is a significant difference in the assessment of the reform that follows two lines: the time that the text was published; and involvement/non-involvement in power structures. For example, representatives of the authorities (members of the legislative assemblies, governors, the Presidential Envoy to the Volga District Sergei Kiriyenko, and Deputy Head of the Presidential Administration Vladislav Surkov) generally had a positive attitude towards the reforms before the law on the merger of Komi-Permyak Autonomous Okrug and Perm Oblast entered into force. All texts that reflect a negative attitude towards the reform were published after the merger in 2005 and were written by people who were not employed in any of the power structures, with the exception of two pieces (one from 2005 and the other from 2015) – both interviews with the last Head of Komi-Permyak Autonomous Okrug Gennady Savelyev (Novy Kompanyon 2005). In 2005, Savelyev, in the presence of Prime Minister of the Russian Federation Mikhail Fradkov, accused Acting Governor of Perm Oblast Oleg Chirkunov of paying insufficient attention to the former autonomous *okrug*, with the promises made before the referendum having been broken. In a 2015 interview with *Parma Novosti* newspaper, Savelyev went even further in his criticism, stating that, "God saved me, ensuring that I did not participate in this shameful process" (Yanovskaya 2015). As a person in power, the last Governor of Parma did not profit from the unification process. On the contrary, he fell victim to it, so it is hardly surprising that he was not happy with it.

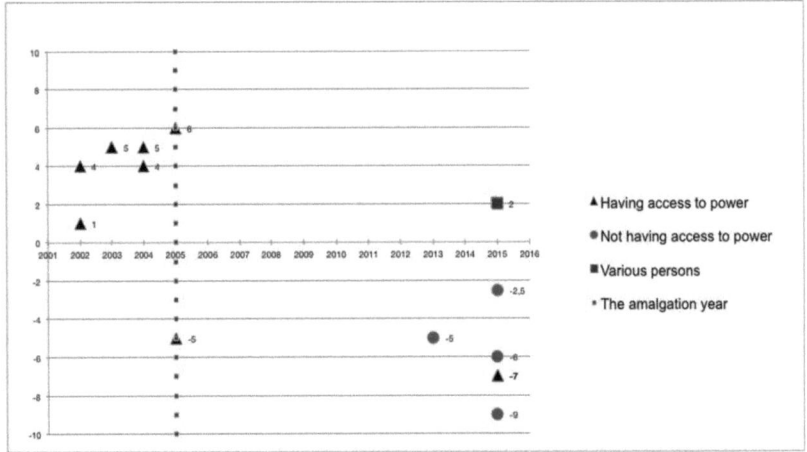

Fig 11. Attitude towards the reform in Komi-Permyak Autonomous Okrug and Perm Oblast (Perm Krai)

What language constructions were used by the supporters and opponents of the reform?

Supporters of the reform stressed the economic feasibility of the project, the opportunity for Parma to become something more than a "timber factory" and improve its own infrastructure (construction projects: a bridge over the Kama River, a gas pipeline, the Syktyvkar–Kudymkar–Grigorievskaya railway; modernization projects: Kudymkar Airport, medical facilities and housing and communal services; and the renovation of the theatre building in Kudymkar). The discourse surrounding the "historical expediency" of the reform is reflected in such terms as "Perm is our big brother" (Yanovskaya 2015), and "togetherness even in times of administrative split".

Critics of the reform used a more extensive arsenal of narratives. In terms of the economic aspect, they stressed "continuing the subsidization of the region" even after the merger and talked about its economic "depression" and it being "turned into a village," noting that Parma was "still a sawmill colony" (Argumenty i fakty 2013). As for the historical aspect, those who were against the merger pointed out that, despite the administrative unity of the two territories during Soviet times, the

Parma economy was not particularly successful and was little more than a "raw material appendage" of Perm. The most noteworthy aspect of the governance of the merged region could be summed up as follows: "The process of merging the two constituent entities is a planned and organized show of the Kremlin puppet masters" (Yanovskiy 2015), which involved a certain redistribution of cashflows, but the corruption and indifference of the authorities nullified any positive changes that may have been achieved.

The frequency with which the national and cultural aspect was brought up is particularly interesting, with only six of the 15 texts examined (or 40%) containing any mention of it, and four of those were in a negative context. Following the merger, people complained that Komi-Permyak culture was being eroded gradually, and events organized by the administration were accused of being a "façade behind which hides a far less rosy picture" (Argumenty i fakty 2013), one where schools had stopped teaching the Komi-Permyak language. That said, the "national" argument was not as prevalent in the discourse in Komi-Permyak Autonomous Okrug as it was in the other cases.

Taymyr Dolgano-Nenets Autonomous Okrug, Evenk Autonomous Okrug and Krasnoyarsk Krai

A similar trend can be observed in this case: a preponderance of positive articles and texts on the part of the establishment before the reform, and negative reaction to the public after the reform. That said, we were able to uncover two texts that looked back on the merger positively, one by former Speaker of the Krasnoyarsk Legislative Assembly Alexander Uss (Newslab.ru 2010), and another by former Speaker of the Evenk Legislative Assembly Anatoly Amosov (TASS 2016), both of which came out at on the anniversary of the merger of the three constituent entities of the Russian Federation. The only negative assessment of the merger on the part of the authorities was expressed in a 2004 interview given by Advisor to the Governor of Evenk Autonomous Okrug Yevgeny Vasiliev in an interview to *Evenk Life* newspaper. His views reflected the position of the Evenk elite, who did not want to go ahead with the merger because they would soon lose their status and power.

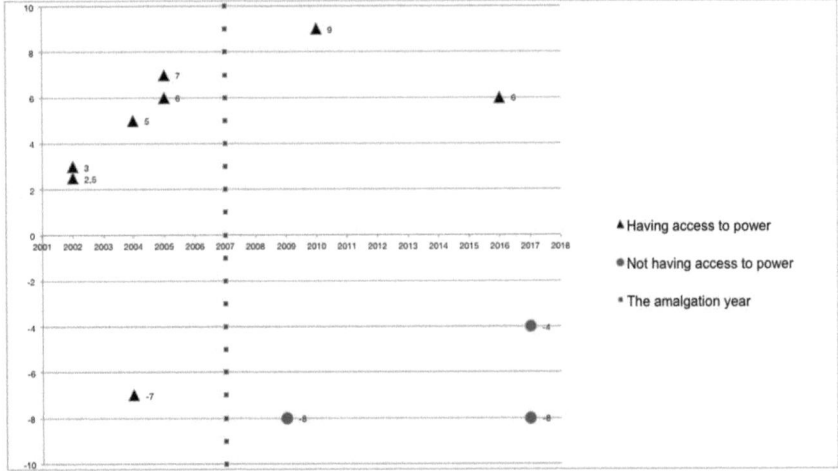

Fig 12. Attitude towards the reform in Taymyr Dolgano-Nenets Autonomous Okrug, Evenk Autonomous Okrug and Krasnoyarsk Krai

Let us take a look at the arguments put forward by both sides.

Supporters of the Merger

The economic aspect. Supporting such small regions as Taymyr Dolgano-Nenets Autonomous Okrug and Evenk Autonomous Okrug is wasteful. The merger is important in terms of fiscal equalization, as is increasing the efficiency of spending on the state apparatus.

The managerial aspect. Opponents of the reform are "individuals who are more concerned with their own future than with what will happen to the territories they currently control" (Alexander Khloponin) (REGNUM 2004b). The federal and local authorities are ready to merge, because they are all part of the same *matryoshka* territories. Merger is thus a natural and fitting step.

The national and cultural aspect. In this case, those in favour of the merger were better able to use the national and cultural aspect to defend their position. They explained that, first of all, the indigenous peoples would not lose out because of the merger. On the contrary, they would profit from it, because the new region would be richer, and the Evenks, Dolgans and Nenets would receive benefits. Second, the national question, in their opinion, is not of major importance within the framework of the new constituent entity if we think on the scale of the whole of Russia: "We live in one state and in a single society, and a person's national or ethnic background is not important. You can't bury your head in the sand. At the same time, we must ensure that not a single ethnic group is lost," Presidential Envoy to the Siberian Federal District Anatoly Kvashnin noted (Ryabinskaya 2005).

The geopolitical aspect also appears in here, which is somewhat unique among the cases we are examining. Specifically, it was mentioned in an interview with Alexander Uss, who outlined it as follows: "What happened was that, having felt our weakness, forces abroad started to call on the indigenous people to build the so-called Finno-Ugric Belt. This was a move that was aimed at creating a divide between the northern territories and the centre, that is, Russia. So, in addition to our own domestic problems, we also faced a geopolitical threat" (Newslab.ru 2010). Such verbiage is particularly important for our study, as it appeals to the category of spatiality – places and their significance for Russia. The category of *other* and the discourse of a force being opposed to Russia and "abroad" (whether this means the West or other forces is irrelevant) are also used to justify the administrative and territorial reform.

Opponents of the Merger

The economic aspect. The key points here are: criticism of the plan to turn two subsidized and one donor region into a single donor region, as rearranging the terms does not change the sum or the terms themselves; criticism of the policy of megaprojects, where several "major construction projects" (such as the Evenk Hydroelectric Power Plant project) are supposed to solve the problems of the entire region; the insinuation that Moscow will continue its "colonial policy" in relation to Evenk Autonomous

Okrug and Taymyr Dolgano-Nenets Autonomous Okrug, which are seen as raw materials appendages; as well as complaints about job cuts following the mergers (Verkhoturov 2007a).

The managerial aspect. Members of the public noted that the quality of governance was poor both before and after the reform (Kosacheva 2017), as residents faced difficulties accessing public services and losing direct access to local issues at the federal level.

The national and cultural aspect. Critics of the reform cited this issue, and while nothing specific about the decline of national cultures after the reform could be found in the texts, the following argument was put forward: the status of autonomous *okrug* gives the indigenous peoples the opportunity to develop, something they did not have before. Thus, the current level of culture, particularly among the Evenks, is the result of a long period of neglect – including in the economic sphere – of the Evenk people and their problems. What is more, one of the texts examined included an attempt to make the problems of an indigenous people international: "The issues faced by Evenk Autonomous Okrug are of a federal, even international, level, and not at all a municipal one. We are talking about preserving a unique set of forests, the conservation of biological diversity, the use of the Tunguska coal basin, which has only been explored superficially, and much more. In order for these issues to be resolved in a fair and just manner, the Evenk people need representation at the federal level" (Verkhoturov 2009).

Consequently, we can identify common pattern both in changes in the assessment of reforms and in the arguments related to economics, public administration and national policy. However, the case of Krasnoyarsk Krai, Taymyr Dolgano-Nenets Autonomous Okrug and Evenk Autonomous Okrug is interesting due to the following reasons: a) mentions of the importance and strategic position of the territories; b) attempts to move the problems of small-numbered peoples and their environment to the international level; and c) the "colonial" discourse surrounding the autonomous *okrug*.

Koryak Autonomous Okrug and Kamchatka Oblast

The case of Koryak Autonomous Okrug and Kamchatka Oblast is less typical, but there are still similarities with the other examples we have looked at: massive support from the establishment, dissatisfaction of those who stand to lose power and resources as a result of the merger, and the gradual decline in the assessments of the merger over time.

Fig 13. Attitude towards the reform in Koryak Autonomous Okrug and Kamchatka Oblast (Kamchatka Krai)

However, certain points should be noted here. In particular, a 2005 text that is rated −4 on our scale contains a negative assessment by Former Governor of Krasnoyarsk Krai Alexander Khloponin regarding the possible unification of Koryak Autonomous Okrug and Kamchatka Oblast. According to him, the reform should only be carried out if it is economically expedient to do so, and thus "poor regions" such as Kamchatka Oblast and Koryak Autonomous Okrug should not be merged (Newdaynews.ru 2005). This is a rare example of a reform being assessed by someone in a different constituent entity of the Russian Federation, rather than from within the federal/local authorities. Khloponin's statement suggests that there is a competition of sorts between different options for unification. He stresses that the "unification of

Krasnoyarsk Krai will produce a positive economic result not only for the region itself, but also for the entire east of Russia."

Another text, rated 3 on our scale and dated 2013, is attributed to the first Governor of Kamchatka Krai Aleksey Kuzmitsky and was published to mark the fifth anniversary of the establishment of the constituent entity (the interview was reprinted a year later). Since the ex-governor is unlikely to give a negative assessment of his own activities, the content of the interview should be regarded as "window dressing": Kuzmitsky is trying to present events in the most favourable light. He places a particular emphasis on the difficulties he faced: "It was an extremely difficult period – it was the first time that two largely impoverished constituent entities had been merged. Yet the merger did not lead to a sharp increase in the coffers." Quite the opposite, according to Kuzmitsky, "new debts were uncovered on a daily basis," but the situation gradually changed for the better – infrastructure projects went ahead, social facilities were renovated, and production of canned fish resumed in Koryak Okrug (Kamchatka Inform 2014). Special emphasis was placed on the fact that the assistance provided by Vladimir Putin and his team was vital to the success of the merger. This is a rare instance where assistance from the federal centre is mentioned directly.

One text from 2017 contains data on an online poll conducted by the Kam 24 news agency on its website asking users whether they would support the merger of Kamchatka Oblast and Koryak Autonomous Okrug if the referendum were to take place today. The results showed that 50% of the people would vote against the merger, 39% would vote for it, while 10% answered "don't know" (Kam 24 2017). A total of 250 people took part in the poll, and while online voting such be taken with a grain of salt, in this case it is a fresh indicator of the mood in Kamchatka Krai.

Ust-Orda Buryat Autonomous Okrug and Irkutsk Oblast

The last two cases do not quite fit into the patterns we have identified thus far, as the texts by people who are not involved in the power structures are almost exclusively negative about the reform, both after the merger (which is typical for all cases) and before it. This can be explained by the fact that there was a pronounced Buryat national factor in the case of Ust-Orda Buryat Autonomous Okrug and Irkutsk Oblast (as there was in Agin-Buryat Autonomous Okrug and Chita Oblast). Buryat public figures and journalists who sympathized with them were categorically against the idea of merging the two regions.

The arguments against the merger can be divided into the following blocks:

First, the discourse on the economically "unequal marriage," in which Ust-Orda Buryat Autonomous Okrug is presented as the affluent constituent entity, and Irkutsk Oblast is seen as the economically "depressed" one. One of the texts we examined used the following metaphor: "a poor Russian elder brother married a rich ethnic girl" (Dmitriev 2007). The same rhetoric was used in a text about Agin-Buryat Autonomous Okrug.

Second, the element of a shared history and the "victim" narrative. Those who were against the reform repeatedly brought up the supposedly "illegal" division of Buryat-Mongol Autonomous Soviet Socialist Republic, where the Ust-Orda and Aginsky districts were torn away and attached to Irkutsk and Chita oblasts, respectively. Thus, the pro-Buryat camp positions its territories, and the Buryat people as a whole, as a victim of the wilfulness of the centre (Dmitriev 2007).

Third, the national and cultural aspect. Before the merger, the pro-Buryat camp noted its concerns about the loss of its national culture. Afterwards, however, it openly talked about the decline of its culture and the fake concern of the authorities about the indigenous peoples, where "upholding national and cultural identity" essentially amounted to the "holding of sporting and cultural events" (Basaev 2016).

Fourth, the opponents of the reform did not forget about the managerial aspect of the merger. However, the arguments are similar to those put forward in the other cases we have looked at and concern the lack of representation and indifference of the Irkutsk authorities to the problems of the former constituent entity.

Our sample contains four texts with a positive rating, two of which are attributed to members of the public, which is also unusual.

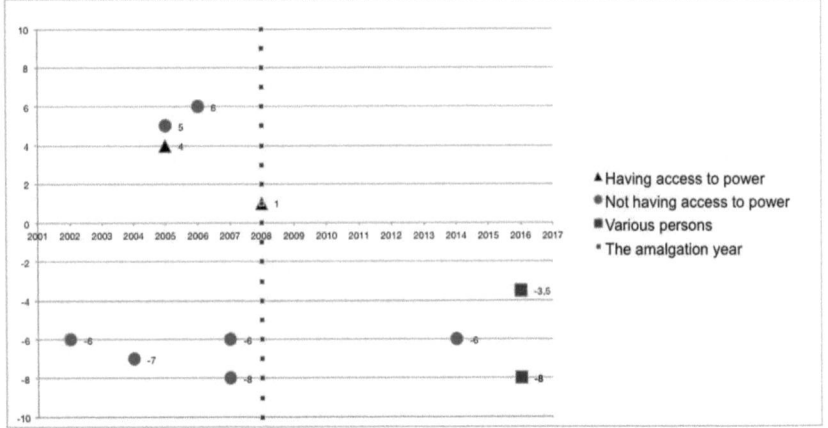

Fig 14. Attitude towards the reform in Ust-Orda Buryat Autonomous Okrug and Irkutsk Oblast

One of the texts aims to create a positive image of Irkutsk Governor Alexander Tishanin (Sobakina 2005), while the second is patently propagandistic and talks about the creation of the "Peoples of Baikal Region for Unification" referendum group and the development of a coherent national policy in Irkutsk Oblast, which is home to more than 100 peoples whose interests are safe and secure (REGNUM. 2006b). It is also noteworthy that there were no messages after the reform that spoke positively of the move, as if its initiators decided that there was no need for PR support after the fact.

We can thus state that resistance to the merger was more pronounced than in the other cases we have examined, and the activities of the authorities in building a positive agenda around the merger were half-hearted and apathetic.

Agin-Buryat Autonomous Okrug and Chita Oblast

We were only able to find six texts about the merger of these two regions, which points to the low level of interest in the issue. That notwithstanding, a similar trend can be discerned in this case to that of the merger of Ust-Orda Buryat Autonomous Okrug and Irkutsk Oblast in that the reform was perceived negatively both before and after it took place. The attitude of those in the power structures in the two regions was somewhat surprising, as we could not find a single mention of the reform before it was carried out. The only material we managed to uncover was an interview with the head of Agin-Buryat Autonomous Okrug, Ananda Dondokov, which is little more than a typical window-dressing piece with an official who waxes lyrical about the success of the merger and paints himself in the most favourable light (Kolokolova 2016). The text is also interesting because Dondokov lays out the reasons why it was necessary to merge Agin-Buryat Autonomous Okrug with Chita Oblast:

- historical community ("our children went to Chita universities," "the adult population worked in the districts of the *oblast*");
- it made sense from an economic point of view (Agin-Buryat Okrug is an exclusively agricultural territory and could learn a lot from Chita Oblast);
- "it's what the people wanted" (Dondokov is referring to the referendum here).

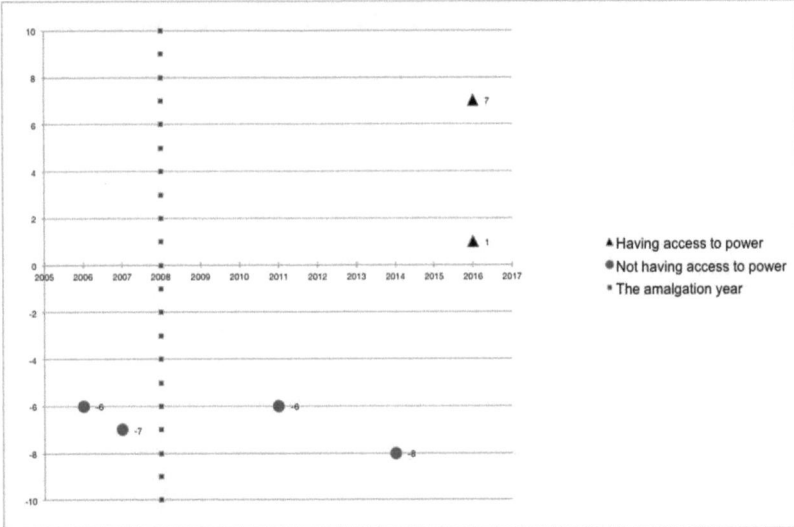

Fig 15. Attitude towards the reform in Agin-Buryat Autonomous Okrug and Chita Oblast (Zabaykalsky Krai).

Those who opposed the merger were far more aggressive and proactive in their stance, and they used arguments that resembled those used in the case of Ust-Orda:

- The difference in the economic potentials of the prosperous Agin-Buryat Autonomous Okrug and the impoverished Chita Oblast. As one of the articles we looked at points out, "Agin-Buryat Autonomous Okrug is the only region in Siberia that receives minimal subsidies from the government, with assistance from the federal centre amounting to just 6.43%. Meanwhile, as much as 45% the budget of the region that was set to absorb it – Chita Oblast – was made up of federal assistance (Zabinfo.ru 2011).
- The historical argument and "victim" narrative – we are, after all, dealing with the Buryat people and the same story about the wilful division of the Buryat territories.
- Unmet expectations: the quality of life in the region declined; Agin-Buryat Autonomous Okrug did not become more industrialized; and all the promises were nothing more than enticing slogans from the central authorities which, in addition to the local "corrupt" officials, used the

administrative resource during the referendum to get the result they wanted. (The local authorities turned out to be "corrupt" because they had initially spoken out against the merger and were then "convinced" to support it. Most prominent among these officials were the governor of Agin-Buryat Autonomous Okrug Bair Zhamsuev and the *okrug*'s representative in the State Duma I. Kobzon.)
- National-cultural reasons. Here, reform is seen as the "epic of erasing two Buryat autonomies" and the danger of the Buryat people losing their national identity.

Moscow came under heavy criticism in the cases of the two former Buryat autonomous *okrug*s: negative statements were more to the point ("the lure of the federals") (Zabinfo.ru 2011), and the government was accused of "pushing the reform through." At the same time, there are similarities in the materials on the merger that took place in Zabaykalsky Krai with the unsuccessful attempts to unite the Republic of Adygea and Krasnodar Krai, as well as those to unite Altai Krai and the Altai Republic. These regions were able to resist the pressure of the centre and retain their status. The authors lamented the lack of civic activity on the part of the people of Agin-Buryat Autonomous Okrug and the dearth of political leaders who could rally protest sentiments around them to fight the merger (Verkhoturov 2007a).

Takeaways:

1. What we see in most cases is initial enthusiasm on the part of the authorities were about the mergers before they took place (although this is not true for those in the power structures who did not stand to benefit from the move), which then gives way to more negative assessments of the reform that typically appear around the time that the respective constituent entity is marking an anniversary of the merger.

2. The cases of Agin-Buryat Autonomous Okrug and Ust-Orda Buryat Autonomous Okrug do not follow this general pattern due to the strong national component that is present in these regions. We can thus conclude that Buryat identity is stronger than that of the Komi-Permyaks, Koryaks, Dolgano-Nenets and Evenks, and it was this that led to more active resistance in the media.
3. A common thread in all the cases was the discourse about "unmet expectations" and unfulfilled promises in the economic and social spheres, and, less frequently, in terms of the preservation of national culture. What is more, when politicians talk about the lack of success (and outright failures) of the mergers, they usually cite the 2008 financial crisis as the reason, while the people tend to blame the local authorities rather than the central government.
4. The reform only really affected the consciousness of the people living in the formerly autonomous regions: there is a very small corpus of texts discussing the respective mergers in Perm, Krasnoyarsk, Kamchatka and Zabaykalsky krais and Irkutsk Oblast, and the most noticeable feature of them is an indifference to the events and their former neighbours.

Analysis of Opinion Polls

Maria Tislenko & Igor Okunev

The issue of spatial inequality is rather sensitive in Russia, and awareness of this problem exists both within the academia and at the governmental level. In this regard, regional policy can be divided into two main types according to the measures that underlie it: equalizing and stimulating. The desire in Russia for convergence of the country's regions was even set out in a separate federal target programme entitled "Reducing Differences in the Socio-Economic Development of the Regions of the Russian Federation (2002–2010 and up to 2015)," which was completed ahead of schedule in 2006.

Regional convergence is possible, including through formal means, by reducing the number of constituent entities. This was partially justified for the Russian Federation in the early 2000s, since a number of administrative and territorial units remained as rudiments of the Soviet system of administrative and territorial division. These constituent entities were determined according to the dominant nationality/ethnicity in each region, although territorially, they turned out to be *matryoshka* regions located inside larger and economically stronger entities. This was the background for the reform of the administrative and territorial division of the Russian Federation that took part in the mid-2000s, which involved 11 constituent entities being merged into five regions.

Nevertheless, as researchers, we are still faced with the question of what the reform aimed to achieve – whether the goals were purely political, i.e., aimed at building a vertical of power, or economic, which is what was proclaimed during the public rallies for the mergers. To this end, we attempted to analyse the causes and consequences of the administrative and territorial reform carried out in Russia in the mid-2000s through an assessment of public opinion. After all, any reform affects the lives of ordinary people, and the reforms we are looking at were carried out for the people, to improve their quality of life and increase the wellbeing of society. This is why the assessment of the reform by ordinary citizens is so important, as any changes initiated "from above" inevitably encounter resistance and the desire to maintain the *status quo*, no matter how unfavourable it may be (Davies 1962).

We offer the hypothesis that residents responded negatively to the merger of constituent entities of the Russian Federation because they were not initially presented with a single, understandable goal, which is what makes an objective assessment of the achievement of this goal impossible. The people in the former constituent entities of the Russian Federation are even harsher in their judgements, because losing their status has meant that they are now neglected by the federal centre and have been deprived of the opportunity to lobby their economic and political interests. As a result, everyone measures the success of the reform with the changes that have affected them the most (political controllability, the socioeconomic situation, national identity, perhaps even transport accessibility, etc.) and thus gives a unique assessment of the process – from very positive to extremely negative.

To assess the consequences of the reform, we made research trips to villages, former centres of constituent entities that ceased to exist (Kudymkar, Dudinka, Tura, Ust-Ordynsky, Aginsky and Palana), and cities that now serve as the centres of the enlarged entities (Perm, Krasnoyarsk, Irkutsk, Chita and Petropavlovsk-Kamchatsky). We carried out a telephone-based opinion poll in each city.

A total of 3 382 telephone interviews were conducted, and 555 complete and 48 incomplete questionnaires were collected (data is only provided for the completed questionnaires): 50 questionnaires each in Petropavlovsk-Kamchatsky, Chita, Irkutsk, Kudymkar and Aginsky; 51 each in Krasnoyarsk, Perm, Ust-Ordynsky and Palana; 63 in Dudinka; and 38 in Tura. We wanted to collect 50 questionnaires for each city. However, this was impossible for Tura, as we could not find the required number of respondents among the small population of 5493 people. The number was made up by Dudinka, as the former constituent entities to which these cities belonged – Taymyr Dolgano-Nenets Autonomous Okrug and

Evenk Autonomous Okrug – were both merged into Krasnoyarsk Krai, so they can be seen as two parts of the same case.

The authors acknowledge the existence of objective limitations, such as the decline in the number of landline telephones in big cities and the difficulty searching phone number databases in such small towns as Palana, Tura and Dudinka, as well as the relative distrust among the population in opinion polls. Given that the sample is in no way representative, the results we offer are only estimations and, statistically, not strictly observable. They are thus interpreted from the standpoint of qualitative sociology.

The telephone questionnaire was made up of 34 questions divided into a number of blocks which assess:

- the goals and consequences of the reform;
- the level of satisfaction with certain aspects of life in the region;
- the level of trust in various institutions of government and civil society;
- the level of the political "wellbeing" of respondents in the current political field of Russia;
- information about the respondent (age and gender).

All this notwithstanding, our focus in this work is on the results of the first block.

Results. This is dedicated directly to assessing the goals and consequences of the reform. One of the key questions for our entire study is: "What goals did the reform pursue?" In this regard, the administrative and territorial reforms that took place in the Russian Federation in the 2000s offer us a wide range of subtopics, because the reasons and goals are not as obvious as they may seem at first glance. The assumption that the reforms pursued socioeconomic goals was supported by the statements of high-ranking officials such as Vladislav Surkov (Semyonov 2003). However, our in-depth interviews with people who held key positions within the constituent entities of the Russian Federation at the time revealed misunderstanding and bewilderment on the part of the respondents: hypothetical explanations were never extensive for them, so many of these officials had their own vision of reform, and the populations was offered various options for activism during the referendum campaign. A number of assumptions thus appeared as to why the reform was necessary: to ensure the economic development of the newly formed constituent entities, especially the smaller regions that were being assimilated into larger ones; to reduce the number of constituent entities in the Russian Federation and increase governability from the federal centre; to overcome the centrifugal tendencies of the 1990s and build a vertical of power; and to reduce the influence of national minorities whose desire to maintain autonomy could turn into separatist sentiments and even lead to military conflicts.

In this connection, we identified the four main types of answers:

1. "Improving the governability of the regions from the centre";
2. "The socioeconomic development of the regions";
3. "The elimination of national *okrugs*":
4. "Don't know."

Representatives of the government authorities often went for "Improving the governability of the regions from the centre," as they are associated the reforms with building a vertical of power and the trends towards its consolidation, which replaced the centrifugal tendencies of the 1990s. That said, most of the respondents (almost 41%) saw the goal of the reform as being the socioeconomic development of the regions (Fig. 16). In many ways, this is very much in line with the propagandistic discourse, which was used to convince the people to turn up to vote for the merger of the regions. What is more, a presidential decree containing a list of facilities to be created in each constituent entity was drawn up for each reform.

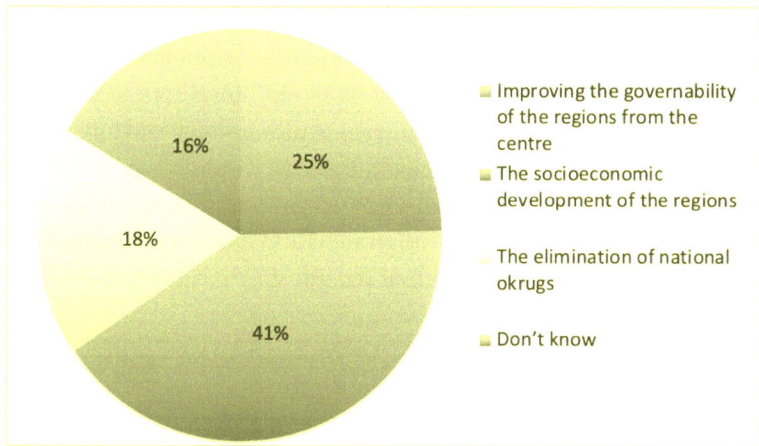

Fig. 16. Answers to the question: "What was the main goal of the reform?", %

People living in the cities that became the administrative centres of the enlarged regions are more convinced that the goal of the reforms was the socioeconomic development of the regions than the residents whose constituent entities ceased to exist as independent entities after the mergers – 51.6% compared to 31.6% (Fig. 17).

One possible explanation for this is that the larger, richer regions were expected to "pull" the weaker *matryoshka* regions out of their economic doldrums, which would involve a redistribution of financial flows within the new constituent entity, and the more efficient use of finances by reducing spending on maintaining the bureaucracy and infrastructure projects funded by the federal centre. This is perhaps the reason that respondents in large cities saw behind the reforms, seeing their region as a "benefactor." However, this explanation does not pan out in at least two cases, namely, Zabaykalsky Krai and Kamchatka Krai. Agin-Buryat Autonomous Okrug flourished compared to Chita Oblast thanks to its special tax status, while 45% of the Chita budget was made up of federal subsidies (compared to 6.43% in Agin-Buryat Autonomous Okrug during the final years before the merger) (Tvortsov 2011). This, we believe, is what explains the high proportion of respondents in Chita Oblast citing the second option as the goal of the reform (60%). Judging by what the people of Chita told us in the in-depth interviews, we can say that they believed that if they voted in favour of the merger, investments would start flowing into the region, or at least the "old" investors (companies with a legal address in Agin-Buryat Autonomous Okrug) would not leave. The situation in Kamchatka was different, as one of the poorest *oblast*s in the Russian Federation was absorbing an even poorer autonomous *okrug*, so alignment and assistance through the redistribution of funds was out of the question – Kamchatka Oblast was itself in need of serious economic assistance.

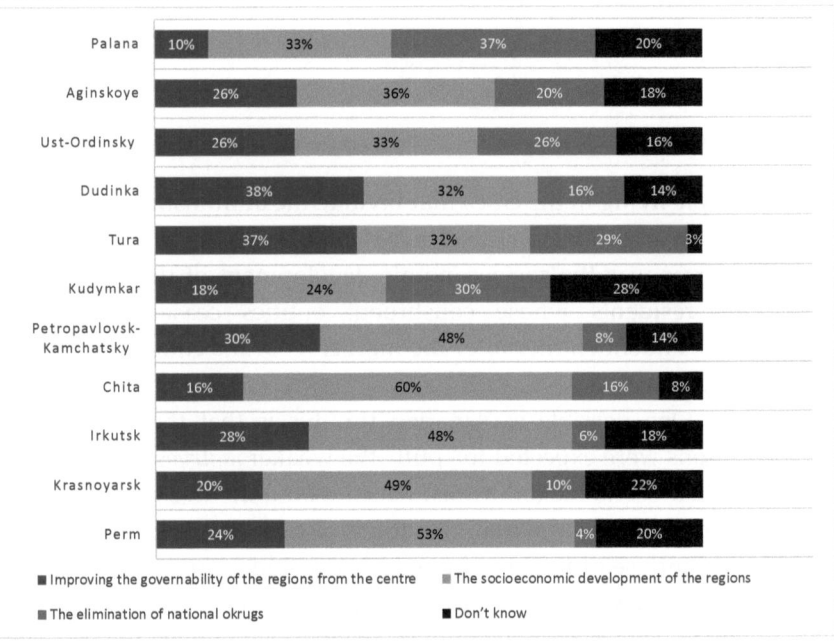

Fig. 17. Answers to the question: "What was the main goal of the reform?" by city, %

Respondents who said that the main goal of the reforms was to improve the governability of the regions from the centre. Two former administrative centres can be singled out here, Dudinka and Tura, both of which were merged with Krasnoyarsk Krai. A rather high percentage of respondents in Petropavlovsk-Kamchatsky cited this reason, even though only 9.85% of people in Palana (in the former Koryak Autonomous Okrug) who took part in the poll gave this answer. What is more, the most popular response in

Koryak Okrug was "The elimination of national *okrugs*": 37.3% compared to 8% in Petropavlovsk-Kamchatsky, although the national question was not as prominent as it was in the Buryat territories that were absorbed into larger regions and did not generally appear in the rhetoric for or against the reform in the public statements made by officials or in the media. The opinion that the reform was carried out in order to eliminate national autonomies was expressed most frequently by those who saw the mergers as an attack on federalism, the desire to control everything from the federal centre at the expense of the rights of small-numbered indigenous peoples and the suppression of any attempts to foster national separatist movements. The explanation resonated with an average of 17% of all people who took part in the poll and was more pronounced in the former administrative centres of the constituent entities of the Russian Federation: Kudymkar (30%), Tura (slightly less than 29%), and Ust-Ordinsky (25.5%).

Thus, there was greater disagreement among the people in the smaller constituent entities of the Russian Federation that the main goal of the reform was socioeconomic development. The answers given by respondents are far more varied, unlike those given by the residents of the enlarged regions. This is almost certainly due to the fact that the *matryoshka* entities did not really see any of the improvements they had been promised following the mergers.

Assessment of the consequences of the reform.

Respondents were asked to give a score from 1 (extremely negative) to 10 (extremely positive). Opinions are very much polarized here (Fig. 18): half of the respondents chose either 1 or 10, with the proportion of those who are completely dissatisfied with the merger being higher be 0.5% – 25.2% (140 people) compared to 24.7% (135 people). One fifth of all respondents gave scores of between 5 and 10. In order to divine what is behind the ratings in each particular case we will conduct a pairwise comparison of the former and current administrative centres.

Having divided the cities into two groups according to the criterion we mentioned, we see a sharp cleavage between them (Fig.

19): in the former administrative centres, 34.88% of respondents offered extremely negative appraisals of the reform, and 12.42% were extremely positive; meanwhile, in the current administrative centres of the enlarged regions, 9.14% of those who took part in the poll rated the reform a 1, and 39.32% gave it a score of 10.

The most pessimistic group of respondents was found in Kudymkar, where 52% gave a score of 1, compared to 7.8% in Perm. This was the first in the series of mergers, and, being an experimental step, it was not thought out carefully, which ultimately led to greater disappointment among the population of the "pioneering" region that had been promised much for its courage.

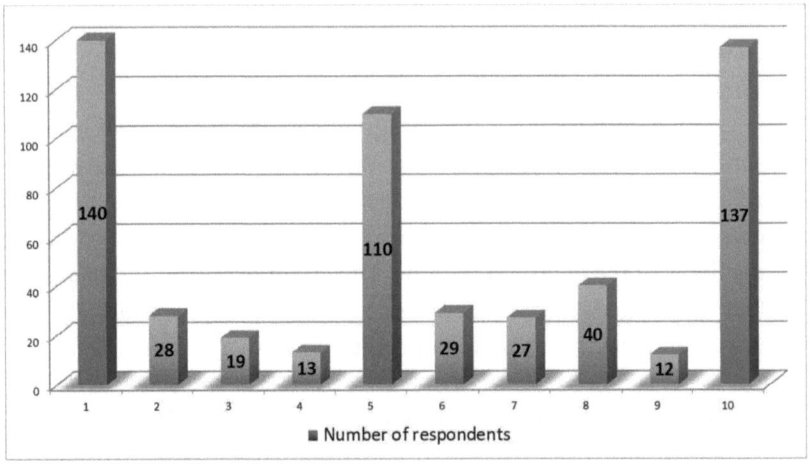

Fig. 18. Answers to the question: "How do you assess the results of the federal reform in Russia that saw your autonomous *okrug* merge with larger regions?" (number of respondents who gave scored between 1 and 10)

In Dudinka, 46% of respondents expressed their extreme dissatisfaction with the reform, compared to 24% in Tura, and 5.9% in Krasnoyarsk (the current centre of the region that assimilated Taymyr Dolgano-Nenets Autonomous Okrug and Evenk Autonomous Okrug), which is 7.5 times less than in Dudinka and the lowest among all regions for this answer. More than half of the respondents in Krasnoyarsk and Tura gave scores of 6 or above, compared to just 23.8% in Dudinka.

Zabaykalsky Krai is an interesting case, given that it is the respondents in the current administrative centre, Chita, who are the most negative about the reform (20%). That said, pessimism does not distort the overall picture, where the residents of the former *matryoshka* region are mostly dissatisfied (68% of respondents rated the merger 1 to 5), and the population of the new administrative centre is positive in its assessments (56% rated it 6 to 10). On the one hand, the inhabitants of Zabaykalsky Krai (excluding the territories of the former Agin-Buryat Autonomous Okrug) are not particularly happy with the results of the reform. On the other hand, there is reason to believe that the merger was unavoidable, especially for Agin-Buryat Autonomous Okrug, whose special tax status as a guarantee of the region's economic wellbeing was bound to change sooner or later, turning it into a classic agricultural region that specializes in risky farming. Accordingly, the Agin Buryat people, even if they were aware of all the limitations, still believe that it is better to live as an isolated entity with its own budget, despite the promises of the federal centre and the Chita authorities.

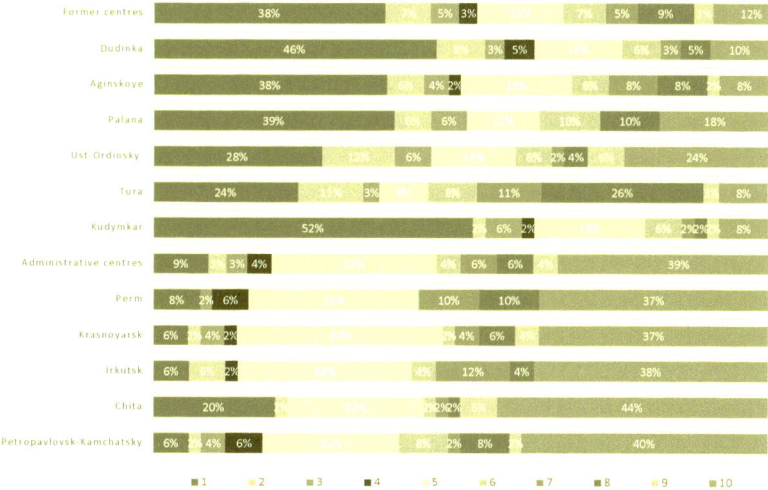

Fig. 19. Distribution of assessments of the results of the reform by city (share of respondents who gave scored between 1 and 10)

As for Kamchatka Krai and Irkutsk Oblast, they fit into the described pattern without any notable statistical anomalies, except for the former Ust-Orda Buryat Autonomous Okrug, where respondents had a more positive view of the results of the reform compared to the other former administrative centres.

Thus, our preliminary conclusion based on the results of an analysis of the two tables is as follows: most respondents believe that the mergers of regions were initiated in order to give an impetus to the socioeconomic development of the territories. However, assessments of the consequences differ: the constituent entities that ceased to exist as independent regions see the results of the reform negatively, while the regions that absorbed them are more optimistic.

Nevertheless, the overall assessment is made up of several components that can also be assessed as independent criteria. In view of this, we identified five components that correspond to different areas of public life:

1. The quality of the work of the government bodies.
2. The level of economic development of the region.
3. The degree of social support provided by the government.
4. Stability and peace in inter-ethnic relations.
5. The level of government support for the national culture and language.

We will take a separate look at each pair of cities whose subjects were enlarged for the purposes of a comparative analysis (three cities are included in one of the cases – Krasnoyarsk, Dudinka and Tura).

Perm and Kudymkar

It is here where views on the reform to merge Perm Oblast and Komi-Permyak Autonomous Okrug into Perm Krai demonstrate the highest degree of polarization (Table 64). Thus, 50% of respondents from Kudymkar believe that the quality of work of the government bodies has deteriorated either slightly or significantly, compared to 15.7% of respondents in Perm. Meanwhile, 47.1% of the respondents in Perm noted that they had not seen any changes in the work of the government bodies. This negative assessment is actually typical of all the former administrative centres, since losing their status as constituent entities of the Russian Federation meant the liquidation of their territorial government bodies such as the departments of the Federal Tax Service and the prosecutor's office, causing some civil servants to lose their jobs and certain public services to become more difficult to obtain, which thus requires people to travel to the new administrative centre. At the same time, the percentage of Komi-Permyaks who noticed significant improvements in the quality of the work of bureaucratic structures is twice that of Perm residents, and a similar discrepancy in assessments is observed in the answers provided by respondents from Zabaykalsky Krai and Krasnoyarsk Krai (Tura and Krasnoyarsk, excluding Dudinka) and Irkutsk Oblast. Hypothetically, this can be put down to an increase in transparency and a decrease in "feudalist" tendencies in small regions, which, due to their size, importance and remoteness from the federal centre, were "black boxes" of sorts with higher corruption risks.

Table 64: Distribution of answers to the question: "To what extent has the situation changed in individual spheres of life as a result of the federal reform?" in Perm Krai, %

Responses	Assessment of respondents				
	Government bodies	Economy	Social welfare	Inter-ethnic relations	National culture
Perm					
Deteriorated significantly	5.9	3.9	11.8	2.0	3.9
Most likely deteriorated	9.8	17.6	25.5	5.9	2.0
No change	47.1	41.2	23.5	21.6	25.5
Most likely improved	31.4	33.3	33.3	39.2	43.1

Improved significantly	5.9	3.9	5.9	31.4	25.5
Kudymkar					
Deteriorated significantly	32.0	32.0	16.0	12.0	4.0
Most likely deteriorated	18.0	20.0	14.0	4.0	4.0
No change	32.0	30.0	36.0	32.0	28.0
Most likely improved	6.0	16.0	24.0	22.0	42.0
Improved significantly	12.0	2.0	10.0	30.0	22.0

Economic development is an important topic for the Komi-Permyak territories, as the region's economy was always – at least during the Soviet period and the period of existence of Komi-Permyak Autonomous Okrug – focused on the export of raw materials, namely timbre, which earned it the nickname of a "sawmill colony." It has been over ten years since the merger, during which time the situation has not changed radically. This may explain why 52% of Komi-Permyaks believe that things have got worse for them, 32% believe that nothing has changed, and only 18% noted positive changes in terms of economic development. The opinions of respondents from Perm are distributed in an entirely different manner: approximately 20% feel that things have got worse, 41.2% believe that no changes have occurred as such, and 37.2% noticing improvements in the economy.

In terms of social welfare, the people of Perm demonstrate a greater degree of dissatisfaction with the changes in the social sphere than the people of Komi-Permyak Autonomous Okrug: 37.3%, compared to 30%. This is likely not due to the reform, as other factors in Perm Krai influence the "social wellbeing" indicator. In Komi-Permyak Autonomous Okrug, 36% of respondents believe that no changes have taken place, while 34% believe that the situation has most likely improved or even improved significantly. That is quite comparable with Perm, where the respective figure was 39.2%.

The two remaining indicators concern the national identity aspects of the people in the Komi-Permyak and Komi communities

– peace in inter-ethnic relations and the level of state support for national cultures and languages. The inter-ethnic aspect is associated with the inevitable migration processes that take place in the context of the transformation of centre–periphery relations in the regions. In the *matryoshka* regions, the administrative centre was alluring because of the expanded life opportunities it afforded. But, following the merger, it was just another city, and the "focus of hopes" moved to the new administrative centre, or these hopes intensified even more. Not just a "brain drain," but the fact that the national minority also leaves its ancestral territory and "dissolves" into the new host community, thus losing an important part of its national culture and identity. However, it is not a given that events will unfold "diffusely": hostility and competition may arise between the two cultures, reinforced by the "Us and Them" dichotomy, even if the cultures are objectively quite similar. This is why we asked about inter-ethnic relations in our poll. We learned that 70% of Perm natives and over 50% of Komi-Permyaks believed that inter-ethnic relations in the region had improved, despite the fact that 12% of Komi-Permyaks noted a significant deterioration in this area. Unfortunately, we were unable to determine what meaning the respondents attributed to the term "improvement of interethnic relations" – was about reducing conflict or was it about something else? Nevertheless, both sides are satisfied and believe that the positive changes have come about as a result of the reform.

Positive dynamics are also observed in the state support for national culture, which in this case refers to the culture of the national minority, the Komi-Permyaks. Assessments are almost the same for both cities: the vast majority (over 60%) of respondents in Perm and Kudymkar believe that state support for Komi-Permyak culture has increased. Checking this against available data, we can see that greater funds have indeed been allocated for culture and education in the national language. What is more, they have become more popular among the local population, and it has become quite fashionable among the Komi-Permyak people, including the youth, to learn more about their origins. We should take this into consideration when assessing the successes in the cultural sphere and be somewhat reticent to attribute them exclusively to the merger of the two regions.

To sum up the case of the creation of Perm Krai, we should note the extreme pessimism of the Komi-Permyak people when assessing the consequences of the reform in such areas as the quality of the work of the government bodies and economic development, while respondents in Perm tended to see the situation as remaining the same. In terms of social development, certain positive dynamics are observed in the assessments, and they are characterized by a convergence of the positions of respondents in Perm and Kudymkar. As for national and cultural issues, residents of both cities generally note positive changes, although citing these metrics to identify the relationship between the positive assessments and the transformations that took place during and after the reform presents certain difficulties.

Krasnoyarsk, Dudinka and Tura

This case serves as an example of greater homogeneity in the assessments of the reforms (Table 65), with certain reservations, and a demonstration of the opinion that the merger was just a rearrangement of the components, with the result remaining the same – that is, the answer "No change" dominated in our survey. And this, even though the share of respondents in Dudinka who assessed the reform extremely negatively was among the highest in the entire opinion poll (46%, compared to 23.7% in Tura and 5.9% in Krasnoyarsk).

Assessing the quality of work of the government bodies after the reform, the majority of respondents did not see any changes in this criterion in the 11 years since the merger: 41.3% in Dudinka and 64% in Krasnoyarsk, while the most popular answer among respondents in Tura was "Improved significantly" (34.2%).

Table 65: Distribution of answers to the question: "To what extent has the situation changed in individual spheres of life

as a result of the federal reform?" in Krasnoyarsk Krai, %

Responses	Assessment of respondents				
	Government bodies	Economy	Social welfare	Inter-ethnic relations	National culture
Krasnoyarsk					
Deteriorated significantly	3.9	9.8	9.8	0.0	0.0
Most likely deteriorated	13.7	23.5	23.5	2.0	2.0
No change	64.7	41.2	27.5	54.9	45.1
Most likely improved	11.8	23.5	31.4	21.6	31.4
Improved significantly	5.9	2.0	7.8	21.6	21.6
Dudinka					
Deteriorated significantly	22.2	22.2	7.9	0.0	3.2
Most likely deteriorated	15.9	15.9	11.1	0.0	0.0
No change	41.3	41.3	22.2	6.3	4.8
Most likely improved	17.5	17.5	39.7	33.3	17.5
Improved significantly	3.2	3.2	19.0	60.3	74.6
Tura					
Deteriorated significantly	15.8	10.5	5.3	5.3	2.6
Most likely deteriorated	10.5	7.9	10.5	2.6	2.6
No change	26.3	52.6	26.3	18.4	13.2
Most likely improved	34.2	21.1	52.6	28.9	31.6
Improved significantly	13.2	7.9	5.3	44.7	50.0

That notwithstanding, there are plenty of dissatisfied people in Dudinka, where, according to 22% of respondents, the quality of work of the government bodies deteriorated noticeably following the reform. This can be attributed to the fact that, as we noted earlier, many public services have become inaccessible to Taymyr residents, who must now travel at the very least to Norilsk (two hours by car from Dudinka) to obtain various permits and licenses, which is especially difficult for those who live in remote areas of Taymyr, for example, in Dikson and Khatanga, where the main transport connection with large settlements is by helicopter.

As for the economic development indicator, the most common answer was "No change" (41% in both Krasnoyarsk and Dudinka, and 52.6% in Tura). At the same time, a curious picture is observed in Dudinka: 22% of respondents gave a score of 1 here, and there is reason to believe that these are the same people. Such coincidences are quite common in the case of Krasnoyarsk Krai, which speaks to the consistency of respondents in their assessments, except for instances where it is difficult to deny achievements or failures.

Social welfare has increased, more so in Tura and Dudinka (52.6% and 39.7%, respectively) than in Krasnoyarsk (31.4%), which indicates that respondents attribute their improved social wellbeing with the merger.

The answers to the block of questions relating to inter-ethnic relations and the cultures of national minorities are just as interesting: the people of Dudinka and Tura are more positive in their assessments of the changes in this area than the people of Krasnoyarsk, and by a significant margin. For example, 74.6% of respondents from Dudinka noted that inter-ethnic relations had become more stable, and 81.6% agreed that support for national culture had increased. These figures were even higher for Tura, at 93.6% and 92.1%, respectively. Such unanimity is not evident in any other region. Efforts have indeed been stepped up over the past ten years to support the cultural development of the Dolgans and Nenets in Taymyr, including the publication of school readers in the languages of the Indigenous Peoples of the North.

As a result, respondents in Krasnoyarsk Krai overwhelmingly stated that the situation had not changed significantly in the 11 years since the reform, with the exception that inter-ethnic ties had become more stable and peaceful and government support for the Indigenous Peoples of the North had increased. The people of Dudinka were particularly sceptical due to the geographical location and harsh climatic conditions, exacerbating the problems of quality of life and governability of this vast subarctic territory whose area is greater than that of any European country.

Petropavlovsk-Kamchatsky and Palana

As we mentioned earlier, the merger of the two constituent entities into Kamchatka Krai is an unusual case in many respects, since there were no objective economic prerequisites for it to take place: Kamchatka Oblast was itself in need of development and thus was not able to boost the Koryak Autonomous Okrug economy, as was the case in Krasnoyarsk Krai in relation to Evenk Autonomous Okrug and Taymyr Dolgano-Nenets Autonomous Okrug. Even during the planning stages, it was clear that huge financial injections would be required for the development of the newly united territory, which is why the corresponding decree of the President of the Russian Federation contained nine points, compared to the usual six for decrees on the development of new territories. Some of these points were only implemented in 2017–2018 (the completion of the reconstruction of the marine terminal in Petropavlovsk-Kamchatsky and the construction of a low-capacity combined heat and power plant in the village of Tilichiki. Table 66 illustrates how the respondents in Petropavlovsk-Kamchatsky and Palana assessed the results of the reform.

The people of Petropavlovsk-Kamchatsky and Palana generally had good things to say about the merger, and the level of satisfaction with the reform was higher in Kamchatka Krai than in any other region in all aspects: 28.73% of respondents noted that the situation had most likely improved, and 22.98% even noted a significant improvement. Looking at each aspect separately, we see that, in terms of the quality of work of the public authorities, 53% of the respondents from Palana did not notice any serious changes, 23.5% noted a regression, and 23.5% stated that improvements had indeed been made. The people of Petropavlovsk-Kamchatsky were more optimistic in their assessments of the reform (28%, 54% and 18%, respectively), although this is likely not connected with the merger itself, nor is it a result of a general increase in the level of work of the government bodies in Russia.

In terms of economic development, the majority of respondents in both settlements noticed no significant change: 40% of respondents from Petropavlovsk-Kamchatsky, and 35% of respondents from Palana. That said, there are fewer sceptics than there are "optimists" here, approximately 37–38% in both.

Respondents were divided on the issue of social welfare, where the people of Palana were more positive: 26% of respondents in Petropavlovsk-Kamchatsky noticed at least some deterioration, compared to 9.8% of those in Palana. A total of 34% of the people of Petropavlovsk-Kamchatsky and 33.3% of the people of Palana did not see any changes. That said, almost 57% of respondents in Palana noted at least some improvements, compared to 40% among those from Petropavlovsk-Kamchatsky.

Table 66: Distribution of answers to the question: "To what extent has the situation changed in individual spheres of life as a result of the federal reform?" in Kamchatka Krai, %

Responses	Assessment of respondents				
	Government bodies	Economy	Social welfare	Inter-ethnic relations	National culture
Petropavlovsk-Kamchatsky					
Deteriorated significantly	40	6.0	10.0	0.0	0.0
Most likely deteriorated	14.0	16.0	16.0	4.0	2.0
No change	28.0	40.0	34.0	24.0	30.0
Most likely improved	32.0	22.0	24.0	38.0	34.0
Improved significantly	22.0	16.0	16.0	34.0	34.0
Palana					

Deteriorated significantly	13.7	15.7	5.9	3.9	2.0
Most likely deteriorated	9.8	11.8	3.9	3.9	2.0
No change	52.9	35.3	33.3	29.4	31.4
Most likely improved	15.7	25.5	39.2	29.4	27.5
Improved significantly	7.8	11.8	17.6	33.3	37.3

As for stability and peace in inter-ethnic relations, the answers given to a great extent coincided, but not in every respect. Residents of Petropavlovsk-Kamchatsky tended to give higher scores than those of Palana, with 72% noticing improvements, compared to 63% in Palana (30% of respondents answered "No change").

A similar picture is observed in terms of the level of government support for national culture and language – that is, the people of the current administrative centre see more positive changes than those in Palana. This is most likely an indication of an increase in the "visibility" of Koryak culture in the capital of Kamchatka, although it is difficult to say with complete certainty that this was a result of the reform: it is possible that exhibitions of Koryak culture and concerts by Koryak national ensembles have become more popular because interest in them has grown naturally, and not because uniting the Koryak people within a single constituent entity of the Russian Federation has brought them "closer" to one another.

The people of Kamchatka Krai are generally more positive about the results of the reform than those in the other regions. That said, it would seem that they are unsure about why this is the case, so it is likely that they are evaluating the changes in general, rather than the consequences of the reform. This is particularly evident in Petropavlovsk-Kamchatsky, where it is unlikely that such positive changes in the quality of work of the government bodies could have taken place solely as a result of a change in status from an *oblast* to a *krai*, which cannot be said of Palana. It is thus important to note for the purposes of this study that respondents are not always able to differentiate those transformations that have occurred as a result of the merger from those that have occurred in spite of it.

Irkutsk and Ust-Ordinsky

In many ways, the enlargement of Irkutsk Oblast and Ust-Orda Buryat Autonomous Okrug appeared justified: the agrarian economy of Ust-Orda Buryat Autonomous Okrug was already focused on supplying products to the Irkutsk market, and the region's economic growth rates made it possible to assume that Irkutsk Oblast, along with aid from the federal government and the transfer of budgetary flows from Ust-Orda Buryat Autonomous Okrug (which are always spent effectively), would solve all of Ust-Orda's problems, specifically those of water supply and the availability of roads. Not everyone in Irkutsk was delighted with the *oblast*'s new role as a "tow-boat," as it had barely got back on its feet. But there was not much resistance either, as, according to respondents, the merger would simply fix the already existing state of affairs between the two regions.

Based on the results of our telephone survey in Irkutsk and Ust-Ordinsky (Table 67), we can say that opinions on the merger are divided: some in the previously autonomous territories are dissatisfied, and the same can be said of some in the current administrative centre. In addition, certain indicators for Irkutsk are surprising and raise questions.

When asked about the quality of work of the government bodies, 42% of Irkutsk respondents and 31.4% of those from Ust-Ordinsky did not notice any changes. At the same time, however, many answered that they believed the situation to have deteriorated significantly (25.5%, which puts it among the top responses). The high level of scepticism can be explained by the fact that a great number of people from Ust-Ordinsky worked as government officials and, accordingly, lost their jobs after the merger, when the state institutions of Ust-Orda Buryat Autonomous Okrug were abolished. Not everyone was able to take part in the "elite transfer" of personnel to Irkutsk or adapt to the new reality. But residents of the region suffered too, as the representatives of the tax, supervisory and other authorities that remained there mostly provide advisory functions. The more serious public services are only available in Irkutsk, and travelling there places a heavy burden on the already low incomes of the local population. In this sense, the quality of work of the government bodies may have improved (as noted by 35.3% of respondents) in terms of transparency and reduced corruption in government structures, but it has become less accessible due to a number of functions transferred to Irkutsk.

Table 67: Distribution of answers to the question: "To what extent has the situation changed in individual spheres of life as a result of the federal reform?" in Irkutsk Oblast, %

Responses	Assessment of respondents				
	Government bodies	Economy	Social welfare	Inter-ethnic relations	National culture
Irkutsk					
Deteriorated significantly	12.0	14.0	18.0	0.0	0.0
Most likely deteriorated	12.0	4.0	16.0	6.0	4.0
No change	42.0	54.0	38.0	36.0	32.0
Most likely improved	28.0	24.0	26.0	40.0	44.0
Improved significantly	6.0	4.0	2.0	18.0	20.0
Ust-Ordinsky					
Deteriorated significantly	25.5	25.5	7.8	5.9	2.0
Most likely deteriorated	7.8	11.8	23.5	0.0	3.9
No change	31.4	41.2	19.6	23.5	25.5
Most likely improved	19.6	13.7	27.5	25.5	23.5
Improved significantly	15.7	7.8	21.6	45.1	45.1

A similar picture emerges with regard to economic development: 54% of respondents in Irkutsk and 41.2% in Ust-Ordinsky do not feel that the economic situation has changed following the merger. However, 28% of Irkutsk residents see at least some positive transformations, compared to almost 20% in Ust-Ordinsky, while 37.3% of residents in latter believe the economic situation has deteriorated. This may be due in part to the fact that, according to the Ust-Buryats, the region has not experienced a qualitative leap in its economy, and although the Irkutsk markets for agricultural products have allegedly become more accessible for Ust-Orda Buryat Autonomous Okrug farmers, they still have to deal with resellers in order to make use of this increased access.

When asked about the level of state social support, one third of Irkutsk residents stated that the situation has worsened, while almost half of those in Ust-Ordinsky noted improvements. What could account for such a striking difference? One reason is that the merger made it easier for Ust-Orda Buryat Autonomous Okrug residents to access medical services in Irkutsk Oblast, and healthcare is a vital issue for people in the *okrug* due to the low quality of services provided there. Treatment was available at Irkutsk Regional Clinical Hospital before the merger, but with some restrictions and a certain reluctance on the part of Irkutsk doctors. Some of these restrictions may remain, but Ust-Ordinsky residents acknowledge that social benefits have increased and are now on a par with those that residents of the *oblast* receive.

According to both Irkutsk and Ust-Orda residents, there are no problems to mention regarding the situation with national and cultural development. In addition, more respondents in Ust-Orda are positive about the changes that have taken place in inter-ethnic relations and in the level of state support for national culture than in Irkutsk. Meanwhile, the people of Irkutsk mention the large number of mixed marriages between Russians and Ust-Buryats, and the concerts put on by groups from Ust-Orda that are just as good as those from Ulan-Ude.

Chita and Aginskoye

The merger of Chita Oblast and Agin-Buryat Autonomous Okrug into Zabaykalsky Krai is another non-standard case that does not fit into the logic of the socioeconomic development of a backward *matryoshka* region. As we noted earlier, the standard of living and social wellbeing in Agin-Buryat Autonomous Okrug was higher than that of Chita Oblast thanks to its special tax status, which meant that the people of the *okrug* were initially against the merger. Without tax revenues boosting its budget, Agin-Buryat Autonomous Okrug is a typical agricultural region that specializes in animal husbandry that has never shown any significant industrial potential. As for Chita Oblast, its border position during Soviet times meant that industrial potential was not developed here, and the uranium that was mined here was exported to the Urals for processing and further use. Thus, the Chita economy was highly dependent on the military units located in its territory, the number of which decreased after the Siberian Military District headquartered in Chita was closed in 2010. In this sense, both regions were decidedly "average" in terms of their resource potential for socioeconomic development.

Our opinion poll revealed that the people of Chita and Aginskoye are extremely pessimistic about the results of the reform. What is most surprising is that the greatest scepticism was observed in Chita, rather than Aginskoye (Table 68). This is most likely because the society in the former Agin-Buryat Autonomous Okrug is closed and conservative, strictly observes Buryat traditions and holds the authorities in high esteem. As such, they try not to make critical statements about their leaders, especially to outsiders. While the residents of Aginskoye have good reason to believe that a "girl from a rich Buryat family would not voluntarily marry a poor Russian man," Chita residents were also underwhelmed, as it could not secure large-scale investments and development projects because of the global financial crisis. In their communications, officials at various levels often put the failures of the merger down to the 2008 crisis, although we cannot state with any certainty that events in Zabaykalsky Krai would have developed differently if these cyclical fluctuations in the global and Russian economies had not taken place. So, despite the idiosyncrasies of the Agin worldview, 24.4% of respondents noted partial or significant deterioration in various spheres, which is similar to the results for Perm Krai.

When asked about the quality of work of the government bodies, 22% of Chita residents said they believed the situation had deteriorated significantly, while 16% said they had noticed some deterioration, and 44% said they had not noticed any changes. The figures were approximately the same for Aginskoye, at 12%, 22% and 44%, respectively. In other words, the people of Chita no longer like the changes that have taken place. That notwithstanding, 22% of Agin-Buryats note that positive transformations have occurred.

Table 68: Distribution of answers to the question: "To what extent has the situation changed in individual spheres of life as a result of the federal reform?" in Zabaykalsky Krai, %

Responses	Assessment of respondents				
	Government bodies	Economy	Social welfare	Inter-ethnic relations	National culture
Chita					
Deteriorated significantly	22.0	32.0	20.0	0.0	2.0
Most likely deteriorated	16.0	30.0	18.0	2.0	6.0
No change	44.0	28.0	42.0	34.0	36.0
Most likely improved	14.0	6.0	16.0	30.0	36.0
Improved significantly	4.0	4.0	4.0	34.0	20.0
Aginskoye					
Deteriorated significantly	12.0	18.0	14.0	2.0	0.0

Most likely deteriorated	22.0	20.0	4.0	0.0	4.0
No change	44.0	48.0	22.0	30.0	24.0
Most likely improved	12.0	12.0	50.0	34.0	38.0
Improved significantly	10.0	2.0	10.0	34.0	34.0

Economic development turned out to be a sore point for those who took part in the survey in both localities, with 62% of Chita residents believing that the economic situation in the region has deteriorated partially or significantly following the merger. The figure is lower for Aginskoye, at 38%, with 48% noting that the situation has not changed in any way (compared to 28% in Chita). That said, it is difficult to say whether or not the assessments of Chita residents are connected to the merger – as in previous cases, there are doubts that Chita respondents are able to distinguish the consequences of the reform from other events.

As for assessments of social welfare, the results here cannot be called anything but paradoxical: 60% of respondents in Agin-Buryat Autonomous Okrug believe that the situation in this area has improved significantly, yet 38% of these people rated the reform a 1. We know for certain that after the merger, and after the former Agin-Buryat Autonomous Okrug lost its special tax status, the social situation got progressively worse due to the reduction in budget spending on social institutions in Agin-Buryat Okrug. It thus follows that the generally high assessment of respondents raises very serious doubts as to their "sincerity." As for Chita, 42% of respondents did not see significant changes, 38% noted changes for the worse, and 20% noted changes for the better.

In terms of inter-ethnic relations and the level of support for national culture in Zabaykalsky Krai, a trend has appeared whereby respondents greatly appreciate the changes that have taken place in these areas, and representatives of national minorities give higher scores compared to those from the new administrative centre. As a result, no statistical anomalies were found in this area.

Preliminary conclusions

First, assessments of the mergers are polarized: approximately one quarter of those who took part in the opinion poll described the results of the reform in an extremely negative light; and roughly the same number saw it as a positive. However, if we take a closer look and break the overall assessment down into individual criteria, we find that the respondents are not so divided and not so gloomy in their assessments of the transformations in such areas as the quality of work of the government bodies, economic development, social welfare, and stability and peace in inter-ethnic relations and support for national cultures. This could suggest that a certain stereotype has appeared where reform is seen as a negative phenomenon that has brought discord into the order that existed before. This is especially true for the former administrative centres, while the attitude towards the reform in the new administrative centres is more balanced and even positive. This means that the merger did not affect them very much and very likely fixed in their minds the image of a "benefactor" for small *matryoshka* regions.

Second, we suspect that respondents find it difficult to differentiate between changes caused by the reform and changes caused by other factors, in particular the natural course of political and socioeconomic development. This leads to both positive and negative distortions, which we ostensibly saw in the case of Kamchatka Krai and Zabaykalsky Krai. If we look at the in-depth interviews with representatives of the government bodies taken during our field trips to these cities, we will notice that officials often try to explain negative outcomes away – that is, certain negative phenomena or reactions are interpreted not so much as the consequences of a poorly thought-out policy devised by the regional or federal authorities, but rather as the result of the intervention of external forces or the "evil fate," with the most oft-cited culprit being the 2008 financial crisis. The limited format of surveys means that the respondents in our particular study could not make such distinctions, and we should take this into account.

Third, based on the results of our telephone surveys with residents of 11 cities, we can conclude that public perception of the success of the mergers varies, from positive to not so positive. The most "satisfied" respondents live in Kamchatka Krai, while the least satisfied live in Perm and Zabaykalsky krais. At the same time, there is a clear cleavage in the assessments of respondents living in the current and former administrative centres, which is quite understandable: the former centres of *matryoshka* regions lost their status and political and economic significance when they were absorbed into the new constituent entities, and not a single infrastructure project aimed at developing the territories was able to compensate for this loss of status, considering how long they were implemented.

Fourth, according to the overwhelming majority of respondents, inter-ethnic relations did not suffer as a result of the mergers, even though there was a very real danger of this happening, as it was the national autonomies that were absorbed into larger constituent entities. What is more, those who took part in the survey in both the current and former administrative centres agreed that the level of state support for the culture of national minorities had increased, which can be explained, among other things, by the efforts of the regional and federal authorities. In this sense, the risk of the cultures of national minorities being systematically wiped out due to the loss of their autonomy never panned out.

Why does our survey suggest such polarized attitudes towards the reform among the public? We put forward the following factors as possible explanations.

First, despite the fact that the reform was initiated by the federal centre, in practice, it was proposed as a common institutional model for the integration of the regions, and they were given a free hand to put forward their own formulas for future interaction with the *okrug*s they absorbed. At the same time, those who voted in the referendums saw the reform as a deliberate policy of Moscow to solve issues of socioeconomic development, governability and security, which is why they supported it. When unification processes stalled (for example, the planned merger of Nenets Autonomous Okrug and Arkhangelsk Oblast, much like that of Republic of Adygea and Krasnodar Krai, never went ahead), the federal centre lost interest in the idea and, as a result, the special status that had been promised to the territories that had been assimilated into larger constituent entities turned out to be more of an empty title than something specific that was backed by administrative and financial resources.

This brings us to the second reason for dissatisfaction with the reform – the people feel that they have been deceived. They saw the reform as a "super-task" of the state – something that they would support, and in return for their loyalty, they would receive special attention from the government. But the opposite happened – the *okrug*s that had been assimilated disappeared from the federal agenda completely, and their lobbying efforts in Moscow stopped working, effectively making them hostages to the situation in their region.

Ultimately, it turned out that the subjective psychologies of respondents played a key role in their assessments of the consequences of the reform: regardless of the actual results of the development of a territory, the reform is viewed more positively by people in those constituent entities of the Russian Federation that acquired a higher status (all of the regions were promoted to the status of *krai*, except for Irkutsk Oblast and Krasnoyarsk Krai, which already had that status). Conversely, the reform was negatively assessed by those in regions that lost their status (especially in Taymyr Dolgano-Nenets Autonomous Okrug and Evenk Autonomous Okrug, where the status of *okrug* has not been preserved even at the symbolic level, as they have both simply become municipal districts). In this regard, the residents of the regions that have been absorbed into larger constituent entities now attribute their many problems to the reform. These problems had existed beforehand, and their newfound status did nothing to address them, especially those connected with the living conditions in the Far North and issues of transport isolation.

Analysis of In-Depth Interviews

Petr Oskolkov & Igor Okunev

A total of 125 interviews were conducted as part of the study. Respondents were asked ten questions:

1. In the 2000s, Russia underwent a federal reform, during which the autonomous *okrug*s became part of larger regions. What do you think about the reform's implications for Russia in general, and for your region in particular?
2. What was the main goal of the reform in your opinion? Has it achieved what it set out to achieve?
3. To what extent has the quality of the work of the public authorities changed following the merger of the regions?
4. Have the people become more politically engaged since the merger? Do they now have greater or lesser trust in the authorities?
5. To what extent has the economic situation in the region changed since the federal reform?
6. What changes have occurred in terms of social welfare since the merger of the regions?
7. How has the level of support for ethnic culture and language changed since the merger of the regions?
8. How would you assess inter-ethnic relations in the region? Has the situation changed significantly since the merger?
9. If you could go back to the beginning of the reform, what changes do you think would need to be made in terms of its implementation?
10. Should Russia continue to reform the administrative and territorial structure of the country?

An analysis of the answers we obtained allows us to draw a number of preliminary conclusions about attitudes towards the reform in the regions it affected.

Before we go any further, we should note a number of general trends.

First, the respondents ignored some of the questions outright or gave purely perfunctory answers to them (for example, if the issue in question was not within their professional expertise). The question about social welfare provided the least useful answers in terms of their substance, which is quite natural seeing as specialized knowledge is required in order to give a detailed answer.

Second (and this is also natural), in most cases, the content and quality of the answers were conditioned by the position of the respondent in respect to the government authorities. Employees in two institutions (located in Ust-Orda Buryat Okrug and Agin-Buryat Okrug) refused in principle to talk to members of the research team even after agreeing to give an interview; in others, they delegated one representative to "give out" brief answers that had clearly been prepared beforehand. Special attention should be given to those cases where, after getting the "official" part out of the way, the government official moved on to give their personal, often emotional, opinion of the reform. However, for ethical reasons, we cannot use these answers in our study, as they were made after the respondent asked us to stop recording. In cases where the respondent had no connection to the authorities, his or her answers largely depended on their personal involvement in the transformation process and the extent to which the outcome of the reform affected them or the institution they represent.

Finally, as could be expected once again, the answers given differ significantly in different regions on the one hand, and within the "*oblast/krai* capital – *okrug/raion* capital" pairs on the other. The vast majority of respondents in the capitals of *oblast*s and *krai*s saw the reform and everything it brought as a plus, while those in the *okrug/raion* capitals demonstrate a much broader range of opinions. Regional discrepancies can be explained by the differences in the initial conditions in the regions that were assimilated. Clearly, people in the former Komi-Permyak Autonomous Okrug, one of the most subsidized constituent entities of the Russian Federation, would view the reform differently to people in the prosperous

Agin-Buryat Autonomous Okrug, for example.[1] Much also depends on the political culture of the region in question – whether this implies unconditional loyalty to the executive branch or leaves room for organized protest.

The answers to the first question (one of the most general in the list) are the broadest in terms of views on the reform – ranging from positive to negative. While the majority of respondents agree that the mergers were a good thing for the Russian Federation ("This has been a very positive change for Russia, for the Russian state, in the sense that various procedures have been simplified" [member of the clergy, Ust-Ordinsky]), their consequences for individual regions are assessed very differently. In particular, the opinion was expressed that, "the merger was to the detriment of the national *okrugs*" [member of the clergy, Ust-Ordinsky], "the changes […] have caused people more irritation than they have brought positive emotions" [journalist, Petropavlovsk-Kamchatsky]. The following assessment was also offered: "The merger didn't do much" [government representative, Chita].

There is a relative consensus on the issue of the main goal of the reform, with most respondents believing it was to increase governability by way of reducing the number of constituent entities of the Russian Federation and strengthening the "power vertical": "When there are too many regions, governance suffers" [journalist, Aginskoye]. And while other goals were also mentioned – improving the wellbeing of the subsidized regions, reducing the importance of the ethnic factor in the territorial structure of the Russian Federation ("National elites should be dissolved into large regions so that they don't feel like separate pieces" [journalist, Chita]; "reducing the size of the administrative apparatus" [educator, Kudymkar]), and maximizing the benefits of industrial companies ("So that they don't abandon the region, so that they've got investment projects […] to get easier access to the subsoil of the former autonomous *okrugs* [NGO representative, Dudinka]) –

---

1 "Agin-Buryat Okrug was the rich younger brother who was envied" [journalist, Chita].

improving governability was the clear winner. Opinions differ on whether this goal was actually achieved.

As for the impact of the reform on the quality of work of the government bodies, some respondents did not notice any changes in this area, because "the people remained the same" [cultural worker, Ust-Ordinsky]. At the same time, most respondents noted that the quality of work had deteriorated, at least in those territories that had lost their status as constituent entities of the Russian Federation, as their powers had been greatly reduced. This led to the emergence of many intermediate links and the need for all decisions to be additionally coordinated with the new centres of power:

> "When there was a separate constituent entity, it was possible to work directly with the federal centre [...] It was easier to resolve issues directly, but now it's up to the government of the krai to decide" [journalist, Aginskoye].
> "The money was transferred, but the rulemaking wasn't. So, whenever we come against difficulties ... we have to go to the Krasnoyarsk authorities, explain to them why we need to make changes, or why certain orders or resolutions need to be adopted" [NGO representative, Dudinka].

Respondents pointed to the inconveniences faced by residents of the structural elements of the former *okrug*'s as a result of key decision-making centres being displaced:

> "The powers that the okrug had now belong to the krai. The district's powers have been transferred to Dudinka, and the villages in the district have been left without any powers" [government representative, Dudinka].
> "Even if the governor worked 20 hours a day, he would only be able to give 15 minutes of his time per day to Taymyr. In the past, he would give 20 hours per day" [government representative, Krasnoyarsk].
> "To get a driver's license or a weapons permit, to pass a medical test to work in healthcare or as a school and pre-school teacher, and so on, you need to go to Dudinka… That's around 12,000–15,000 roubles [...] There's no [urine] analyser in Dudinka. So, you have to go to Norilsk [...] If the coroner goes on vacation ... then we have to keep the dead bodies for months" [NGO representative, Dudinka].
> "We had almost everything we needed in our village. The mail isn't delivered here anymore, since the merger, it gets delivered to some far-off corner now. It's the same with the hospital and the school" [educator, Palana].

"Olenprom, the most important enterprise in the region, is located here in Petropavlovsk. Whenever a problem arises, they come here, to the city, to sort it out. Of course, the executives want to live comfortably here, but there aren't any executives in the far north, they almost never go there. This is your pain in the neck, the north, so let it stay that way. All they do here is ask for reports and give orders. This is an ugly situation with Olenprom" [educator, Petropavlovsk-Kamchatsky].

It is obvious that the reform hit the local administrative elite the hardest, and only a small number of them remained in their positions. This raises doubts as to the justification for maintaining a separate *okrug* administration (in Ust-Orda Buryat Okrug and Agin-Buryat Okrug) given the sharp reduction in its powers:

"District administrations work quite well, but I don't understand the need for this okrug administration, this appendage. What is its function?" [government representative, Chita].
"People don't have any reason to go there. The officials don't decide anything, they don't have a budget of their own. It's just a label… The okrug administration is nothing but a name" [member of the clergy, Ust-Ordinsky].
"The administration doesn't do anything; it doesn't have any powers. This is mostly for the people not to get disappointed – look, you've got the administration of Koryak Okrug here, – but there's just about ten people left" [NGO representative, Petropavlovsk-Kamchatsky].

The reduction of powers has led, among other things, to the indigenous peoples losing a sense of their former administrative integrity, of their representation in the administrative landscape of Russia:

"The Koryak people rightly believe that they are no longer represented as a nation […] There is no national self-consciousness, not a single politician among them who could articulate questions and conduct an equal dialogue with the governor […] The elites note that in the past they openly raised concerns about poverty, but this is not the case anymore. And they're right" [journalist, Petropavlovsk-Kamchatsky].

Most respondents were cautious when making statements about trust in the authorities, citing the lack of data for qualified conclusions. We came across the following position quite frequently:

"Looking at the election results, it would seem that everything is fine and dandy, that we have absolute trust in the authorities. But if you listen to what the people are saying on the street, then a completely different picture emerges" [government representative, Kudymkar].

Some assessments were far more critical:

"We don't have any trust in the authorities of the krai since the merger" [cultural worker, Aginskoye].
"People have become extremely suspicious of the actions of the authorities" [entrepreneur, Ust-Ordinsky].

According to respondents, political activity in the regions that have been merged has mostly decreased due to the closing of the regional branches of political parties. Almost none of them mentioned the mobilization of protest activity during the reform. Exceptions here include Komi-Permyak Okrug, where interview participants noted protest sentiments among the ruling elites, not the general population, and Taymyr Dolgano-Nenets Municipal Raion, where one of the people interviewed mentioned *"the mobilization of part of the population [...] who demand a referendum on breaking away from Krasnoyarsk Krai"* [government representative, Dudinka]. When asked to clarify about the presence of politically active NGOs, participants replied that the activities of NGOs are exclusively of a cultural and educational nature. In a number of cases, respondents noted that the respective regions "do not have political movements or opposition forces" [journalist, Aginskoye].

The biggest criticisms of the reform came when the interviewees were asked about the economic consequences of the merger. They pointed to unfulfilled promises (the construction of mining and processing plants in Agin-Buryat Okrug, social facilities in Ust-Orda Buryat Okrug, and roads to Syktyvkar in Komi-Permyak Okrug), the outflow of the population, and the transformation of the regions into "commuter settlements":

"They went ahead with the merger, but didn't really give us anything in return" [cultural worker, Kudymkar].
"People's wellbeing suffered a little, of course, because [...] we didn't have as many niches in which we could work – mostly federal structures that kept their representative offices in the region. They closed them down, and a lot

of young people were left without work, so they left for Chita and other regions" [journalist, Aginskoye].

"In the past, university graduates came back to work here, since there was at least some money in the region. But the situation deteriorated after the merger and people started to leave en masse" [entrepreneur, Aginskoye].

"The decline in the number of jobs in federal structures and district services led to an outflow of the most prominent experts" [cultural worker, Kudymkar].

We also came across some very harsh assessments:

"The quality of life of residents of Agin-Buryat Okrug today is worse than it has ever been" [cultural worker, Aginskoye].

However, it is worth repeating that the assessment of the consequences of the reform for the economy largely depends on the wellbeing of the region before the merger. And certain aberrations are observed here too. Thus, Agin-Buryat Autonomous Okrug's financial wellbeing was largely determined by its position as a "domestic offshore" with reduced income taxes. Losing this position would inevitably mean economic decline, even if the *okrug* were to retain its status as an autonomy. Many interviewees noted (positively) that the "large" region now considers the *okrug* as part of its territory and earmarks money for its development. At the same time, critics pointed out that the *okrug*s that had lost their autonomy had their own budgets and thus the ability to independently determine priority areas for financing:

"If the krai allocates certain funds, then they are for the krai in general. Before, money was allocated from the federal government for our own budget" [journalist, Aginskoye].

"Now, we've got to call Irkutsk, we've got to go there and ask them for money, convince them that we need it" [member of the clergy, Ust-Ordinsky].

"A different status means different financing. In the past, we received money and were free to use it for our own needs. Now, we are forced to beg for every penny in the Ministry of Krasnoyarsk Krai, we have to fight for every single kopeck" [public servant, Tura].

It is worth noting that the people of Ust-Orda and Kudymkar are generally happier about this state of affairs, given the high level of corruption that existed before the merger:

> "The requirements [of municipalities] are more stringent because there is a feeling that the regional authorities [...] now exercise greater control" [lawyer, Kudymkar].

As we noted earlier, many of the people we interviewed avoided answering the question about changes in social support, citing their own lack of expertise in this area. According to one of the people we talked to, an expert in issues of social security, "nothing can get worse there, because we are making efforts to ensure that our employees perform their functions to the fullest" [government representative, Dudinka]. At the same time, a number of respondents noted positive changes in healthcare, as the people in the former autonomies gained access to medical services in the *krais/oblasts*:

> "As a resident of Ust-Ordinsky, it has become easier for me to travel to Irkutsk to receive medical treatment. When it was an okrug [...] no one would have treated you" [entrepreneur, Ust-Ordinsky].

According to most respondents, government support for ethnic cultures has either not changed, or has even increased (which we believe is due to the desire of the federal/*krai*/*oblast* authorities to somehow compensate for depriving the former autonomous regions of their former status):

> "The merger of the regions had nothing to do with it [culture], because it [culture] is higher than that" [cultural worker, Aginskoye].
> "There are far more opportunities to receive support, there's much more money" [government representative, Kudymkar].
> "I believe that the merger, on the contrary, gave a much-needed boost to efforts to preserve our culture and language" [government representative, Kudymkar].

At the same time, activities in this area are often carried out "for show," with very little significance:

> "Questions are raised, forums, congresses and conferences are frequently organized, and I have the feeling that everything discussed at these roundtables stays there" [cultural worker, Ust-Ordinsky].

Many of the people we talked to from among the representatives of ethnic groups of the regions that bore their names are concerned about the declining status and prestige of their language and education in inter-ethnic communication (this is common for the ethnic intelligentsia):

> "Some even think that my generation will be the last to speak the Buryat language" [member of the clergy, Ust-Ordinsky].

However, this trend goes back to Soviet times and has nothing to do with the reform (which, by the way, the respondents also noted). And if the *krai/oblast* authorities do not make the necessary efforts to maintain ethnic languages, this does not mean that things were different when the autonomies still existed:

> "Parents [...] believe that their children don't need it. They don't need to speak the Komi-Permyak language, because they're going to leave the region anyway" [cultural worker, Kudymkar].

Almost everyone we interviewed described inter-ethnic relations in the regions we are looking at as problem-free. Only one person mentioned obvious nationalism of the titular nation (which is probably due to subjective perceptions):

> "Buryat nationalism is flourishing right now. I grew up among the Buryat people, but I never made the distinction between who's Russian and who's Buryat. But they do" [entrepreneur, Ust-Ordinsky].

Many respondents noted the absence of nationalist organizations (while such organizations do exist in Buryatia, attempts to extend their activities to Ust-Orda Buryat Okrug and Agin-Buryat Okrug were unsuccessful). Those from Perm, however, noted a certain disregard for the Komi-Permyaks on the "mainland," although this has never led to ethnic violence. Almost all those interviewed saw this as being connected to the difficult climatic conditions in their regions:

> "The people manage to live in such difficult, harsh conditions. If they start fighting for scarce resources, they won't survive" [journalist, Aginskoye].
> "The North has its own rules governing the co-existence of peoples, it helps to smooth out difficult situations" [journalist, Petropavlovsk-Kamchatsky].

If any inter-ethnic tensions were found then it was only in relation to migrants from Central Asia and the Caucasian republics:

> "We had a number of high-profile conflicts that could be called inter-ethnic, but this has less to do with the merger than it does with migration processes in general, with the fact that the new diasporas from the Central Asian and Caucasian republics are appearing" [government representative, Kudymkar]; "we need to train and nurture our own cadres, not bring them in from the outside, so that we're not overrun with Kyrgyz, we're not against them coming, but still… sorry" [cultural worker, Tura].

In response to the "speculative" question about what could have been done differently when implementing the reform, many people we talked to mentioned the need for the competencies of the *okrug/raion* and *krai/oblast* to be delimited more strictly and for the concept of "administrative-territorial unit with a special status" to be clarified:[2]

> "The first thing I would do is define what 'special status' means and what it entails, so that people understand what they are voting for or against […] Basically, we bought a pig in a poke. 'Special status' appears to be a giant secret" [government representative, Kudymkar].
> "There was not a word in the federal constitutional law about what a special status actually is. So, the people in Irkutsk Oblast could not understand what it was for a long time after the merger" [law enforcement official, Ust-Ordinsky].
> "Koryak Okrug retained its status; it is spelled out in the charter – a territory with a special status. But what is that status? Perhaps it is on paper only? We still have no idea what it means. As far as I understand it, 'special status' implies the preservation of economic activity, that the indigenous people and their families have somewhere to fish…" [cultural worker, Petropavlovsk-Kamchatsky].

Some also believe that it was necessary, first of all, to improve the economic situation in regions that are being merged (for example, to establish large-scale production to provide jobs), and then to actually go ahead with the merger:

> "The reform can't be carried out until we've got to the core problem. And the core problem is the economy […] First, we need to pull the two regions

---

2　The lack of a clear definition of "special status" is also criticized by specialists on Russian Federalism (see, for example, Kynev 2010a).

out of poverty, and only then can we start patching other things up" [entrepreneur, Aginskoye].

At the same time, some stated that the reform shouldn't have been carried out at all:

> "I wouldn't merge such massive territories, and I wouldn't merge the south and the north" [government official, Dudinka].
> "It should never have happened. Autonomy was necessary, because, as they say, we are small, but we are proud" [cultural worker, Ust-Ordinsky].

The question of the advisability of further reforms of the administrative and territorial structure of the country did not interest the participants in our in-depth interviews. Some refused to answer it outright, citing their lack of expertise. Others noted the need to take the economic and ethno-political situation in regions that could be merged into account. Some suggested that the reform could be expanded to include non-ethnic constituent entities of the Russian Federation. Only people from the regional centres (of *krai*s and *oblast*s) spoke favourably about the possibility of further consolidating the structure of the Russian Federation:

> "The premise was spot on, and I've got no idea why everything stopped all of a sudden!" [journalist, Chita].
> "It was a miscalculation on the part of the federal government to not continue with the process" [government official, Chita].

Our in-depth interviews allow us to identify the official and unofficial goals of the federal reform carried out in the 2000s – as they are seen by the respondents. The former include reducing economic imbalances by attaching subsidized regions to donor regions and increasing the efficiency of public administration by reducing the number of sparsely populated regions with an extremely high share of public sector institutions and an extremely small share of private sector institutions. The unofficial goals include strengthening centripetal forces in Russian federalism by squeezing its ethnic component (for the federal centre), and increasing the budget and status of the region (for the political class in the *oblast*/*krai*). As the reform progressed, the official goals that dominated the first stage (the accession of Komi-Permyak

Autonomous Okrug to Perm Oblast) increasingly gave way to the unofficial goals, which is one of the reasons why it was suspended.

The interviews also allowed us to determine the pros and cons of the reform for the regions that absorbed the former autonomies entities, as well as for these entities themselves. The benefits obtained by the former included increasing their status and weight in Russian politics and gaining full control over financial flows and executive power in the *okrugs*. The downside was the compensatory redistribution of budget funds from the *krai/oblast* to the *okrug*. The advantages for the entities that were assimilated into larger regions were the completion (or partial completion) of a number of infrastructure projects, a sizeable increase in the funds earmarked for supporting the national culture and language, and access to regional programmes, primarily in the field of medicine. The disadvantages included diminished status (the transformation from full-fledged constituent entities of the Russian Federation into administrative-territorial units with an undefined "special status"), the severance of direct ties with Moscow, and the weakening of the human resource potential.

Why are assessments of the reform so ambiguous, sometimes even polarized? While we do not profess to be able to give a comprehensive answer to this question, we can outline a number of factors that have influenced its perception in the *okrugs* that were absorbed by other regions.

First, it is mostly people in the expert community who view the reform as a reform. Both the government and the media spun the mergers as local initiatives supported by the centre, which eliminated the need to propose some kind of general institutional integration model. This made it possible to delegate the development of a formula for future interaction with the former autonomous *okrugs* to the regions. In turn, the *okrugs* saw the mergers as a deliberate policy pursued by Moscow that was designed to help solve national (federal) problems. This is why the people there supported the reform, ignoring local interests. When the process of merging regions stalled (three regions of dual subordination did not agree to mergers), the centre lost interest, and the "special status" that had been promised to the territories that had been absorbed into the larger regions turned out to be mainly "for show" and not backed by administrative or financial resources. As a result, people felt deceived: they viewed reform as a "super-task" of the state, and supporting it would have brought them increased attention from the centre. But in practice, the former autonomous *okrug*s disappeared from the federal agenda completely, and their lobbying efforts in Moscow stopped working, effectively making them hostages to the situation in their region.

Second, the fact that the reform lacked a clearly defined goal means that residents of the regions in question could not assess its outcomes. While governability in the former Taymyr Dolgano-Nenets Autonomous Okrug, for instance, has certainly increased (in the logic of a single vertical of power), Komi-Permyak and Ust-Orda Buryat Autonomous Okrugs have seen the introduction of intermediate authorities whose powers are unclear, and this has only complicated the power vertical.

In terms of socioeconomic development, the situation in Taymyr Dolgano-Nenets Municipal Raion and Ust-Orda Buryat Okrug has improved thanks to the launch of a number of regional investment projects, while Agin-Buryat Okrug has benefited from the redistribution of financial flows to the region. In Komi-Permyak and Ust-Orda Buryat Okrugs, support for the local ethnic culture has increased significantly, while the ethnic component in many other constituent entities (most notably the former Evenk and Koryak Autonomous Okrugs) continues to weaken because of migration processes. That is, the reform has been a mixed bag in terms of the political, socioeconomic and ethno-cultural development of the regions affected by the mergers. And this inevitably colours perceptions of the success of the reform, since people tend to judge such processes by the degree to which they have been personally affected by them.

And last but not least, there is a psychological aspect to the reform that should not be ignored. Regardless of the real consequences for the territories affected by the mergers, their outcomes are typically rated more highly by those who acquired a higher status after they were launched, while those who lost their status are more critical. Our study showed that issues of status, even if purely symbolic, are sometimes more important for people than certain material changes in their lives. As a result, residents of the regions that have been assimilated now attribute even those problems that had existed previously and are in no way connected with the presence or absence of their status as a constituent entity of the Russian Federation to the reform.

Conclusions and Recommendations

Igor Okunev

Any reform is a targeted measure and, as such, they are impossible to analyse without first defining the goals of the transformations. In the course of our analysis of the federal reform that was carried out in the Russian Federation in the 2000s, we determined the official and unofficial goals of the merger of the regions. The former include reducing economic imbalances by attaching subsidized regions to donor regions and increasing the efficiency of public administration by reducing the number of sparsely populated regions with an extremely high share of public sector institutions and an extremely small share of private sector institutions. Unofficial goals include strengthening centripetal forces in Russian federalism by squeezing its ethnic component (for the federal centre), and increasing the budget and status of the region (for the political class in the oblast/krai). We found that, as the reform progressed, the official goals that dominated the first stage (Komi-Permyak Autonomous Okrug) increasingly gave way to the unofficial goals (Agin-Buryat Autonomous Okrug), which is why it was suspended.

The model highlighted the pros and cons of the reform for both the acceptor and donor regions. Areas that have not undergone significant changes as a result of the reform include inter-ethnic relations, security and law enforcement, and human rights and freedoms. The advantages for the acceptor regions (*oblast*s and *krai*s) consisted in a higher status (the promotion from *oblast* to *krai*), greater clout in Russian politics, and the acquisition of full control over financial flows and executive power in the *okrug*s. The downside was the compensatory redistribution of budget funds from the *krai* to the *okrug*. As a result, spatial identity strengthened in the acceptor region, which made it easier for residents to continue to support the reform, or be generally indifferent to it, even when there was no obvious improvement in the quality of life.

For the donor regions (autonomous *okrugs*), the downsides included having their status downgraded from region to sub-region, the severance of direct ties with Moscow, the withdrawal of representative offices from federal government bodies, the acquisition of a conditional special status with "show" *okrug*-level government bodies that receive no independent funding, and the weakening of the human resource potential. The benefits included the partial implementation of significant infrastructure projects, a sizeable increase in funding to support the national culture and language, and accesses to regional programmes, including the compulsory health insurance (CHI) programme. This led to a weakening of spatial identity and subsequent disappointment in the reform, even when certain improvements in quality of life were observed.

What all the enlargement scenarios have in common is that the former autonomous *okrugs* have become administrative-territorial units with a special status. That said, there is no indication whatsoever of what exactly this status implies, and it meant different things in each specific case depending on how the political bargaining between the different parts of the complex constituent entity went. All the "enlarged: *okrugs*/districts are represented in the legislative assemblies of their respective *oblasts/krais*, although this representation is extremely uneven – from 20% in Koryakia to 3.3% in Komi Okrug. Two main models can be observed: 1) the transformation of autonomous *okrugs* into districts, where the new entity receives an elected head, a district council and local administration (as in the case of Taymyr Dolgano-Nenets District and Evenk District); and 2) the transformation of autonomous *okrugs* into *okrugs*, where the leadership of the new entity is transferred to the executive power of the *krai/oblast* by including the ministry for the affairs of the *okrug* in question in the structure of the executive power (as with Komi-Permyak Okrug), or an administration with the status of a ministry (Ust-Orda Buryat Okrug, Agin-Buryat Okrug, Koryak Okrug). At the same time, the powers of these ministries/administrations are connected mostly with national and cultural issues, and their head is appointed by the governor (Komi-Permyak Okrug, Koryak Okrug), or is automatically given the position of deputy chairperson of the regional government (Agin-Buryat Okrug,Ust-Orda Buryat Okrug). However, variations can be seen in the second model. In Agin-Buryat Okrug, for instance, a consultative and advisory body was set up under the Legislative Assembly of Zabaykalsky Krai in addition to the administration that was established in accordance with the aforementioned scheme – the Assembly of Representatives of Agin-Buryat Okrug.

A common element in all cases is the narrative about "disappointed expectations" and broken promises in the economic and social spheres and, less often, in the preservation of national culture. What is more, when politicians talk about the lack of success or the numerous failures, they usually blame the 2008 financial crisis, while the general public tends to point the finger at the local authorities that were tasked with carrying out the reform, rather than at the federal authorities. The reform only really affected the consciousness of the people living in the formerly autonomous regions: there is a very small corpus of texts discussing the respective mergers in Perm, Krasnoyarsk, Kamchatka and Zabaykalsky krais and Irkutsk Oblast, and the most noticeable feature of them is an indifference to the events and their former neighbours.

Our analysis of the opinion poll and in-depth interviews reveals a polarization of assessments of the outcomes of the reform. Why is the reform such a polarizing issue among the public? Some of the factors that explain this are common to all the regions that were absorbed into larger entities, while others are specific to individual groups of regions.

First, this is how the reform is generally seen by the expert community: the mergers were presented in governance practice and the media space as unrelated local initiatives that were supported by the federal centre, and in this logic, the centre did not consider itself obliged to offer a common institutional model of integration, leaving it to the regions to come up with their own formulas for future engagement with the regions that had been assimilated into larger entities. At the same time, those who voted in the referendums saw the reform as a calculated policy pursued by Moscow to resolve issues of governability, development and security. This is why they largely supported the initiative and stopped lobbying for local interests. When the reform stalled (three autonomous *okrug*s voted against joining), the federal centre lost interest in the idea and, as a result, the special status that had been promised to the territories that had been assimilated into larger constituent entities turned out to be more of an empty title than something concrete that was backed by administrative and financial resources. This brings us to the second reason for dissatisfaction with the reform – the people feel that they have been deceived. They saw the reform as a "super-task" of the state – something that they would support, and it return for their loyalty, they would receive special attention from the government. But the opposite happened – the *okrug*s that had been assimilated disappeared from the federal agenda completely, and their lobbying efforts in Moscow stopped working, effectively making them hostages to the situation in their region.

Second, the fact that the reform lacked a clearly defined goal means that residents of the regions in question have a hard time assessing its outcomes: while governability in the former Taymyr Dolgano-Nenets Autonomous Okrug, for instance, has certainly increased (in the logic of a single vertical of power), Komi-Permyak and Ust-Orda Buryat autonomous *okrug*s have seen the introduction of intermediate authorities whose powers are unclear, and this has only complicated the power vertical. In terms of socioeconomic development, the situation in Taymyrsky Dolgano-Nenetsky and Ust-Orda Buryat autonomousokrugs has improved thanks to the launch of a number of regional investment projects, whileEvenk Autonomous Okrugand Agin-Buryat Autonomous Okrug have benefited from the redistribution of financial flows to the region. In Komi-Permyak and Ust-Orda Buryat autonomous *okrug*s, support for the national culture has increased significantly, while the ethnic component in many other constituent entities (most notably the former Evenk and Koryak autonomous *okrug*s, which are not included in this study) continues to weaken migration processes. As a result, the reform has been a mixed bag in terms of the political, socioeconomic and national-cultural development of the regions affected by the mergers, and the people in these regions tend to judge such processes by the degree to which they have been personally affected by them.

Third, in assessing the outcomes of the reform, the psychological aspect turned out to be key: regardless of the real consequences for the territories affected by the mergers, the reform is rated more highly by those who acquired a higher status after it was launched (all of the regions were promoted to the status of *krai*, except for Irkutsk Oblast and Krasnoyarsk Krai, which already had that status), while those who lost their status are more critical (especially in Taymyr Dolgano-Nenets Autonomous Okrug and Evenk Autonomous Okrug, where the status of *okrug* has not been preserved even at the symbolic level, as they have both simply become municipal districts). Accordingly, issues of status, even if purely symbolic, are sometimes more important for people than certain changes in their lives. In this regard, the residents of the regions that have been absorbed into larger constituent entities now attribute their many problems (especially those connected with the living conditions in the Far North and issues of transport isolation to the reform, and even more so in Evenk Autonomous Okrug and Koryak Autonomous Okrug, where these issues are combined). These problems had existed beforehand, and their newfound status did nothing to address them.

Based on the results of this study, the following practical recommendations can be formulated for the executive authorities in the event that they are interested in continuing the reform process or mitigating the negative consequences of the past mergers.

First, the administrative division of the Russian Federation does not need simplifying. What is needed is a more comprehensive regional policy on the part of the state and further movement towards decentralization and asymmetry. To deal with the situation surrounding small national *okrug*s that are unable to perform all the functions of a constituent entity of the Russian Federation, we recommend creating a regulatory framework for the creation of second-order autonomous constituent entities – that is, constituent entities that belong to another constituent entity. The can be done by making good on the promises to introduce a federal law on the administrative units with a special status that would regulate the status of the merged *okrug*s. This new law should distribute powers between the acceptor regions and the *okrug*s – at the very least, issues of supporting national culture and language, as well as a share of the taxes collected, should be transferred to the *okrug*s. Legislative and executive authorities should also be created in the second-order autonomous entities, functioning within the framework of the powers delegated to them.

Second, institutions should be set up to allow for the regions that have lost their status to lobby their interests in Moscow – say, in the format of permanent representative offices in the capital. Separate electoral districts should be assigned to these economies for State Duma elections. The issue of granting second-order autonomous entities a seat in the Federal Council could potentially be raised during a possible discussion of amendments to the Constitution.

Finally, all the promised plans for the socioeconomic development of the regions should be implemented, and programmes to improve the human resource potential there should be created – for example, by restoring district branches of universities.

Bibliography

Agnew, J. A. 2003. *Geopolitics: Re-visioning World Politics*. London and New York: Routledge.

Antonova, E., and E. Kalyukov. 2020. "Glava Nenetskogo okruga ob'yasnil golosovanie ego zhiteley protiv popravok". *RBC*, July 2, 2020. https://www.rbc.ru/politics/02/07/2020/5efdc0489a794715acde15d5.

Anuchina, N. 2011a. "Ob'edinenie Chitinskoy oblasti i ABAO: expertnoe mnenie." *Vestnik Chitinskogo gosudarstvennogo universiteta*, no. 12 (79): 61–65.

Anuchina, N. 2011b. "Ob'edinitel'nye reformy v sub'ektakh RF: motivy i posledstvia (na primere integratsii Chitinskoy oblasti i Aginskogo Buryatskogo avtonomnogo okruga)." *Sovremennye issledovaniya sotsialnykh problem*, no. 4. https://cyberleninka.ru/article/n/obedinitelnye-reformy-v-subektah-rf-motivy-i-posledstviya-na-primere-integratsii-chitinskoy-oblasti-i-aginskogo-buryatskogo-avtonomnogo/viewer.

Anuchina, N. 2011c. "Ukrupnenie sub'ektov Rossiyskoy Federatsii na etape reformirovaniya rossiyskogo federalisma." *Vestnik Chitinskogo gosudarstvennogo universiteta*, no. 11 (78): 63–67.

Argumenty i fakty. 2013. "Vosem' let na krayu. Kto izlechit komi-permyatskuyu depressiyu?" November 27, 2013. http://www.perm.aif.ru/politic/inperm/1031928?utm_source=aifrelated&utm_medium=click&utm_campaign=aifrelated.

Artobolevsky, S., and E. Gontmakher, eds. 2010. *Ob'edinenie sub'ektov Rossiyskoy Federatsii: za i protiv*. Moscow: INSOR.

Arutyunov, S. A. 1995. "Etnichnost' – ob'ektivnaya real'nost' (otklik na stat'yu S.V. Cheshko)." *Etnograficheskoe Obozrenie*, no. 5: 7–10.

Badmaeva, I. 2010. "Otnosheniya zhiteley Irkutskoy oblasti i Ust'-Ordynskogo Buryatskogo avtonomnogo okruga k protsessu ob'edineniya." *Vestnik Buryatskogo gosudarstvennogo universiteta*, no. 6: 201–206.

Baikal Info. 2016. "Chetyre ob'ekta po ukazu prezidenta RF ostalis' nedostroennymi v Ust'-Ordynskom okruge." September 29, 2016. http://baikal-info.ru/chetyre-obekta-po-ukazu-prezidenta-rf-ostalis-nedostroennymi-v-ust-ordynskom-okruge.

Baikal Media Consulting Information Agency. 2006. "V Buryatii iz'yaty listovki dvizheniya 'Erkhe', agitiruyushchego protiv ob'edineniya s Ust'-Ordoy" April 10, 2006. http://www.baikal-media.ru/news/conflicts/22992/.

Barnes, T. J., and M. Farish. 2006. "Between regions: science, militarism, and American geography from World War to Cold War". *Annals of the Association of American Geographers* 96, no. 4 (December): 807-826.

Basaev, S. 2016. "Est' li osobyy status u Ust'-Ordy?" *Asiarussia.ru*, February 29, 2016. http://asiarussia.ru/articles/11380/.

Beissinger, M. 2015. "Self-Determination as a Technology of Imperialism: The Soviet and Russian Experiences". *Ethnopolitics* 14, no. 5 (October): 479-487.

Beloborodova, I. 2008. "Traditsionnoe prirodopol'zovanie russkikh Arkhangel'skogo Severa: istoriko-etnologicheskiy podkhod k opredeleniyu issledovatel'skogo polya". *Voprosy istorii i kul'tury severnykh stran i territoriy*, no. 1: 45-68.

Berger, P., and T. Luckmann. 1967. *The social construction of reality: A treatise in the sociology of knowledge.* London and New York: Penguin Books.

Bezformata.ru. 2019. "Reprintъ: Referendum po ob'edineniyu Irkutskoy Oblasti i Ust'-Ordynskogo okruga mozhet ne sostoyat'tsya." January 11, 2019. http://irkutsk.bezformata.ru/listnews/oblasti-i-ust-ordinskogo-okruga/42174041/.

Bogdanova, L. 2005 Ustoichivoe razvitie i sotsial'noe vosproizvodstvo regional'noy obshchnosti. *Vestnik Moskovskogo universiteta. Seriya 5: Geografiya*, no. 6: 9-15.

Bogdanova, L. P., and A. S. Shchukina. 1999. "Territorial'nye interesy obshchnostey raznykh ierarhicheskikh urovney." In *Territorial'nye interesy*, edited by A.A. Tkachenko, 32–55. Tver: Tver State University Press.

Bogdanova, L., and A. S. Shchukina. 2002. "Demograficheskie problemy v regional'nom soznanii naseleniya Tverskoy oblasti." In *Territorial'noe soznanie kak nauchnaya problema*, edited by G. Y. Golovnykh, 9-18. Smolensk: Smolensk State University, Center for Regional Studies, Department of Human Sciences.

Bogoyavlenski, D. 2012. *Dannyye vserossiyskoy perepisi 2010.* Assotsiatsia korennykh malochislennykh narodov Severa, Sibiri i Dal'nego Vostoka. http://www.raipon.info/peoples/data-census-2010/data-census-2010.php.

Bourdieu, P. 1989. "Social space and symbolic power." *Sociological theory* 7, no. 1 (January): 14-25.

Brenner, N., B. Jessop, M. Jones, and G. Macleod, eds. 2008. *State/space: a reader*. John Wiley & Sons.

Busygina, I. M. 2011. "Model' 'tsentr-periferiya', federalism i problema modernizatsii rossiyskogo gosudarstva." *Politicheskaya nauka*, no. 4: 53–70.

Chandra, K. 2012. "Introduction." In *Constructivist Theories of Ethnic Politics*, edited by K. Chandra, 1-50. Oxford: Oxford University Press.

Chebotkova, A. D. 2010. "Territorial'nye osobennosti kachestva i obraza zhizni naseleniya Komi-Permyatskogo okruga Permskogo Kraya". PhD diss., Perm State University.

Clayton, D. 2004. "Imperial geographies." In *A companion to cultural geography*, edited by J. S. Duncan, N. C. Johnson, and R. H. Schein, 449-468. Blackwell Publishing Ltd.

Connor, W. 1984. The National Question in Marxist-Leninist Theory and Strategy. Princeton, NJ: Princeton University Press.

Connor, W. 1994. *Ethnonationalism: The Quest for Understanding*. Princeton, NJ: Princeton University Press.

Current Time. 2017. "Zhiteli Taymyra prosyat Putina vernut' poluostrovu status avtonomnogo okruga." August 16, 2017. https://www.currenttime.tv/a/28679488.html.

Damdinov, B. 2005. *Konstitutsionno-pravovoy status avtonomykh okrugov Rossiyskoy Federatsii: istoriya, sovremennost', perspektivy (na materialakh Aginskogo Buryatskogo i Ust'-Ordynskogo Buryatskogo avtonomnykh okrugov). Irkutsk*: MION.

Damdinov, B. 2009. "Osobyy status Aginskogo Buryatskogo okruga v sostave Zabaikal'skogo kraya: ot kontseptsii k ustavu." *Sibirskiy yuridicheskiy vestnik*, no. 2 (45): 34–42.

Damdinov, B. 2016. "Organizatsiya ispolnitel'noy vlasti v administrativno-territorial'nykh edinitsakh s osobym statusom." *Sibirskiy yuridicheskiy vestnik*, no. 1 (72): 26–31.

Davies, J. C. 1962. "Toward a Theory of Revolution." *American Sociological Review* 27, no. 1 (February): 5–19.

Demidenko, O. 2018a. "Kamchatka vstayot na dyby: nedaleko do bedy?" *REGNUM*, July 30, 2018. https://regnum.ru/news/2455975.html.

Demidenko, O. 2018b. "Nedaleko do bedy? Na Kamchatke davno beda! – kamchattsy o publikatsii IA REGNUM." *REGNUM*, August 3, 2018. https://regnum.ru/news/2458714.html.

Dmitriev, I. 2007. "Federatsiya neravnykh brakov." *Moscow Daily News*, November 7, 2007. http://www.mn.ru/print.php?2007-11-7.

Dobchinov, A. 2017. "K 80-letiyu Aginskogo Buryatskogo okruga." *Aginskaya Pravda*, September 25, 2017. http://www.aginskpravda.ru/blog/k_80_letiju_aginskogo_burjatskogo_okruga/2017-09-25-229.

Dobriakova, M. 1999. "Issledovaniya lokal'nykh soobshchestv v sotsiologicheskoy traditsii." *Sotsiologicheskie issledovaniya*, no. 7: 125-133.

Dorogin, V. 2003. "Zabytyy region, ili pochemu Kamchatka, blagodatnyy kray s unikal'nymi vozmozhnostyami, zhivyot na dotatsiyakh." *Regionalnaya ekonomika: Teoriya i praktika*, no. 2: 2-6.

Drobizheva, L. M. 2002. "Rossiiskaya i etnicheskaya identichnost': protivostoianie ili sovmestimost'." *Rossiya reformiruiushchayasya*, no. 2: 213-244.

Drobizheva, L. M. 2013. *Etnichnost' v social'no-politicheskom prostranstve Rossiyskoy Federatsii: opyt 20 let*. Moscow: Novyi Chronograph.

Drobizheva, L. M. 2017. "Etnicheskaya identichnost'." In *Identichnost': lichnost', obshchestvo, politika*, edited by I. S. Semenenko, 417-423. Moscow: Ves' Mir.

Eco, U. 1986. *Semiotics and the Philosophy of Language*. Bloomington: Indiana University Press.

Fedotova, N. 2015. Territorial'naya identichnost' kak simvolicheskiy resurs regiona. *Vestnik Novgorodskogo gosudarstvennogo universiteta*, no. 7 (90): 105-108.

Filippov, V. 2010. *Sovetskaya teoriya etnosa: istoriograficheskiy ocherk*. Moscow: Institute for African Studies of the Russian Academy of Sciences.

Gasilin, V., and A. Riazanov. 2016. "Tsennosti i idealy formiruiushchegosya rossiyskogo obshchestva: filosofsko-metodologicheskie aspekty." *Vestnik Povolzhskogo instituta upravleniya*, no. 2 (53): 106-114.

Gel'man, V. 2001. "Po tu storonu Sadovogo kol'tsa: opyt politicheskoy regionalistiki Rossii." *Politiya: Analiz. Khronika. Prognoz (Zhurnal politicheskoy filosofii i sotsiologii politiki)*, no. 4: 65-94.

Goncharik, A. 2011. "Regional'naya identichnost' v politicheskom analize protsessov regionalizatsii i formirovaniya regionov." *Politicheskaya nauka*, no. 4: 175-186.

Gorshkov M. K., and V. V. Petukhov, eds. 2015. *Rossiyskoe obshchestvo i vyzovy vremeni. Kniga vtoraya*. Moscow: Ves' Mir.

Gradetskiy, A., G. Marchenko, and A. Shmarov. n.d. "Doklad 'Tri v odnom': ob'edinyonnyy Krasnoyarskiy kray." *Expert RA*. https://raexpert.ru/researches/regions/krasnoyarsk/.

Gritsai, O., G. Ioffe, and A. Treivish. 1991. *Tsentr i periferiya v regional'nom razvitii*. Moscow: Nauka.

Grunt, Z. 1982. "Urbanizatsiya i territorial'naya obshchnost'." In *SSHA glazami amerikanskikh sotsiologov*. Moscow: Nauka.

Guboglo, M. 2017. ""Tri istochnika i tri sostavnye chasti" etnicheskoy identichnosti." *Vestnik antropologii*, no. 2: 113-135.

Hale, H. 2004. "Divided We Stand: Institutional Sources of Ethnofederal State Survival and Collapse." *World Politics* 56, no. 2 (January): 165-193.

Hale, H. 2005. "The makeup and breakup of ethnofederal states: Why Russia survives where the USSR fell." *Perspectives on Politics* 3, no. 1 (March): 55-70.

Harrison, J. 2007. "From competitive regions to competitive city-regions: a new orthodoxy, but some old mistakes." *Journal of Economic Geography* 7, no. 3 (May): 311-332.

Heinemann-Grüder, A. 2007. "Russia's Ethnofederalism: Under-Institutionalized, Not Self-Sustaining." In *Politics in the Russian Regions*, edited by G. Gill, 16-53. London: Palgrave Macmillan.

Henley, D. 1995. "Regional nationalism in a colonial state: a case study from the Dutch East Indies." *Political Geography* 14, no. 1 (January): 31-58.

Hirschon, R., and J. Gold. 1982. "Territoriality and the home environment in a Greek urban community." *Anthropological Quarterly* 55, no. 2 (April): 63-73.

Irkutskaya oblast'. Ofitsial'nyy portal. 2018. *Otchyot o rezul'tatakh deyatel'nosti administratsii Ust'-Ordynskogo Buryatskogo okruga za 2017 god*.http://irkobl.ru/sites/uobo/%D0%BE%D0%B1%D1%89%D0%B8%D0%B9%20%D0%BE%D1%82%D1%87%D0%B5%D1%82%20%D0%BF%D0%BE%20%D1%84%D1%83%D0%BD%D0%BA%D1%86%D0%B8%D1%8F%D0%BC%202017.pdf.

Interfax. 2020. "*Assotsitsiya nenetskogo naroda vystupila protiv obyedineniya s Pomoryem*". May 20, 2020. https://www.interfax.ru/russia/709527.

Ionin, L. 2005. "Novaya magicheskaya epokha." *Logos*, no. 5 (50): 23-40.

Itogi. 2001. "*Komu investor, a komu oligarkh.*" http://www.itogi.ru/archive/2001/3/119757.html.

Ivanov, V. 2008. *Putinskiy federalism. Tsentralizatorskie reformy v Rossii v 2000-2008 godakh*. Moscow: Territoriya Budushchego.

Jonas, A. and S. Pincetl. 2006. "Rescaling regions in the state: The New Regionalism in California." *Political Geography* 25, no. 5 (June): 482–505.

Kam 24. 2017. *"Opros: zhiteli kraya neodnoznachno otnosyatsya k ob'edineniyu Kamchatskoy oblasti i Koryakii."* June 30, 2017. https://www.kam24.ru/news/main/20170630/49656.html.

Kamchatka Inform. 2014. *"Na Kamchatke otmechayut 7 let so dnya ob'edineniya Kamchatskoy oblasti i Koryakskogo okruga."* July 1, 2014. https://kamchatinfo.com/news/politics/detail/5468/.

Kamchatka-Inform. 2014. *"Pri stroitel'stve odnoy iz tak i ne zarabotavshikh mini-TETS na severe Kamchatki 'zloupotrebili' na 53 milliona."* November 20, 2014. https://kamchatinfo.com/news/crimes/detail/7260/.

Kamchatskiy Kray. Ofitsialnyy sayt. 2018. *Na subsidirovanie aviaperelyotov po Kamchatke napravleno poryadka 500 mln rubley.* https://kamgov.ru/news/na-subsidirovanie-aviapereletov-po-kamcatke-napravleno-poradka-500-mln-rublej-15028.

Keating, M. 1998. *The new regionalism in Western Europe: Territorial restructuring and political change.* Cheltenham, UK: E. Elgar.

Khamaganov, Y. 2017. *"Vy molodtsy! Vashi protivniki v Chite i Age gordyatsya vami!"* *AsiaRussiaDaily,* January 16, 2017. http://asiarussia.ru/blogs/14874/.

Khamidullina, Z. 2016. *"Ust'-Orda + Irkutsk: Khronologiya ob'edineniya."* *Ircity.ru,* April 16, 2016. https://ircity.ru/articles/11859/.

Khamutaev, V. 2005. *Buryatskoe natsional'noe dvizhenie, 1980–2000-e gg.* Ulan-Ude: Izdatel'stvo Buryatskogo nauchnogo tsentra SO RAN.

Knight, D. B. 1982. *"Identity and Territory: Geographical Perspectives on Nationalism and Regionalism."* *Annals of the Association of American Geographers* 72, no. 4 (December): 514–531.

Kohn, H. 1965. *Nationalism: Its Meaning and History.* Malabar, Florida: Robert E. Krieger Publishing Company.

Kolmogorova, D. 2010. *"Ukrupnenie rossiyskih regionov."* In *Federalism i etnicheskoe raznoobrazie v Rossii,* edited by I. M. Busygina, and A. Heinemann-Grüder, 149–157. Moscow: Rossiyskaya politicheskaya Entsiklopediya.

Kolokolova, T. 2016. *"Aginskiy Buryatskiy Okrug: 8 let posle ob'edineniya."* *AsiaRussiaDaily,* March 17, 2016. http://asiarussia.ru/persons/11625/.

Kolosov, V., T. Galkina, and A. Krindach. 2001. *"Territorial'naya identichnost' i mezhetnicheskie otnosheniya na primere vostochnykh rayonov Stavropol'skogo kraya."* *Polis. Politicheskie issledovaniya,* no. 2: 61-77.

Komipermyatskiiao.ru. n.d. *Komi-Permyatskiy okrug. Ob'edinenie.* http://www.komipermyatskiiao.ru/about/united/htm.

Komi-Permyatskiy okrug. n.d. "Naselenie Komi-Permyatskogo okruga." https://комиокруг.рф/komi-permyatskiy-okrug.

Kommersant. 2004. "Boris Zolotaryov zashchitil Evenkiyu." March 22, 2004. https://www.kommersant.ru/doc/459418/.

Kommersant. 2015. "Kraevye vlasti ne ostavlyayut popytok prodat' gasoprovod Ochyor–Kudymkar–Kupros." June 24, 2015. https://www.kommersant.ru/doc/2753767.

Kosacheva, T. 2017. "Taymyrskie deputaty ne podderzhali otdelenie ot Krasnoyarskogo Kraya." *Kommersant*, June 22, 2017. https://www.kommersant.ru/doc/3299346.

Kravchenko, M. 2005. "Kamchatskie deputaty odobrili ob'edinenie s Koryakiey na den'gi federal'nogo tsentra." *Kommersant*, April 27, 2005. https://www.kommersant.ru/doc/573820.

Krug, P. 2006. "Kamlanie pered referendumom." *Religii*, April 5, 2006. http://www.ng.ru/ng_religii/2006-04-05/3_kamlanie.html.

Krylov, M., and A. Gritsenko. 2015. "Identichnosti na Ukraine: vyzovy sovremennosti - ekho proshlogo?" *Mir peremen*, no. 2: 142-156.

Kuveneva, T. N., and A. G. Manakov. 2003. "Formirovanie prostranstvennykh identichnostey v porubezhnom regione." *Sotsiologicheskie issledovaniya*, no. 7: 77-84.

Kynev, A. 2004. "Demokratiya v nishchete: Koryakiya izbrala gubernatora bez nadezhdy na luchshee." *Demokratia.ru*, April 28, 2004. http://www.democracy.ru/article.php?id=591.

Kynev, A. 2010a. "Nedostizhimaya simmetriya: ob itogakh 'ukrupneniya' sub'ektov Rossiyskoy Federatsii." *Neprikosnovenny zapas*, no. 3 (71): 123–136.

Kynev, A. 2010b. "Uproshchenie prostranstva." *Gazeta.ru*, April 28, 2010. https://www.gazeta.ru/comments/2010/01/28_x_3317483.shtml.

Kynev, A. n.d. "Vybory Dumy Koryakskogo okruga 19 dekabrya 2004: Elektoral'nye eksperimenty na fone total'nogo krizisa system ZHKH." *Demokratia.ru*. http://www.democracy.ru/library/publications/koriak_elections_2004.html.

Lagendijk, A., and J. Cornford. 2000. "Regional institutions and knowledge – tracking new forms of regional development policy." *Geoforum* 31, no. 2 (May): 209-218.

Latynina, S. 2016. "Effekt sliyaniya. Shto dalo Priangar'yu i Ust'-Ordynskomy okrugu ob'edinenie?" *Argumenty i Fakty*, April 13, 2016. http://www.irk.aif.ru/society/effekt_sliyaniya_chto_poluchili_pri angare_i_ust-ordynskiy_okrug_ot_sliyaniya#id=6311440.

Lebedeva, E. 2012. "*Opyt ob'edineniya sub'ektov v RF: problemy i predvaritel'nye itogi.*" Vestnik Adygeyskogo gosudarstvennogo universiteta. Seriya 1: Regionovedeniye: filosofiya, istoriya, sotsiologiya, yurisprudentsiya, politologiya, kul'turologiya, no. 1: 297-309.

Makarychev, A. 2000. "Federalizm epokhi globalizma: vyzovy dlia regional'noy Rossii." *Polis. Politicheskie issledovaniya*, no. 5: 81-97.

Makhschkeev, A. 2014. "Emigratsiya Agi." *AsiaRussiaDaily*, March 11, 2014. http://asiarussia.ru/blogs/2267/.

Malygina, I. 2011. "Kul'turnaya identichnost' v sovremennoy Rossii: poisk novykh modeley." *Vestnik Moskovskogo gosudarstvennogo universiteta kul'tury i iskusstv*, no. 3 (41): 43-48.

Manakov, A., and S. Evdokimov. 2013. "Skobari: istoricheskaya zrelost' granits i regional'naya identichnost' v Pskovskoy oblasti." *Kul'turnaya i gumanitarnaya geografiya* 2, no. 1: 28-38.

Marcusen, A. 1987. *Regions: The Economics and Politics of Territory*. Totowa, New Jersey: Rowman and Littlefield.

Melnikova, A. 2020. "Proyavlenie neuvazheniya k interesam nenetskogo naroda." *Znak*, May 23, 2020. https://www.znak.com/2020-05-23/v_nao_protestuyut_protiv_obedineniya_s_arhangelskoy_oblast yu.

Milchakov, M. 2007. "Ob'edinenie regionov: analiz sovremennoy praktiki ispol'zovaniya transformatsii administrativno-territorial'nogo deleniya v reshenii sotsial'no-ekonomicheskikh i politicheskikh zadach." *Regional'nye issledovaniya*, no. 5 (15): 33-46.

Milchakov, M. n.d. "Ob'edinenie Permskoy oblasti i KPAO: politicheskie, ekonomicheskie, sotsial'nye konflikty." *Geokonfliktologia*. http://geoconflict.narod.ru/texts/milchakov.html.

Miller, A. 2003. "Tsentr i okraina: Metamorfozy problemy v XVIII-XXI vv. Otnosheniya vlasti i obshchestvennaya mneniya v Rossii k Ukraine i Belorussii." In *Tsentr i regional'nye identichnosti v Rossii*, edited by V. Gel'man, and T. Hopf, 29-46. Saint-Petersburg: Izdatel'stvo Evropeyskogo universiteta; Moscow: Letniy Sad.

Mitin, I. 2015. "Novaya Moskva: konstruirovanie novogo lokal'nogo diskursa." *Labirint. Zhurnal sotsial'no-gumanitarnykh issledovaniy*, no. 2: 71-82.

Mosienko, N, and E. Goryachenko. 2010. *Sotsial'no-territorial'naya struktura prostranstva gorodskoy aglomeratsii*. Novosibirsk: Institut ėkonomiki i organizatsii promyshlennogo proizvodstva SO RAN.

Mukhametshina, E. 2020. "Arkhangel'skaya oblast' i Nenetskiy okrug otkladyvayut ob'edinenie." *Vedomosti*, May 28, 2020. https://www.vedomosti.ru/politics/articles/2020/05/27/831303-arhangelskaya-obedinenie.

Murdock, G. 1949. *Social Structure*. New York: The MacMillan Company.

Nazukina, M. 2014. "Novye tendentsii v politike identichnosti na regional'nom urovne v Rossii: aktory, spetsifika, trendy." *Antinomii* 14, no. 3: 137-150.

Nazukina, M., and O. Podvintsev. 2009. "Stolichnye ambitsii kak otrazhenie regionalizatsii sovremennoy Rossii." *Antinomii*, no. 9: 290-302.

Nechaev, V. 1998. *Regional'nyi mif v politicheskoy kul'ture sovremennoy Rossii*. Moscow: IA RAN.

Newdaynews.ru. 2005. "Khloponin protiv ob'edineniya Koryakii i Kamchatki." April 29, 2005. https://newdaynews.ru/siberia/24717.html.

Newslab.ru. 2010. "5-letie ob'edineniya Krasnoyarskogo kraya, Taimyra i Evenkii." April 17, 2010. http://newslab.ru/zs/tema/311453.

NIA Krasnoyarsk. 2013. "Pereselenie iz zony zatopleniya Boguchanskoy GES zaversheno." January 31, 2013. https://24rus.ru/more.php?UID=93913.

Novy Kompanyon. 2005. "Gennadiy Savel'yev postaralsya razrushit' <raduzhnuyu kartinku> v glazakh Mikhaila Fradkova." September 23, 2005. https://www.newsko.ru/news/nk-168808.html.

O'Driscoll, D., I. Costantini, and S. Al. 2020. "Federal versus Unitary States: Ethnic Accommodation of Tamils and Kurds." *Nationalism and Ethnic Politics* 26, no. 4 (October): 351-368.

O'Tuathail, G. 1999. "Understanding Critical Geopolitics: Geopolitics and Risk Society." *Journal of Strategic Studies* 22, no. 2-3 (June): 107-124.

Okunev, I. Y. 2021. *Political Geography*. Brussels: Peter Lang.

Okunev I. Y., and E. S. Bibina. 2019. "Ob'edinenie Taymyrskogo (Dolgano-Nenetskogo) i Evenkiyskogo avtonomnykh okrugov v sostave Krasnoyarskogo kraya: istoriya izmeneniya statusov i otsenki v SMI." *Pskovskiy regionologicheskiy zhurnal*, no. 1 (37): 46-55.

Okunev, I. Y., and M. I. Tislenko. 2017. "Geopolitical Positioning of Twin Cities: A Case Study of Narva/Ivangorod, Valga/Valka, and Blagoveshchensk/Heihe." *Teorija in Praksa* 54, no. 3-4: 592–605.

Okunev I. Y., and P. V. Oskolkov. 2019. "Posledstviya ob'edineniya rossiyskikh regionov v hode federativnoy reformy 2000-h godov (sravnitel'nyy analiz na osnove ekspertnykh interview)." *Politiya: Analiz. Khronika. Prognoz (Zhurnal politicheskoy filosofii i sotsiologii politiki)*, no. 1 (92): 149-166.

Okunev I. Y., and R. S. Shilovskiy. 2018. "Posledstviya ob'edineniya Kamchatskoy oblasti i Koryakskogo avtonomnogo okruga." *Vestnik Rossiyskogo universiteta druzhby narodov. Seriya: Politologiya* 20, no. 4: 484-495.

Okunev I. Y., and R. S. Shilovskiy. 2018. "Reformy ob'edineniya Ust'-Ordynskogo Buryatskogo avtonomnogo okruga s Irkutskoy oblast'yu i Aginskogo Buryatskogo avtonomnogo okruga s Chitinskoy oblast'yu: motivy i posledstviya." *Pskovskiy regionologicheskiy zhurnal*, no. 1 (33): 10-23.

Okunev, I. Y., M. I. Tislenko, A. Salavatova, and G. Ostapenko. 2016. "Geopolitichsekie kody postsovetskikh etnonatsional'nykh soobshchestv." *Mezhdunarodnye protsessy* 14, no. 1 (44): 156-171.

Okunev I. Y., M. I. Tislenko, and E. S. Bibina. 2018. "Otsenki posledstviy ob'edineniya Permskoy oblasti i Komi-Permyatskogo avtonomnogo okruga." *Istoricheskaya i sotsial'no-obrazovatel'naya mysl'* 10, no. 2-2: 133-147.

Okunev, I. Y., P. V. Oskolkov, and M. I. Tislenko. 2017. "Faktor limitrofnogo geopoliticheskogo pozitsionirovaniya v transformatsii prostranstvennoy identichnosti (na primere Gagauzii i Adzharii)." *Istoricheskaya i sotsial'no-obrazovatel'naya mysl'* 9, no. 2-2: 173-185.

Okunev I. Y., P. V. Oskolkov, and M. I. Tislenko. 2018. "Ob'edinenie regionov Rossiyskoy Federatsii: institutsional'nye i sotsial'nye posledstviya." *Polis. Politicheskie issledovaniya*, no. 2: 8-28.

Okunev I. Y., P. V. Oskolkov, and M. I. Tislenko. 2019. "Transforming the Matryoshka: Merger of Russian Regions." *Regions and Cohesion* 9, no. 3: 29-57.

Okunev I. Y., P. V. Oskolkov, M. I. Tislenko, E. S. Bibina, and R. S. Shilovskiy. 2020. *Ob'edinenie regionov Rossiyskoy Federatsii: sotsiologicheskie dannye, glubinnye interview, sravnitel'nyy analiz*. Moscow: Aspekt Press.

Oracheva, O. I. 1999. "Regional'naya identichnost': mif ili real'nost'?" In *Regional'noe samosoznanie kak faktor formirovaniya politicheskoy kul'tury v Rossii*, edited by M. V. Ilyin, and I. M. Busygina, 36-44. Moscow: MONF.

Oskolkov P. V. 2020. "Merging Russia's Autonomous Entities: Ethnic Aspect." *ICELDS*, June 15, 2020. https://www.icelds.org/2020/06/15/merging-russias-autonomous-entities-ethnic-aspect/.

Oskolkov, P. V. 2022. "Ethnicity and Politics: Terminological Debates and Nodal Points of Intersection." *Herald of the Russian Academy of Sciences* 92, no. 2: 155-160.

Ostrom, V., C. Tiebout, and R. Warren. 1961. "The organization of government in metropolitan areas: a theoretical inquiry." *American political science review* 55, no. 4 (December): 831-842.

Özkırımlı, U. 2010. *Theories of Nationalism: A Critical Introduction*. London: Palgrave Macmillan.

Paasi, A. 2001. "Europe as a social process and discourse: considerations of place, boundaries and identity." *European urban and regional studies* 8, no. 1 (January): 7-28.

Panarin, A. S. 2005. *Revansh istorii: rossiyskaya strategicheskaya initsiativa v XXI veke*. Moscow: Russkiy mir.

Panov, P., and E. Filippova. 2015. "Praktiki raspredeleniya vlastnykh pozitsiy v rossiyskikh 'natsionalnykh respublikakh': problema mezhetnicheskogo balansa." *Bulletin of Perm University. Political Science*, no. 3: 33-50.

Pantin, V., and V. Lapkin. 2015. "Etnopoliticheskie i etnosotsial'nye protsessy na postsovetskom prostranstve (na primere Rossii, Belorussii, Kazakhstana i Ukrainy)." *Polis. Politicheskie issledovaniya*, no. 5: 75-93.

Pavlyuk, S. 2007. "Toponimika grafstv SSHA: geokriptografiya identichnosti." *Izvestiya Rossiiskoy akademii nauk. Seriya geograficheskaya*, no. 1: 53-65.

Perevalova, E. 2019. *Obskiye ugry i nentsy Zapadnoy Sibiri: etnichnost' i vlast'*. St. Petersburg: MAE RAS.

Petrov, N. 2000. "Federalizm po-rossiyski." *Pro et Contra* 5, no. 1: 7-34.

Plotina.Net. n.d. "Istoriya proyekta stroitel'stva Boguchanskoy GES." http://www.plotina.net/experts/history/.

Podosokorsky, N. 2017. "Zhirinovskiy annonsiroval ukrupnenie regionov posle vyborov presidenta v marte 2018 goda." *LiveJournal* (blog), December 30, 2017. https://philologist.livejournal.com/9923452.html.

Polar Trans. n.d. "Morskoy port Dudinka." https://polartrans.ru/information/morskoj-port-dudinka.html.

Popov, A. 2006. "Poslednee Sliyanie." *Expert.ru*, October 6, 2006. http://expert.ru/2006/10/6/slijanie/.

Popov, A. 2013. "Matryoshka-2020." *Expert.ru*, June 26, 2013. http://expert.ru/2013/06/26/matreshka-2020/.

Postanovlenie N 353-pp ob utverzhdenii dolgosrochnoy tselevoy programmy Irkutskoy oblasti 'O sokhranenii i dal'neishem razvitii buryatskogo yazyka v Ust'-Ordynskom Buryatskom okruge' na 2013-2016 gody 2012 (Irkutsk oblast). http://docs.cntd.ru/document/469412958.

Pravitel'stvo Kamchatskogo Kraya. 2011. *Informatsiya o hode realizatsii Ukaza Prezidenta Rossiyskoy Federatsii No. 1227 'O merakh po sotsial'no-ekonomicheskomu razvitiyu Kamchatskoy oblasti i Koryakskogo avtonomnogo okruga'*. http://old.kamgov.ru/oiv_doc/7/11404.doc.

Prikaz No. 25-pr *'Ob utverzhdenii vedomstvennoy tselevoy programmy "Razvitie natsional'nykh i massovykh vidov sporta na territorii Ust'-Ordynskogo Buryatskogo okruga" na 2014-2020 gody'* 2013 (Ust-Orda Buryat Okrug). http://docs.cntd.ru/document/460192010.

Prokhorenko, I. 2012. "O metodologicheskikh problemakh analiza sovremennykh politicheskikh prostranstv." *Polis. Politicheskie issledovaniya*, no. 6: 68-80.

ProPerm. 2015. "Gazoprovod 'Ochyor–Kudymkar–Kupros' prodan bez ob'yavleniya tseny za 3,4 mln rubley." December 22, 2015. https://properm.ru/news/business/116338/.

Proyekt 'Sotsial'nyi atlas rossiyskich regionov'. n.d. *Sotsial'nyi atlas rossiyskich regionov. Portrety regionov: Kamchatskiy Krai.* http://www.socpol.ru/atlas/portraits/kamch.shtml.

Puzanov, K. 2013. "Territorial'nye granitsy gorodskikh soobshchestv." *Sotsiologiya vlasti*, no. 3: 27-38.

Radio Svoboda. 2005. "Byvshyi vitse-gubernator Koryakii prigovoryon k tryom godam lisheniya svobody" July 21, 2005. https://www.svoboda.org/a/109840.html.

Ragulina, M. 2012. "K metodike issledovaniya territorial'noy identichnosti." *Voprosy sovremennoy nauki i praktiki. Universitet im. V.I. Vernadskogo*, no. 3 (41): 10-14.

Redfield, R. 1947. "The folk society." *American Journal of sociology* 52, no. 4 (January): 293-308.

Regional'naya assotsiatsiya korennych malochislennych narodov Severa Krasnoyarskogo Kraya. *Taymyrskiy munitsipal'nyi rayon.* http://www.narodsevera.ru/north/area/tmr/?news_id=69.

REGNUM. 2004a. "Obzor SMI o situatsii v Krasnoyarskom Kraye za 12 oktyabrya 2004." October 12, 2004. https://regnum.ru/news/340434.html.

REGNUM. 2004b. "Po mneniyu gubernatora Krasnoyarskogo Kraya Alexandra Khloponina, ob'edeneniyu regionov protivyatsya te, kto obespokoyen sobstvennymi ambitsiyami." June 3, 2004. https://regnum.ru/news/polit/271608.html.

REGNUM. 2005. "Zhiteli Koryakii neodnoznachno otnosyatsya k ob'edineniyu s Kamchatkoy." April 6, 2005. https://regnum.ru/news/433747.html.

REGNUM. 2006a. *"Irkutsk i Ust'-Orda prishli k referendumu cherez soprotivlenie elity i 'ogolteluyu' agitatsiyu."* April 14, 2006. https://regnum.ru/news/623606.html.

REGNUM. 2006b. *"Sozdana gruppa uchastnikov referenduma 'Narody Pribaykalia za ob'edinenie'."* February 2, 2006. https://regnum.ru/news/583668.html.

REGNUM. 2017. *"Shto stoit za initsiativami ob'edineniya regionov v Rossii?"* December 28, 2017. https://regnum.ru/news/2363481.html.

Relph, E. 1976. *Place and placelessness.* London: Pion.

RIA Deita. 2008. *"Polpred Oleg Safonov raskritikoval rukovodstvo Kamchatskogo kraya."* September 22, 2008. https://deita.ru/ru/news/115482-polpred-oleg-safonov-raskritikoval-rukovodstvo-kamchatskogo-kraja.

RIA Novosti. 2010. *"Alexandr Gennadievich Khloponin. Biographicheskaya spravka."* January 19, 2010. https://ria.ru/politics/20100119/205330234.html.

RIA Novosti. 2015. *"Kitay primet uchastie v stroitel'stve zh/d 'Belkomur'."* September 7, 2015. https://ria.ru/20150907/1234745295.html.

RIA Novy den. 2005. *"Zhiteli Koryakii protiv sliyaniya s Kamchatkoy. Zachem ob'edinyat' 'gologo i nishchego'?"* April 13, 2005. https://newdaynews.ru/fareast/22707.html.

Riazantsev, I. and A. Zavalishin. 2009. *Territorial'noe povedenie rossiian. Istoriko-sotsiologicheskiy analiz.* Moscow: Akademicheskiy proekt.

Robber, M. A., and F. Tilman. 1988. *Psikhologiya individa i gruppy.* Moscow: Progress.

Rokkan, S., and D. Urwin. 1983. *Economy, territory, identity: Politics of West European peripheries.* Sage Publications (CA).

Rosstat. 2010. *Itogi Vserossijskoy perepisi naseleniya 2010 goda v otnoshenii demograficheskikh i social'no-jekonomicheskikh kharakteristik otdel'nykh natsional'nostey.* https://www.gks.ru/free_doc/new_site/perepis2010/croc/results2.html.

Rosstat. n.d. *Regiony Rossii. Sotsial'no-ekonomicheskie pokazateli.* http://www.gks.ru/wps/wcm/connect/rosstat_main/rosstat/ru/statistics/publications/catalog/doc_1138623506156.

Rothschild, J. 1981. *Ethnopolitics: A Conceptual Framework.* New York: Columbia University Press.

Ryabinskaya, Y. 2005. *"Kvashnin: ob'edinenie regionov neobkhodimo."* *RIA Novosti*, September 9, 2005. https://ria.ru/politics/20050909/41346073.html.

Ryazantsev, I. P. 1998. *Sotsial'no-ekonomicheskie otnosheniya 'region-tsentr': teoriya, metodologiya, analiz.* Moscow: Izdatel'stvo Moskovskogo universiteta.

Sayt Ministerstva po delam Komi-Permyatskogo okruga Permskogo kraya. http://minkpo.permkrai.ru/komi-permyatskiy-okrug/obshchie-svedeniya/.

Semenenko, I. 2016. "Politika identichnosti i identichnost' v politike: etnonatsional'nye rakursy, evropeyskiy kontekst." *Polis. Politicheskie issledovaniya,* no. 4: 8-28.

Semyonov, M. 2003. "Kreml' priznal tselesoobraznym ob'edinenie sub'ektov." *Kommersant,* April 18, 2003. https://www.kommersant.ru/doc/377711.

Shabaev, Y. P. 1997. "Komi-Permyatskiy avtonomnyy okrug: etnodemographicheskie problemy." *Region: Ekonimika i Sotsiologiya,* no. 3: 134-142.

Shabaev, Y. P. 2006. "Etnosotsial'nye posledstviya ob'edineniya regionov (iz opyta formirovaniya Permskogo kraya)." *Sotsiologicheskie issledovaniya,* no. 3 (263): 64-71.

Shabaev, Y. P., and K. V. Istomin. 2017. "Territorial'nost', etnichnost', administrativnye i kul'turnye granitsy: komi-izhemtsy (Iz'vatas) i komi-permyaki kak 'drugie' komi." *Etnograficheskoe Obozrenie,* no. 4: 99-114.

Shakkum, M. 2010. "Martin Shakkum: Ob'edinenie regionov – odin iz deystvennykh variantov ukrepleniya vlastnoy vertikali." *Rossiyskaya Gazeta,* May 10, 2010. https://rg.ru/2010/05/11/shakkum.html.

Shibaeva, O. 2011. "Ukrupnenie regionov: problemy i perspektivy." *Vestnik Moskovskogo universiteta. Seriya 21: Upravlenie (Gosudarstvo i obshchestvo),* no. 4: 62-68.

Sidorenko, A. V. 2009. "Etnicheskiy vyzov rossiyskomu federalizmu." *Politicheskaya Ekspertiza* 5, no. 1: 100-115.

Smirnyagin, L. V. 1995. *Kontseptsiya regional'noy sistemy Rossii.* Moscow.

Smirnyagin, L. V. 2005. "Uzlovye voprosy raionirovaniya." *Izvestiya Rossiyskoy akademii nauk. Seriya geograficheskaya,* no. 1: 5-16.

Snyder, J. 2000. *From Voting to Violence: Democratization and Nationalist Conflict.* New York: W.W. Norton.

Sobakina, D. 2005. "Tishanin vosstanavlivaet ravnovesie." *Politcom.ru,* October 17, 2005. http://politcom.ru/1532.html.

Soglashenie 'Ob osobom statuse administrativno-territorial'noy edinitsy v sostave novogo sub'ekta Rossiyskoy Federatsii, obrazovannogo v rezul'tate ob'edineniya Aginskogo Buryatskogo avtonomnogo okruga i Chitinskoy oblasti' 2007 (Chita oblast, Agin-Buryat Autonomous Okrug). http://docs.cntd.ru/document/922209159.

Sokolov, A. 2006. "Kamchatku pugaet ob'edinenie s Koryakiey." *Pravda.ru*, July 18, 2006. https://www.pravda.ru/society/family/purse/18-07-2006/191011-kamchatka-0/.

Sokolovsky, S. 2007. "Pravovoy status i identichnost' korennykh narodov (po materialam Vserossiyskoy perepisi naseleniya 2002 goda)." *Rasy i narody. Sovremennye etnicheskie i rasovye problemy*, no. 33: 11–57.

Soviet Federatsii Federal'nogo Sobraniya Rossiyskoy Federatsii. *Taymyrskiy (Dolgano-Nenetskyy) avtonomnyy okrug*. http://council.gov.ru/services/reference/9420/.

Stefanenko, T. G. 2000. *Etnopsikhologiya*. Moscow: Institut psikhologii RAN.

Stefanenko, T. G. 2009. "Etnicheskaya identichnost': ot etnologii k sotsial'noy psikhologii." *Vestnik Moskovskogo universiteta. Seriia 14. Psikhologiya*, no. 2: 3-17.

Streletskii, V. N. 2008. "Kul'turnaya geografiya v Rossii: osobennosti formirovaniya i puti razvitiya." *Izvestiya Rossiiskoy akademii nauk. Seriya geograficheskaya*, no. 5: 21-33.

Suvorova, I. 2014. "Novoe zdanie Komi-Permyatskogo dramteatra otkrylos' v Kudymkare." *Rossiyskaya gazeta*, January 15, 2014. https://rg.ru/2014/01/15/reg-pfo/kudymkar.html.

Szczepański, J. 1964. "Some characteristics of contemporary Polish society." *The Polish Sociological Bulletin*, no. 10: 5-16.

Taimyrskiy Dolgano-Nenetskiy munitsipal'nyy rayon. n.d. *Obrazovanie Taymyrskogo Dolgano-Nenetskogo avtonomnogo okruga*. https://taimyr24.ru/about/Histori_T/dop_obraz_TAO.php.

Tarasov, G. 2001. "Kogo nazyvaet Taymyr." *Trud*, January 26, 2001. http://www.trud.ru/article/26-01-2001/18540_kogo_nazyvaet_taj myr.html.

TASS. 2015. "Gubernator Irkutskoy oblasti Yeroshchenko ushyol v otstavku." May 13, 2015. https://tass.ru/politika/1966767.

TASS. 2016. "Ob'edinenie Krasnoyarskogo kraya, Taimyra i Evenkii uskorilo osvoenie nedr." April 29, 2016. http://tass.ru/sibir-news/3250295.

TASS. 2017. "Zhirinovskiy predlagaet sozdat' v Rossii 30 guberniy vmesto 85 sub'ektov." December 29, 2017. http://tass.ru/politika/4852275.

TASS. 2018. "Korennye narody Severa prosyat razrabotat' zakonoproyekt ob osobom statuse Evenkii i Taymyra." January 12, 2018. http://tass.ru/v-strane/4869791.

Teleinform. 2016. *"Detdom v posyolke Ust'-Ordynskiy reshili pereprofilirovat' v shkolu."* December 22, 2016. http://i38.ru/obrazovanie-pervie/detdom-v-poselke-ust-ordinskiy-reshili-pereprofilirovat-v-shkolu.

Territorial'nyy organ Federal'noy sluzhby gosudarstvennoy statistiki po Kamchatskomu krayu. n.d. *Ofitsial'naya statistika.* http://kamstat.gks.ru/wps/wcm/connect/rosstat_ts/kamstat/ru/statistics/.

Tikhomirov, V. 2017. "10 let bez prava peresmotra." *Zab.ru*, March 3, 2017. https://zab.ru/articles/5142_10_let_bez_prava_peresmotra.

Tishkov, V. 1997. *Ethnicity, Nationalism and Conflict in and after the Soviet Union: The Mind Aflame.* London: SAGE Publications.

Tishkov, V. 2001. "Etnos ili Etnichnost'?" In *Etnologiya i politika*, edited by V. Tishkov. Moscow: Nauka.

Tishkov, V. 2008. "Natsiya i natsional'naya identichnost' v Rossii." *Vestnik rossiiskoy natsii*, no. 1: 120-128.

Tislenko M. I., and I. Y. Okunev. 2018. "Posledstviya ob'edineniya sub'ektov Rossiyskoy Federatsii: analiz obshchestvennogo mneniya." *Regional'nye issledovaniya*, no. 4 (62): 118-125.

Tkachenko, A. 1995. *Territorial'naya obshchnost' v regional'nom razvitii i upravlenii. Tver':* Tver' State University.

Trubina, E. G. 2013. "Tsentr i periferiya: mezhdu rostom i razvitiem." *Logos*, no. 4 (94): 237-266.

Trud. 2012. *"Pri stroitel'stve mini-TETS 'Manily' na Kamchatke ischezli 38,5 mln rubley."* April 6, 2012. http://www.combienergy.ru/news/1333637340-Pri-stroitelstve-mini-TEC-Manily-na-Kamchatke-ischezli.

Tuan, Y. 1979. "Space and place: humanistic perspective." In *Philosophy in geography*, edited by S. Gale, and G. Olsson, 387-427. Springer, Dordrecht.

Turovsky, R. F. 1999. "Regional'naya identichnost' v sovremennoy Rossii." In *Rossiiskoe obshchestvo: stanovlenie demokraticheskikh tsennostey*, edited by A. Ryabov, and M. Mcfall, 87-136. Moscow: Gandalf.

Turovsky, R. F. 2006a. *Politicheskaya regionalistika.* Moscow: Izdatel'skiy dom GU-VSHE.

Turovsky, R. F. 2006b. *Tsentr i regiony: problemy politicheskikh otnosheniy.* Moscow: GU-VSHE.

Tvortsov, R. 2011. "Khroniki referenduma i ob'edineniya." *Zabinfo.ru*, March 21, 2011. http://zabinfo.ru/a271.

Tvortsov, V. 2021. "Zabaikal'skiy rekviem po mechte." *EastRussia*, March 10, 2021. https://www.eastrussia.ru/material/zabaykalskiy-rekviem-po-mechte/.

Ukaz Presidenta Rossiyskoy Federatsii No. 1227 'O merakh po sotsial'no-ekonomicheskomu razvitiyu Kamchatskoy oblasti i Koryakskogo avtonomnogo okruga' 2005 (Russia). http://kremlin.ru/acts/bank/22968.

Ukaz Presidenta Rossiyskoy Federatsii No. 1283 'O merakh po sotsial'no-ekonomicheskomu razvitiyu Komi-Permyatskogo avtonomnogo okruga i Permskoy oblasti' 2003 (Russia). http://kremlin.ru/acts/bank/20130.

Ukaz Presidenta Rossiyskoy Federatsii No. 260 'O merakh po sotsial'no-ekonomicheskomu razvitiyu Chitinskoy oblasti i Aginskogo Buryatskogo avtonomnogo okruga' 2007 (Russia). http://kremlin.ru/acts/bank/25073.

Ukaz Presidenta Rossiyskoy Federatsii No. 412 'O merakh po sotsial'no-ekonomicheskomu razvitiyu Krasnoyarskogo Kraya, Taymyrskogo (Dolgano-Nenetskogo) avtonomnogo okruga i Evenkiyskogo avtonomnogo okruga' 2005 (Russia). http://kremlin.ru/acts/bank/22251.

Ukaz Presidenta Rossiyskoy Federatsii 'O merakh po sotsial'no-ekonomicheskomu razvitiyu Irkutskoy oblasti i Ust'-Ordynskogo Buryatskogo avtonomnogo okruga' 2006 (Russia). https://docs.cntd.ru/document/901974673.

Ustav Irkutskoy oblasti 2009 (Irkutsk Oblast). http://www.irk.gov.ru/about/basic/charter/.

Ustav Nenetskogo avtonomnogo okruga 1995 (Nenets Autonomous Okrug). https://docs.cntd.ru/document/748300094.

Vakhrin, S. 2014. "Pochyom rodovye obshchiny na Kamchatke?" *Kamchatskoe Vremya*, February 26, 2014. http://kamtime.ru/node/2802.

Vasilyeva, K., and N. Anuchina. 2012. "Ob'edinenie Chitinskoy oblasti i Aginskogo Buryatskogo avtonomnogo okruga: analiz obshchestvennogo mneniya." *Vestnik Zabaykalskogo gosudarstvennogo universiteta*, no. 12 (91): 52–58.

Vendina, O., and A. Zinoviev. 2022. "Pogranichnost' i periferiynost': k voprosu o kontekste formirovaniya kaliningradskoy identichnosti." *Mir Rossii. Sotsiologiya. Etnologiya* 31, no. 2: 118-143.

Verkhoturov, D. 2007a. "Buryaty: natsiya bez liderov?" *Newsbabr.com*, March 17, 2007. http://newsbabr.com/baik/?IDE=36606.

Verkhoturov, D. 2007b. "Nekonkretnoe ob'edinenie." *Expert Online*, January 22, 2007. http://web.archive.org/web/20080129151806/http://www.expert.ru:80/articles/2007/01/22/obed/.

Verkhoturov, D. 2007c. "V tikhom omute." *Expert Online*, March 12, 2007. http://web.archive.org/web/20071101044123/http://www.expert.ru:80/articles/2007/03/12/slijanie/.

Verkhoturov, L. 2009. "Evenkiya dolzhna stat' respublikoy." *APN.ru*, September 4, 2009. http://www.apn.ru/publications/article21918.htm.

Vinokurov, A., M. Litvinova, and L. Kadik. 2020. "Neob'edinyayemyi avtonomnyi okrug." *Kommersant*, May 31, 2020. https://www.kommersant.ru/doc/4364004.

Viperson. 2001. "*Taymyrskiy avtonomnyy okrug.*" January 23, 2001. http://viperson.ru/articles/taymyrskiy-avtonomnyy-okrug.

Vizgalov, D. V. 2007. *Indikativnoe planirovanie v razvitii territoriy*. Moscow: Fond "Institut ekonomiki goroda".

Vizgalov, D. V. 2011. *Brending goroda*. Moscow: Fond "Institut ekonomiki goroda".

Vladimirova, M. 2014. "Takaya vkusnaya olenina, takoe trudnoe olenevodstvo." *Kamchatka Krai*, October 15, 2014. http://kamkray.ru/news/2014/10/15/takaya-vkusnaya-olenina-takoe-trudnoe-olenevodstvo.html.

Vladimirova, M., and D. Korostelev. 2017. "Dmitriy Korostelyov – o roste ekonomiki kraya." *Kamchatka krai*, July 4, 2017. kamkray.ru/news/12168-dmitrii-korostelyov-o-roste-ekonomiki-kraja.html.

Vostochno-Sibirskaya Pravda. 2002. "*Oblast' i okrug ob'edinyat'tsya ne speshat.*" September 11, 2002. http://www.vsp.ru/2002/09/11/oblast-i-okrug-obedinyatsya-ne-speshat.

Yack, B. 1996. "The myth of the civic nation." *Critical Review* 10, no. 2 (March): 193-211.

Yadov, V. A. 1995. "Sotsial'nye i sotsial'no-psikhologicheskie mekhanizmy formirovaniya sotsial'noy identichnosti lichnosti." *Mir Rossii. Sotsiologiya. Etnologiya* 4, no. 3-4: 158-181.

Yadov, V. A., and Tsetsenbileg, eds. 2014. *Identichnosti, protsessy sotsial'noy integratsii i dezintegratsii v transformiruyushchikhsya obshchestvakh. Materialy dokladov mezhdunarodnoy nauchnoy konferentsii, 10-12 avgusta 2014 g., g. Ulan-Bator*. Moscow- Ulaanbaatar: IS RAN; Institut philosophii, sotsiologii i prava AN Mongolii.

Yanovskiy, Y. 2015. "'Eto vsyo – obman.' Komi-Permyaki ob ob'edinenii s Permskoy oblast'yu." *Properm.ru*, December 1, 2015. https://properm.ru/news/society/115232/.

Yanovskaya, Y. 2015. "Gennadiy Savel'ev, eks-glava Komi-Permyatskogo avtonomnogo okruga rasskazyvaet pro gody u vlasti." *Parma Novosti*, September 28, 2015. http://parmanews.ru/index.php/temy/item/2293-eks-glava-komi-permyatskogo-avtonomnogo-okruga-rasskazyvaet-pro-gody-u-vlasti/.

Yarskaya, V. et al. 2004. *Prostranstvo i vremya sotsial'nykh izmeneniy.* Saratov: Izdatel'stvo "Nauchnaya kniga".

Yusupova, G. 2018. "Cultural Nationalism and Everyday Resistance in an Illiberal Nationalizing State: Ethnic Minority Nationalism in Russia." *Nations and Nationalism* 24, no. 1 (November): 624-647.

Zab.ru. 2016. "V Zabaykal'e vmesto 31 rayona optimal'no sozdat' 10 okrugov – Geniatulin." March 3, 2016. https://zab.ru/news/83975_v_zabajkale _vmesto_31_rajona_optimalno_sozdat_10_okrugov___geniatulin.

Zabinfo.ru. 2011. "Khroniki referenduma i ob'edineniya" http://www.zabinfo .ru/modules.php?op=modload&name=Sections&file=index&req=p rintpage&artid=271.

Zakon Aginskoy Buryatskoy okruzhnoy Dumy Aginskogo Buryatskogo avtonomnogo okruga No. 799-ZAO 2007 (Agin-Buryat Autonomous Okrug). https://www.lawmix.ru/zakonodatelstvo/2264675.

Zakon Irkutskoy oblasti No. 121-OZ 'Ob Ust'-Ordynskom Buryatskom okruge kak administrativno-territorial'noy edinitse Irkutskoy oblasti s osobym statusom 2010 (Irkutsk oblast). http://docs.cntd.ru/document/ 469402091.

Zakon Zabaykal'skogo kraya No. 125-33K 'Ustav Zabaykal'skogo kraya' (s izmeneniyami i dopolneniyami) 2009 (Zabaykalsky Krai). http://constitution.garant.ru/region/ustav_zabaikal/.

Zamyatin, D. 2014. "Soprostranstvennost', territorial'naya identichnost' i mesto: k ponimaniyu politik postmoderna." *Arktika XXI vek. Gumanitarnye nauki*, no. 2 (3): 4-36.

Zamyatina, N. 2012. "Problemnoe pole territorial'noy identichnosti v kontekste organizatsii i samoorganizatsii sotsial'nykh struktur." *Mir psikhologii*, no. 1 (69): 123-137.

Zaslavskaya, T., A. Aganbegian, and R. Ryvkina. 1991. *Sotsiologiya ekonomicheskoy zhizni: Ocherki teorii.* Novosibirsk: Nauka.

Zaslavskaya, T., and V. Yadov. 2008. "Sotsial'nye transformatsii v Rossii v epokhu global'nykh izmeneniy." *Sotsiologicheskiy zhurnal*, no. 4: 8-22.

Zinoviev, A. n.d. "My opyat' vmeste: khronika obrazovaniya Permskogo kraya." *Arkhiv goroda Permi.* http://www.permarchive.ru/index. php?page=my-opyat-vmeste-hronika-obrazovaniya-permskogo-kraya.

Zisserman-Brodsky, D. 2003. *Constructing Ethnopolitics in the Soviet Union: Samizdat, Deprivation and the Rise of Ethnic Nationalism.* London: Palgrave Macmillan.

APPENDICES

Appendix 1

Questions for the Sociological Survey

Interviewer: Hello! I'm a member of a group of researchers from MGIMO University carrying out a sociological survey to assess the degree of development of Russia's regions. Would you be able to answer a few questions for us today? It'll only take a few minutes.

1. Please rate your level of satisfaction with various aspects of life in your region on a scale of 1 to 5, with 1 meaning completely dissatisfied and 5 meaning completely satisfied.

	Completely satisfied	Mostly satisfied	Neither satisfied nor dissatisfied	Mostly dissatisfied	Completely dissatisfied
Quality of work of the public authorities	5	3	3	2	1
Level of economic development of the region	5	3	3	2	1
Level of social welfare provided by the state	5	3	3	2	1
Stability and peace in inter-ethnic relations	5	3	3	2	1
Degree of support for ethnic culture and language	5	3	3	2	1

2. How often do you feel a sense of community with the following groups of people?

	Often	Sometimes	Almost never
People living in your city/village	1	2	3
People with the same ethnicity as you	1	2	3
People living in your region	1	2	3
Russians in general	1	2	3
The global community	1	2	3

3. Do you trust these political and social institutions? (1 – yes / 2 – no)

	Yes	No
The President of Russia	1	2
The federal authorities	1	2
The governor of your region	1	2
The local authorities	1	2
The federal media	1	2
The local media	1	2
Political parties	1	2
Local branches of political parties	1	2
Community-based organizations in your area	1	2

4. I'm going to read you a series of statements. Please rate, on a 5-point scale, the degree with which you agree to them, with 5 meaning completely agree, and 1 meaning completely disagree.

	Completely agree	Mostly agree	No opinion	Mostly disagree	Completely disagree
I have a fairly good idea of what is going on in politics and current affairs	5	4	3	2	1
People should be more involved in political life and government affairs	5	4	3	2	1
I know how to make my voice heard when it comes to important government decisions	5	4	3	2	1
People like me don't have the power to influence the government's actions	5	4	3	2	1
People of my ethnicity have the power to influence the government's actions	5	4	3	2	1

5. How would you assess the consequences of the federal reform in Russia to merge the autonomous *okrug*s with larger regions, as happened in your region? Please rate the reform on a scale of 1 to

10, with 1 meaning that you do not support the reform, and 10 meaning that you fully support the reform.

6. What, in your opinion, was the main goal of the reform?
    1. To improve the governability of the regions from the federal centre.
    2. The socioeconomic development of the regions.
    3. To dissolve the ethnic *okrug*s.
    4. I don't know.

7. To what extent has the situation in certain areas of life changed as a result of the federal reform?

	Significantly improved	Mostly improved	No change	Mostly worsened	Significantly worsened
Quality of work of the public authorities	5	4	3	2	1
Level of economic development of the region	5	4	3	2	1
Level of social welfare	5	4	3	2	1
Stability and peace in inter-ethnic relations	5	4	3	2	1
State support for ethnic culture and language	5	4	3	2	1

8. Gender: 1) Male; 2) Female
9. Age: 1) 16–35; 2) 36–55; 3) 56 and older.

Appendix 2

In-Depth Interview Questions

1. In the 2000s, Russia underwent a federal reform, during which the autonomous okrugs became part of larger regions. What do you think about the results of the form for Russia in general, and for your region in particular?
2. What was the main goal of the reform in your opinion? Has it achieved what it set out to achieve?
3. To what extent has the quality of the work of the public authorities changed following the merger of the regions?
4. Have the people become more politically engaged since the merger? Do they now have greater or lesser trust in the authorities?
5. To what extent has the economic situation in the region changed since the federal reform?
6. What changes have occurred in terms of social welfare since the merger of the regions?
7. How has the level of support for national culture and language changed since the merger of the regions?
8. How would you assess inter-ethnic relations in the region? Has the situation changed significantly since the merger?
9. If you could go back to the beginning of the reform, what changes do you think would need to be made in terms of its implementation?
10. Should Russia continue to reform the administrative and territorial structure of the country? If yes, then in what areas?

APPENDIX

SOVIET AND POST-SOVIET POLITICS AND SOCIETY
Edited by Dr. Andreas Umland | ISSN 1614-3515

1   Андреас Умланд (ред.) | Воплощение Европейской конвенции по правам человека в России. Философские, юридические и эмпирические исследования | ISBN 3-89821-387-0

2   Christian Wipperfürth | Russland – ein vertrauenswürdiger Partner? Grundlagen, Hintergründe und Praxis gegenwärtiger russischer Außenpolitik | Mit einem Vorwort von Heinz Timmermann | ISBN 3-89821-401-X

3   Manja Hussner | Die Übernahme internationalen Rechts in die russische und deutsche Rechtsordnung. Eine vergleichende Analyse zur Völkerrechtsfreundlichkeit der Verfassungen der Russländischen Föderation und der Bundesrepublik Deutschland | Mit einem Vorwort von Rainer Arnold | ISBN 3-89821-438-9

4   Matthew Tejada | Bulgaria's Democratic Consolidation and the Kozloduy Nuclear Power Plant (KNPP). The Unattainability of Closure | With a foreword by Richard J. Crampton | ISBN 3-89821-439-7

5   Марк Григорьевич Меерович | Квадратные метры, определяющие сознание. Государственная жилищная политика в СССР. 1921 – 1941 гг | ISBN 3-89821-474-5

6   Andrei P. Tsygankov, Pavel A. Tsygankov (Eds.) | New Directions in Russian International Studies | ISBN 3-89821-422-2

7   Марк Григорьевич Меерович | Как власть народ к труду приучала. Жилище в СССР – средство управления людьми. 1917 – 1941 гг. | С предисловием Елены Осокиной | ISBN 3-89821-495-8

8   David J. Galbreath | Nation-Building and Minority Politics in Post-Socialist States. Interests, Influence and Identities in Estonia and Latvia | With a foreword by David J. Smith | ISBN 3-89821-467-2

9   Алексей Юрьевич Безугольный | Народы Кавказа в Вооруженных силах СССР в годы Великой Отечественной войны 1941-1945 гг. | С предисловием Николая Бугая | ISBN 3-89821-475-3

10 Вячеслав Лихачев и Владимир Прибыловский (ред.) | Русское Национальное Единство, 1990-2000. В 2-х томах | ISBN 3-89821-523-7

11 Николай Бугай (ред.) | Народы стран Балтии в условиях сталинизма (1940-е – 1950-е годы). Документированная история | ISBN 3-89821-525-3

12 Ingmar Bredies (Hrsg.) | Zur Anatomie der Orange Revolution in der Ukraine. Wechsel des Elitenregimes oder Triumph des Parlamentarismus? | ISBN 3-89821-524-5

13 Anastasia V. Mitrofanova | The Politicization of Russian Orthodoxy. Actors and Ideas | With a foreword by William C. Gay | ISBN 3-89821-481-8

14 Nathan D. Larson | Alexander Solzhenitsyn and the Russo-Jewish Question | ISBN 3-89821-483-4

15 Guido Houben | Kulturpolitik und Ethnizität. Staatliche Kunstförderung im Russland der neunziger Jahre | Mit einem Vorwort von Gert Weisskirchen | ISBN 3-89821-542-3

16 Leonid Luks | Der russische „Sonderweg"? Aufsätze zur neuesten Geschichte Russlands im europäischen Kontext | ISBN 3-89821-496-6

17 Евгений Мороз | История «Мёртвой воды» – от страшной сказки к большой политике. Политическое неоязычество в постсоветской России | ISBN 3-89821-551-2

18 Александр Верховский и Галина Кожевникова (ред.) | Этническая и религиозная интолерантность в российских СМИ. Результаты мониторинга 2001-2004 гг. | ISBN 3-89821-569-5

19 Christian Ganzer | Sowjetisches Erbe und ukrainische Nation. Das Museum der Geschichte des Zaporoger Kosakentums auf der Insel Chortycja | Mit einem Vorwort von Frank Golczewski | ISBN 3-89821-504-0

20 Эльза-Баир Гучинова | Помнить нельзя забыть. Антропология депортационной травмы калмыков | С предисловием Кэролайн Хамфри | ISBN 3-89821-506-7

21 Юлия Лидерман | Мотивы «проверки» и «испытания» в постсоветской культуре. Советское прошлое в российском кинематографе 1990-х годов | С предисловием Евгения Марголита | ISBN 3-89821-511-3

22 Tanya Lokshina, Ray Thomas, Mary Mayer (Eds.) | The Imposition of a Fake Political Settlement in the Northern Caucasus. The 2003 Chechen Presidential Election | ISBN 3-89821-436-2

23 Timothy McCajor Hall, Rosie Read (Eds.) | Changes in the Heart of Europe. Recent Ethnographies of Czechs, Slovaks, Roma, and Sorbs | With an afterword by Zdeněk Salzmann | ISBN 3-89821-606-3

24 Christian Autengruber | Die politischen Parteien in Bulgarien und Rumänien. Eine vergleichende Analyse seit Beginn der 90er Jahre | Mit einem Vorwort von Dorothée de Nève | ISBN 3-89821-476-1

25 Annette Freyberg-Inan with Radu Cristescu | The Ghosts in Our Classrooms, or: John Dewey Meets Ceauşescu. The Promise and the Failures of Civic Education in Romania | ISBN 3-89821-416-8

26 John B. Dunlop | The 2002 Dubrovka and 2004 Beslan Hostage Crises. A Critique of Russian Counter-Terrorism | With a foreword by Donald N. Jensen | ISBN 3-89821-608-X

27 Peter Koller | Das touristische Potenzial von Kam''janec'–Podil's'kyj. Eine fremdenverkehrsgeographische Untersuchung der Zukunftsperspektiven und Maßnahmenplanung zur Destinationsentwicklung des „ukrainischen Rothenburg" | Mit einem Vorwort von Kristiane Klemm | ISBN 3-89821-640-3

28 Françoise Daucé, Elisabeth Sieca-Kozlowski (Eds.) | Dedovshchina in the Post-Soviet Military. Hazing of Russian Army Conscripts in a Comparative Perspective | With a foreword by Dale Herspring | ISBN 3-89821-616-0

29 Florian Strasser | Zivilgesellschaftliche Einflüsse auf die Orange Revolution. Die gewaltlose Massenbewegung und die ukrainische Wahlkrise 2004 | Mit einem Vorwort von Egbert Jahn | ISBN 3-89821-648-9

30 Rebecca S. Katz | The Georgian Regime Crisis of 2003-2004. A Case Study in Post-Soviet Media Representation of Politics, Crime and Corruption | ISBN 3-89821-413-3

31 Vladimir Kantor | Willkür oder Freiheit. Beiträge zur russischen Geschichtsphilosophie | Ediert von Dagmar Herrmann sowie mit einem Vorwort versehen von Leonid Luks | ISBN 3-89821-589-X

32 Laura A. Victoir | The Russian Land Estate Today. A Case Study of Cultural Politics in Post-Soviet Russia | With a foreword by Priscilla Roosevelt | ISBN 3-89821-426-5

33 Ivan Katchanovski | Cleft Countries. Regional Political Divisions and Cultures in Post-Soviet Ukraine and Moldova | With a foreword by Francis Fukuyama | ISBN 3-89821-558-X

34 Florian Mühlfried | Postsowjetische Feiern. Das Georgische Bankett im Wandel | Mit einem Vorwort von Kevin Tuite | ISBN 3-89821-601-2

35 Roger Griffin, Werner Loh, Andreas Umland (Eds.) | Fascism Past and Present, West and East. An International Debate on Concepts and Cases in the Comparative Study of the Extreme Right | With an afterword by Walter Laqueur | ISBN 3-89821-674-8

36 Sebastian Schlegel | Der „Weiße Archipel". Sowjetische Atomstädte 1945-1991 | Mit einem Geleitwort von Thomas Bohn | ISBN 3-89821-679-9

37 Vyacheslav Likhachev | Political Anti-Semitism in Post-Soviet Russia. Actors and Ideas in 1991-2003 | Edited and translated from Russian by Eugene Veklerov | ISBN 3-89821-529-6

38 Josette Baer (Ed.) | Preparing Liberty in Central Europe. Political Texts from the Spring of Nations 1848 to the Spring of Prague 1968 | With a foreword by Zdeněk V. David | ISBN 3-89821-546-6

39 Михаил Лукьянов | Российский консерватизм и реформа, 1907-1914 | С предисловием Марка Д. Стейнберга | ISBN 3-89821-503-2

40 Nicola Melloni | Market Without Economy. The 1998 Russian Financial Crisis | With a foreword by Eiji Furukawa | ISBN 3-89821-407-9

41 Dmitrij Chmelnizki | Die Architektur Stalins | Bd. 1: Studien zu Ideologie und Stil | Bd. 2: Bilddokumentation | Mit einem Vorwort von Bruno Flierl | ISBN 3-89821-515-6

42 Katja Yafimava | Post-Soviet Russian-Belarussian Relationships. The Role of Gas Transit Pipelines | With a foreword by Jonathan P. Stern | ISBN 3-89821-655-1

43 Boris Chavkin | Verflechtungen der deutschen und russischen Zeitgeschichte. Aufsätze und Archivfunde zu den Beziehungen Deutschlands und der Sowjetunion von 1917 bis 1991 | Ediert von Markus Edlinger sowie mit einem Vorwort versehen von Leonid Luks | ISBN 3-89821-756-6

44 Anastasija Grynenko in Zusammenarbeit mit Claudia Dathe | Die Terminologie des Gerichtswesens der Ukraine und Deutschlands im Vergleich. Eine übersetzungswissenschaftliche Analyse juristischer Fachbegriffe im Deutschen, Ukrainischen und Russischen | Mit einem Vorwort von Ulrich Hartmann | ISBN 3-89821-691-8

45 Anton Burkov | The Impact of the European Convention on Human Rights on Russian Law. Legislation and Application in 1996-2006 | With a foreword by Françoise Hampson | ISBN 978-3-89821-639-5

46 Stina Torjesen, Indra Overland (Eds.) | International Election Observers in Post-Soviet Azerbaijan. Geopolitical Pawns or Agents of Change? | ISBN 978-3-89821-743-9

47 Taras Kuzio | Ukraine – Crimea – Russia. Triangle of Conflict | ISBN 978-3-89821-761-3

48 Claudia Šabić | „Ich erinnere mich nicht, aber L'viv!" Zur Funktion kultureller Faktoren für die Institutionalisierung und Entwicklung einer ukrainischen Region | Mit einem Vorwort von Melanie Tatur | ISBN 978-3-89821-752-1

49 *Marlies Bilz* | Tatarstan in der Transformation. Nationaler Diskurs und Politische Praxis 1988-1994 | Mit einem Vorwort von Frank Golczewski | ISBN 978-3-89821-722-4

50 *Марлен Ларюэль (ред.)* | Современные интерпретации русского национализма | ISBN 978-3-89821-795-8

51 *Sonja Schüler* | Die ethnische Dimension der Armut. Roma im postsozialistischen Rumänien | Mit einem Vorwort von Anton Sterbling | ISBN 978-3-89821-776-7

52 *Галина Кожевникова* | Радикальный национализм в России и противодействие ему. Сборник докладов Центра «Сова» за 2004-2007 гг. | С предисловием Александра Верховского | ISBN 978-3-89821-721-7

53 *Галина Кожевникова и Владимир Прибыловский* | Российская власть в биографиях I. Высшие должностные лица РФ в 2004 г. | ISBN 978-3-89821-796-5

54 *Галина Кожевникова и Владимир Прибыловский* | Российская власть в биографиях II. Члены Правительства РФ в 2004 г. | ISBN 978-3-89821-797-2

55 *Галина Кожевникова и Владимир Прибыловский* | Российская власть в биографиях III. Руководители федеральных служб и агентств РФ в 2004 г.| ISBN 978-3-89821-798-9

56 *Ileana Petroniu* | Privatisierung in Transformationsökonomien. Determinanten der Restrukturierungs-Bereitschaft am Beispiel Polens, Rumäniens und der Ukraine | Mit einem Vorwort von Rainer W. Schäfer | ISBN 978-3-89821-790-3

57 *Christian Wipperfürth* | Russland und seine GUS-Nachbarn. Hintergründe, aktuelle Entwicklungen und Konflikte in einer ressourcenreichen Region| ISBN 978-3-89821-801-6

58 *Togzhan Kassenova* | From Antagonism to Partnership. The Uneasy Path of the U.S.-Russian Cooperative Threat Reduction | With a foreword by Christoph Bluth | ISBN 978-3-89821-707-1

59 *Alexander Höllwerth* | Das sakrale eurasische Imperium des Aleksandr Dugin. Eine Diskursanalyse zum postsowjetischen russischen Rechtsextremismus | Mit einem Vorwort von Dirk Uffelmann | ISBN 978-3-89821-813-9

60 *Олег Рябов* | «Россия-Матушка». Национализм, гендер и война в России XX века | С предисловием Елены Гощило | ISBN 978-3-89821-487-2

61 *Ivan Maistrenko* | Borot'bism. A Chapter in the History of the Ukrainian Revolution | With a new Introduction by Chris Ford | Translated by George S. N. Luckyj with the assistance of Ivan L. Rudnytsky | Second, Revised and Expanded Edition ISBN 978-3-8382-1107-7

62 *Maryna Romanets* | Anamorphosic Texts and Reconfigured Visions. Improvised Traditions in Contemporary Ukrainian and Irish Literature | ISBN 978-3-89821-576-3

63 *Paul D'Anieri and Taras Kuzio (Eds.)* | Aspects of the Orange Revolution I. Democratization and Elections in Post-Communist Ukraine | ISBN 978-3-89821-698-2

64 *Bohdan Harasymiw in collaboration with Oleh S. Ilnytzkyj (Eds.)* | Aspects of the Orange Revolution II. Information and Manipulation Strategies in the 2004 Ukrainian Presidential Elections | ISBN 978-3-89821-699-9

65 *Ingmar Bredies, Andreas Umland and Valentin Yakushik (Eds.)* | Aspects of the Orange Revolution III. The Context and Dynamics of the 2004 Ukrainian Presidential Elections | ISBN 978-3-89821-803-0

66 *Ingmar Bredies, Andreas Umland and Valentin Yakushik (Eds.)* | Aspects of the Orange Revolution IV. Foreign Assistance and Civic Action in the 2004 Ukrainian Presidential Elections | ISBN 978-3-89821-808-5

67 *Ingmar Bredies, Andreas Umland and Valentin Yakushik (Eds.)* | Aspects of the Orange Revolution V. Institutional Observation Reports on the 2004 Ukrainian Presidential Elections | ISBN 978-3-89821-809-2

68 *Taras Kuzio (Ed.)* | Aspects of the Orange Revolution VI. Post-Communist Democratic Revolutions in Comparative Perspective | ISBN 978-3-89821-820-7

69 *Tim Bohse* | Autoritarismus statt Selbstverwaltung. Die Transformation der kommunalen Politik in der Stadt Kaliningrad 1990-2005 | Mit einem Geleitwort von Stefan Troebst | ISBN 978-3-89821-782-8

70 *David Rupp* | Die Rußländische Föderation und die russischsprachige Minderheit in Lettland. Eine Fallstudie zur Anwaltspolitik Moskaus gegenüber den russophonen Minderheiten im „Nahen Ausland" von 1991 bis 2002 | Mit einem Vorwort von Helmut Wagner | ISBN 978-3-89821-778-1

71 *Taras Kuzio* | Theoretical and Comparative Perspectives on Nationalism. New Directions in Cross-Cultural and Post-Communist Studies | With a foreword by Paul Robert Magocsi | ISBN 978-3-89821-815-3

72 *Christine Teichmann* | Die Hochschultransformation im heutigen Osteuropa. Kontinuität und Wandel bei der Entwicklung des postkommunistischen Universitätswesens | Mit einem Vorwort von Oskar Anweiler | ISBN 978-3-89821-842-9

73 *Julia Kusznir* | Der politische Einfluss von Wirtschaftseliten in russischen Regionen. Eine Analyse am Beispiel der Erdöl- und Erdgasindustrie, 1992-2005 | Mit einem Vorwort von Wolfgang Eichwede | ISBN 978-3-89821-821-4

74   Alena Vysotskaya | Russland, Belarus und die EU-Osterweiterung. Zur Minderheitenfrage und zum Problem der Freizügigkeit des Personenverkehrs | Mit einem Vorwort von Katlijn Malfliet | ISBN 978-3-89821-822-1

75   Heiko Pleines (Hrsg.) | Corporate Governance in post-sozialistischen Volkswirtschaften | ISBN 978-3-89821-766-8

76   Stefan Ihrig | Wer sind die Moldawier? Rumänismus versus Moldowanismus in Historiographie und Schulbüchern der Republik Moldova, 1991-2006 | Mit einem Vorwort von Holm Sundhaussen | ISBN 978-3-89821-466-7

77   Galina Kozhevnikova in collaboration with Alexander Verkhovsky and Eugene Veklerov | Ultra-Nationalism and Hate Crimes in Contemporary Russia. The 2004-2006 Annual Reports of Moscow's SOVA Center | With a foreword by Stephen D. Shenfield | ISBN 978-3-89821-868-9

78   Florian Küchler | The Role of the European Union in Moldova's Transnistria Conflict | With a foreword by Christopher Hill | ISBN 978-3-89821-850-4

79   Bernd Rechel | The Long Way Back to Europe. Minority Protection in Bulgaria | With a foreword by Richard Crampton | ISBN 978-3-89821-863-4

80   Peter W. Rodgers | Nation, Region and History in Post-Communist Transitions. Identity Politics in Ukraine, 1991-2006 | With a foreword by Vera Tolz | ISBN 978-3-89821-903-7

81   Stephanie Solywoda | The Life and Work of Semen L. Frank. A Study of Russian Religious Philosophy | With a foreword by Philip Walters | ISBN 978-3-89821-457-5

82   Vera Sokolova | Cultural Politics of Ethnicity. Discourses on Roma in Communist Czechoslovakia | ISBN 978-3-89821-864-1

83   Natalya Shevchik Ketenci | Kazakhstani Enterprises in Transition. The Role of Historical Regional Development in Kazakhstan's Post-Soviet Economic Transformation | ISBN 978-3-89821-831-3

84   Martin Malek, Anna Schor-Tschudnowskaja (Hgg.) | Europa im Tschetschenienkrieg. Zwischen politischer Ohnmacht und Gleichgültigkeit | Mit einem Vorwort von Lipchan Basajewa | ISBN 978-3-89821-676-0

85   Stefan Meister | Das postsowjetische Universitätswesen zwischen nationalem und internationalem Wandel. Die Entwicklung der regionalen Hochschule in Russland als Gradmesser der Systemtransformation | Mit einem Vorwort von Joan DeBardeleben | ISBN 978-3-89821-891-7

86   Konstantin Sheiko in collaboration with Stephen Brown | Nationalist Imaginings of the Russian Past. Anatolii Fomenko and the Rise of Alternative History in Post-Communist Russia | With a foreword by Donald Ostrowski | ISBN 978-3-89821-915-0

87   Sabine Jenni | Wie stark ist das „Einige Russland"? Zur Parteibindung der Eliten und zum Wahlerfolg der Machtpartei im Dezember 2007 | Mit einem Vorwort von Klaus Armingeon | ISBN 978-3-89821-961-7

88   Thomas Borén | Meeting-Places of Transformation. Urban Identity, Spatial Representations and Local Politics in Post-Soviet St Petersburg | ISBN 978-3-89821-739-2

89   Aygul Ashirova | Stalinismus und Stalin-Kult in Zentralasien. Turkmenistan 1924-1953 | Mit einem Vorwort von Leonid Luks | ISBN 978-3-89821-987-7

90   Leonid Luks | Freiheit oder imperiale Größe? Essays zu einem russischen Dilemma | ISBN 978-3-8382-0011-8

91   Christopher Gilley | The 'Change of Signposts' in the Ukrainian Emigration. A Contribution to the History of Sovietophilism in the 1920s | With a foreword by Frank Golczewski | ISBN 978-3-89821-965-5

92   Philipp Casula, Jeronim Perovic (Eds.) | Identities and Politics During the Putin Presidency. The Discursive Foundations of Russia's Stability | With a foreword by Heiko Haumann | ISBN 978-3-8382-0015-6

93   Marcel Viëtor | Europa und die Frage nach seinen Grenzen im Osten. Zur Konstruktion ‚europäischer Identität' in Geschichte und Gegenwart | Mit einem Vorwort von Albrecht Lehmann | ISBN 978-3-8382-0045-3

94   Ben Hellman, Andrei Rogachevskii | Filming the Unfilmable. Casper Wrede's 'One Day in the Life of Ivan Denisovich' | Second, Revised and Expanded Edition | ISBN 978-3-8382-0044-6

95   Eva Fuchslocher | Vaterland, Sprache, Glaube. Orthodoxie und Nationenbildung am Beispiel Georgiens | Mit einem Vorwort von Christina von Braun | ISBN 978-3-89821-884-9

96   Vladimir Kantor | Das Westlertum und der Weg Russlands. Zur Entwicklung der russischen Literatur und Philosophie | Ediert von Dagmar Herrmann | Mit einem Beitrag von Nikolaus Lobkowicz | ISBN 978-3-8382-0102-3

97   Kamran Musayev | Die postsowjetische Transformation im Baltikum und Südkaukasus. Eine vergleichende Untersuchung der politischen Entwicklung Lettlands und Aserbaidschans 1985-2009 | Mit einem Vorwort von Leonid Luks | Ediert von Sandro Henschel | ISBN 978-3-8382-0103-0

98   Tatiana Zhurzhenko | Borderlands into Bordered Lands. Geopolitics of Identity in Post-Soviet Ukraine | With a foreword by Dieter Segert | ISBN 978-3-8382-0042-2

99 Кирилл Галушко, Лидия Смола (ред.) | Пределы падения – варианты украинского будущего. Аналитико-прогностические исследования | ISBN 978-3-8382-0148-1

100 Michael Minkenberg (Ed.) | Historical Legacies and the Radical Right in Post-Cold War Central and Eastern Europe | With an afterword by Sabrina P. Ramet | ISBN 978-3-8382-0124-5

101 David-Emil Wickström | Rocking St. Petersburg. Transcultural Flows and Identity Politics in the St. Petersburg Popular Music Scene | With a foreword by Yngvar B. Steinholt | Second, Revised and Expanded Edition | ISBN 978-3-8382-0100-9

102 Eva Zabka | Eine neue „Zeit der Wirren"? Der spät- und postsowjetische Systemwandel 1985-2000 im Spiegel russischer gesellschaftspolitischer Diskurse | Mit einem Vorwort von Margareta Mommsen | ISBN 978-3-8382-0161-0

103 Ulrike Ziemer | Ethnic Belonging, Gender and Cultural Practices. Youth Identitites in Contemporary Russia | With a foreword by Anoop Nayak | ISBN 978-3-8382-0152-8

104 Ksenia Chepikova | ‚Einiges Russland' - eine zweite KPdSU? Aspekte der Identitätskonstruktion einer postsowjetischen „Partei der Macht" | Mit einem Vorwort von Torsten Oppelland | ISBN 978-3-8382-0311-9

105 Леонид Люкс | Западничество или евразийство? Демократия или идеократия? Сборник статей об исторических дилеммах России | С предисловием Владимира Кантора | ISBN 978-3-8382-0211-2

106 Anna Dost | Das russische Verfassungsrecht auf dem Weg zum Föderalismus und zurück. Zum Konflikt von Rechtsnormen und -wirklichkeit in der Russländischen Föderation von 1991 bis 2009 | Mit einem Vorwort von Alexander Blankenagel | ISBN 978-3-8382-0292-1

107 Philipp Herzog | Sozialistische Völkerfreundschaft, nationaler Widerstand oder harmloser Zeitvertreib? Zur politischen Funktion der Volkskunst im sowjetischen Estland | Mit einem Vorwort von Andreas Kappeler | ISBN 978-3-8382-0216-7

108 Marlène Laruelle (Ed.) | Russian Nationalism, Foreign Policy, and Identity Debates in Putin's Russia. New Ideological Patterns after the Orange Revolution | ISBN 978-3-8382-0325-6

109 Michail Logvinov | Russlands Kampf gegen den internationalen Terrorismus. Eine kritische Bestandsaufnahme des Bekämpfungsansatzes | Mit einem Geleitwort von Hans-Henning Schröder und einem Vorwort von Eckhard Jesse | ISBN 978-3-8382-0329-4

110 John B. Dunlop | The Moscow Bombings of September 1999. Examinations of Russian Terrorist Attacks at the Onset of Vladimir Putin's Rule | Second, Revised and Expanded Edition | ISBN 978-3-8382-0388-1

111 Андрей А. Ковалёв | Свидетельство из-за кулис российской политики I. Можно ли делать добро из зла? (Воспоминания и размышления о последних советских и первых послесоветских годах) | With a foreword by Peter Reddaway | ISBN 978-3-8382-0302-7

112 Андрей А. Ковалёв | Свидетельство из-за кулис российской политики II. Угроза для себя и окружающих (Наблюдения и предостережения относительно происходящего после 2000 г.) | ISBN 978-3-8382-0303-4

113 Bernd Kappenberg | Zeichen setzen für Europa. Der Gebrauch europäischer lateinischer Sonderzeichen in der deutschen Öffentlichkeit | Mit einem Vorwort von Peter Schlobinski | ISBN 978-3-89821-749-1

114 Ivo Mijnssen | The Quest for an Ideal Youth in Putin's Russia I. Back to Our Future! History, Modernity, and Patriotism according to Nashi, 2005-2013 | With a foreword by Jeronim Perović | Second, Revised and Expanded Edition | ISBN 978-3-8382-0368-3

115 Jussi Lassila | The Quest for an Ideal Youth in Putin's Russia II. The Search for Distinctive Conformism in the Political Communication of Nashi, 2005-2009 | With a foreword by Kirill Postoutenko | Second, Revised and Expanded Edition | ISBN 978-3-8382-0415-4

116 Valerio Trabandt | Neue Nachbarn, gute Nachbarschaft? Die EU als internationaler Akteur am Beispiel ihrer Demokratieförderung in Belarus und der Ukraine 2004-2009 | Mit einem Vorwort von Jutta Joachim | ISBN 978-3-8382-0437-6

117 Fabian Pfeiffer | Estlands Außen- und Sicherheitspolitik I. Der estnische Atlantizismus nach der wiedererlangten Unabhängigkeit 1991-2004 | Mit einem Vorwort von Helmut Hubel | ISBN 978-3-8382-0127-6

118 Jana Podßuweit | Estlands Außen- und Sicherheitspolitik II. Handlungsoptionen eines Kleinstaates im Rahmen seiner EU-Mitgliedschaft (2004-2008) | Mit einem Vorwort von Helmut Hubel | ISBN 978-3-8382-0440-6

119 Karin Pointner | Estlands Außen- und Sicherheitspolitik III. Eine gedächtnispolitische Analyse estnischer Entwicklungskooperation 2006-2010 | Mit einem Vorwort von Karin Liebhart | ISBN 978-3-8382-0435-2

120 Ruslana Vovk | Die Offenheit der ukrainischen Verfassung für das Völkerrecht und die europäische Integration | Mit einem Vorwort von Alexander Blankenagel | ISBN 978-3-8382-0481-9

121 *Mykhaylo Banakh* | Die Relevanz der Zivilgesellschaft bei den postkommunistischen Transformationsprozessen in mittel- und osteuropäischen Ländern. Das Beispiel der spät- und postsowjetischen Ukraine 1986-2009 | Mit einem Vorwort von Gerhard Simon | ISBN 978-3-8382-0499-4

122 *Michael Moser* | Language Policy and the Discourse on Languages in Ukraine under President Viktor Yanukovych (25 February 2010–28 October 2012) | ISBN 978-3-8382-0497-0 (Paperback edition) | ISBN 978-3-8382-0507-6 (Hardcover edition)

123 *Nicole Krome* | Russischer Netzwerkkapitalismus Restrukturierungsprozesse in der Russischen Föderation am Beispiel des Luftfahrtunternehmens „Aviastar" | Mit einem Vorwort von Petra Stykow | ISBN 978-3-8382-0534-2

124 *David R. Marples* | 'Our Glorious Past'. Lukashenka's Belarus and the Great Patriotic War | ISBN 978-3-8382-0574-8 (Paperback edition) | ISBN 978-3-8382-0675-2 (Hardcover edition)

125 *Ulf Walther* | Russlands „neuer Adel". Die Macht des Geheimdienstes von Gorbatschow bis Putin | Mit einem Vorwort von Hans-Georg Wieck | ISBN 978-3-8382-0584-7

126 *Simon Geissbühler (Hrsg.)* | Kiew – Revolution 3.0. Der Euromaidan 2013/14 und die Zukunftsperspektiven der Ukraine | ISBN 978-3-8382-0581-6 (Paperback edition) | ISBN 978-3-8382-0681-3 (Hardcover edition)

127 *Andrey Makarychev* | Russia and the EU in a Multipolar World. Discourses, Identities, Norms | With a foreword by Klaus Segbers | ISBN 978-3-8382-0629-5

128 *Roland Scharff* | Kasachstan als postsowjetischer Wohlfahrtsstaat. Die Transformation des sozialen Schutzsystems | Mit einem Vorwort von Joachim Ahrens | ISBN 978-3-8382-0622-6

129 *Katja Grupp* | Bild Lücke Deutschland. Kaliningrader Studierende sprechen über Deutschland | Mit einem Vorwort von Martin Schulz | ISBN 978-3-8382-0552-5

130 *Konstantin Sheiko, Stephen Brown* | History as Therapy. Alternative History and Nationalist Imaginings in Russia, 1991-2014 | ISBN 978-3-8382-0665-3

131 *Elisa Kriza* | Alexander Solzhenitsyn: Cold War Icon, Gulag Author, Russian Nationalist? A Study of the Western Reception of his Literary Writings, Historical Interpretations, and Political Ideas | With a foreword by Andrei Rogatchevski | ISBN 978-3-8382-0589-2 (Paperback edition) | ISBN 978-3-8382-0690-5 (Hardcover edition)

132 *Serghei Golunov* | The Elephant in the Room. Corruption and Cheating in Russian Universities | ISBN 978-3-8382-0570-0

133 *Manja Hussner, Rainer Arnold (Hgg.)* | Verfassungsgerichtsbarkeit in Zentralasien I. Sammlung von Verfassungstexten | ISBN 978-3-8382-0595-3

134 *Nikolay Mitrokhin* | Die „Russische Partei". Die Bewegung der russischen Nationalisten in der UdSSR 1953-1985 | Aus dem Russischen übertragen von einem Übersetzerteam unter der Leitung von Larisa Schippel | ISBN 978-3-8382-0024-8

135 *Manja Hussner, Rainer Arnold (Hgg.)* | Verfassungsgerichtsbarkeit in Zentralasien II. Sammlung von Verfassungstexten | ISBN 978-3-8382-0597-7

136 *Manfred Zeller* | Das sowjetische Fieber. Fußballfans im poststalinistischen Vielvölkerreich | Mit einem Vorwort von Nikolaus Katzer | ISBN 978-3-8382-0757-5

137 *Kristin Schreiter* | Stellung und Entwicklungspotential zivilgesellschaftlicher Gruppen in Russland. Menschenrechtsorganisationen im Vergleich | ISBN 978-3-8382-0673-8

138 *David R. Marples, Frederick V. Mills (Eds.)* | Ukraine's Euromaidan. Analyses of a Civil Revolution | ISBN 978-3-8382-0660-8

139 *Bernd Kappenberg* | Setting Signs for Europe. Why Diacritics Matter for European Integration | With a foreword by Peter Schlobinski | ISBN 978-3-8382-0663-9

140 *René Lenz* | Internationalisierung, Kooperation und Transfer. Externe bildungspolitische Akteure in der Russischen Föderation | Mit einem Vorwort von Frank Ettrich | ISBN 978-3-8382-0751-3

141 *Juri Plusnin, Yana Zausaeva, Natalia Zhidkevich, Artemy Pozanenko* | Wandering Workers. Mores, Behavior, Way of Life, and Political Status of Domestic Russian Labor Migrants | Translated by Julia Kazantseva | ISBN 978-3-8382-0653-0

142 *David J. Smith (Eds.)* | Latvia – A Work in Progress? 100 Years of State- and Nation-Building | ISBN 978-3-8382-0648-6

143 *Инна Чувычкина (ред.)* | Экспортные нефте- и газопроводы на постсоветском пространстве. Анализ трубопроводной политики в свете теории международных отношений | ISBN 978-3-8382-0822-0

144 *Johann Zajaczkowski* | Russland – eine pragmatische Großmacht? Eine rollentheoretische Untersuchung russischer Außenpolitik am Beispiel der Zusammenarbeit mit den USA nach 9/11 und des Georgienkrieges von 2008 | Mit einem Vorwort von Siegfried Schieder | ISBN 978-3-8382-0837-4

145 *Boris Popivanov* | Changing Images of the Left in Bulgaria. The Challenge of Post-Communism in the Early 21st Century | ISBN 978-3-8382-0667-7

146 *Lenka Krátká* | A History of the Czechoslovak Ocean Shipping Company 1948-1989. How a Small, Landlocked Country Ran Maritime Business During the Cold War | ISBN 978-3-8382-0666-0

147 *Alexander Sergunin* | Explaining Russian Foreign Policy Behavior. Theory and Practice | ISBN 978-3-8382-0752-0

148 *Darya Malyutina* | Migrant Friendships in a Super-Diverse City. Russian-Speakers and their Social Relationships in London in the 21st Century | With a foreword by Claire Dwyer | ISBN 978-3-8382-0652-3

149 *Alexander Sergunin, Valery Konyshev* | Russia in the Arctic. Hard or Soft Power? | ISBN 978-3-8382-0753-7

150 *John J. Maresca* | Helsinki Revisited. A Key U.S. Negotiator's Memoirs on the Development of the CSCE into the OSCE | With a foreword by Hafiz Pashayev | ISBN 978-3-8382-0852-7

151 *Jardar Østbø* | The New Third Rome. Readings of a Russian Nationalist Myth | With a foreword by Pål Kolstø | ISBN 978-3-8382-0870-1

152 *Simon Kordonsky* | Socio-Economic Foundations of the Russian Post-Soviet Regime. The Resource-Based Economy and Estate-Based Social Structure of Contemporary Russia | With a foreword by Svetlana Barsukova | ISBN 978-3-8382-0775-9

153 *Duncan Leitch* | Assisting Reform in Post-Communist Ukraine 2000–2012. The Illusions of Donors and the Disillusion of Beneficiaries | With a foreword by Kataryna Wolczuk | ISBN 978-3-8382-0844-2

154 *Abel Polese* | Limits of a Post-Soviet State. How Informality Replaces, Renegotiates, and Reshapes Governance in Contemporary Ukraine | With a foreword by Colin Williams | ISBN 978-3-8382-0845-9

155 *Mikhail Suslov (Ed.)* | Digital Orthodoxy in the Post-Soviet World. The Russian Orthodox Church and Web 2.0 | With a foreword by Father Cyril Hovorun | ISBN 978-3-8382-0871-8

156 *Leonid Luks* | Zwei „Sonderwege"? Russisch-deutsche Parallelen und Kontraste (1917-2014). Vergleichende Essays | ISBN 978-3-8382-0823-7

157 *Vladimir V. Karacharovskiy, Ovsey I. Shkaratan, Gordey A. Yastrebov* | Towards a New Russian Work Culture. Can Western Companies and Expatriates Change Russian Society? | With a foreword by Elena N. Danilova | Translated by Julia Kazantseva | ISBN 978-3-8382-0902-9

158 *Edmund Griffiths* | Aleksandr Prokhanov and Post-Soviet Esotericism | ISBN 978-3-8382-0963-0

159 *Timm Beichelt, Susann Worschech (Eds.)* | Transnational Ukraine? Networks and Ties that Influence(d) Contemporary Ukraine | ISBN 978-3-8382-0944-9

160 *Mieste Hotopp-Riecke* | Die Tataren der Krim zwischen Assimilation und Selbstbehauptung. Der Aufbau des krimtatarischen Bildungswesens nach Deportation und Heimkehr (1990-2005) | Mit einem Vorwort von Swetlana Czerwonnaja | ISBN 978-3-89821-940-2

161 *Olga Bertelsen (Ed.)* | Revolution and War in Contemporary Ukraine. The Challenge of Change | ISBN 978-3-8382-1016-2

162 *Natalya Ryabinska* | Ukraine's Post-Communist Mass Media. Between Capture and Commercialization | With a foreword by Marta Dyczok | ISBN 978-3-8382-1011-7

163 *Alexandra Cotofana, James M. Nyce (Eds.)* | Religion and Magic in Socialist and Post-Socialist Contexts. Historic and Ethnographic Case Studies of Orthodoxy, Heterodoxy, and Alternative Spirituality | With a foreword by Patrick L. Michelson | ISBN 978-3-8382-0989-0

164 *Nozima Akhrarkhodjaeva* | The Instrumentalisation of Mass Media in Electoral Authoritarian Regimes. Evidence from Russia's Presidential Election Campaigns of 2000 and 2008 | ISBN 978-3-8382-1013-1

165 *Yulia Krasheninnikova* | Informal Healthcare in Contemporary Russia. Sociographic Essays on the Post-Soviet Infrastructure for Alternative Healing Practices | ISBN 978-3-8382-0970-8

166 *Peter Kaiser* | Das Schachbrett der Macht. Die Handlungsspielräume eines sowjetischen Funktionärs unter Stalin am Beispiel des Generalsekretärs des Komsomol Aleksandr Kosarev (1929-1938) | Mit einem Vorwort von Dietmar Neutatz | ISBN 978-3-8382-1052-0

167 *Oksana Kim* | The Effects and Implications of Kazakhstan's Adoption of International Financial Reporting Standards. A Resource Dependence Perspective | With a foreword by Svetlana Vlady | ISBN 978-3-8382-0987-6

168 *Anna Sanina* | Patriotic Education in Contemporary Russia. Sociological Studies in the Making of the Post-Soviet Citizen | With a foreword by Anna Oldfield | ISBN 978-3-8382-0993-7

169 *Rudolf Wolters* | Spezialist in Sibirien Faksimile der 1933 erschienenen ersten Ausgabe | Mit einem Vorwort von Dmitrij Chmelnizki | ISBN 978-3-8382-0515-1

170 *Michal Vít, Magdalena M. Baran (Eds.)* | Transregional versus National Perspectives on Contemporary Central European History. Studies on the Building of Nation-States and Their Cooperation in the 20th and 21st Century | With a foreword by Petr Vágner | ISBN 978-3-8382-1015-5

171 *Philip Gamaghelyan* | Conflict Resolution Beyond the International Relations Paradigm. Evolving Designs as a Transformative Practice in Nagorno-Karabakh and Syria | With a foreword by Susan Allen | ISBN 978-3-8382-1057-5

172 *Maria Shagina* | Joining a Prestigious Club. Cooperation with Europarties and Its Impact on Party Development in Georgia, Moldova, and Ukraine 2004–2015 | With a foreword by Kataryna Wolczuk | ISBN 978-3-8382-1084-1

173 *Alexandra Cotofana, James M. Nyce (Eds.)* | Religion and Magic in Socialist and Post-Socialist Contexts II. Baltic, Eastern European, and Post-USSR Case Studies | With a foreword by Anita Stasulane | ISBN 978-3-8382-0990-6

174 *Barbara Kunz* | Kind Words, Cruise Missiles, and Everything in Between. The Use of Power Resources in U.S. Policies towards Poland, Ukraine, and Belarus 1989–2008 | With a foreword by William Hill | ISBN 978-3-8382-1065-0

175 *Eduard Klein* | Bildungskorruption in Russland und der Ukraine. Eine komparative Analyse der Performanz staatlicher Antikorruptionsmaßnahmen im Hochschulsektor am Beispiel universitärer Aufnahmeprüfungen | Mit einem Vorwort von Heiko Pleines | ISBN 978-3-8382-0995-1

176 *Markus Soldner* | Politischer Kapitalismus im postsowjetischen Russland. Die politische, wirtschaftliche und mediale Transformation in den 1990er Jahren | Mit einem Vorwort von Wolfgang Ismayr | ISBN 978-3-8382-1222-7

177 *Anton Oleinik* | Building Ukraine from Within. A Sociological, Institutional, and Economic Analysis of a Nation-State in the Making | ISBN 978-3-8382-1150-3

178 *Peter Rollberg, Marlene Laruelle (Eds.)* | Mass Media in the Post-Soviet World. Market Forces, State Actors, and Political Manipulation in the Informational Environment after Communism | ISBN 978-3-8382-1116-9

179 *Mikhail Minakov* | Development and Dystopia. Studies in Post-Soviet Ukraine and Eastern Europe | With a foreword by Alexander Etkind | ISBN 978-3-8382-1112-1

180 *Aijan Sharshenova* | The European Union's Democracy Promotion in Central Asia. A Study of Political Interests, Influence, and Development in Kazakhstan and Kyrgyzstan in 2007–2013 | With a foreword by Gordon Crawford | ISBN 978-3-8382-1151-0

181 *Andrey Makarychev, Alexandra Yatsyk (Eds.)* | Boris Nemtsov and Russian Politics. Power and Resistance | With a foreword by Zhanna Nemtsova | ISBN 978-3-8382-1122-0

182 *Sophie Falsini* | The Euromaidan's Effect on Civil Society. Why and How Ukrainian Social Capital Increased after the Revolution of Dignity | With a foreword by Susann Worschech | ISBN 978-3-8382-1131-2

183 *Valentyna Romanova, Andreas Umland (Eds.)* | Ukraine's Decentralization. Challenges and Implications of the Local Governance Reform after the Euromaidan Revolution | ISBN 978-3-8382-1162-6

184 *Leonid Luks* | A Fateful Triangle. Essays on Contemporary Russian, German and Polish History | ISBN 978-3-8382-1143-5

185 *John B. Dunlop* | The February 2015 Assassination of Boris Nemtsov and the Flawed Trial of his Alleged Killers. An Exploration of Russia's "Crime of the 21st Century" | ISBN 978-3-8382-1188-6

186 *Vasile Rotaru* | Russia, the EU, and the Eastern Partnership. Building Bridges or Digging Trenches? | ISBN 978-3-8382-1134-3

187 *Marina Lebedeva* | Russian Studies of International Relations. From the Soviet Past to the Post-Cold-War Present | With a foreword by Andrei P. Tsygankov | ISBN 978-3-8382-0851-0

188 *Tomasz Stępniewski, George Soroka (Eds.)* | Ukraine after Maidan. Revisiting Domestic and Regional Security | ISBN 978-3-8382-1075-9

189 *Petar Cholakov* | Ethnic Entrepreneurs Unmasked. Political Institutions and Ethnic Conflicts in Contemporary Bulgaria | ISBN 978-3-8382-1189-3

190 *A. Salem, G. Hazeldine, D. Morgan (Eds.)* | Higher Education in Post-Communist States. Comparative and Sociological Perspectives | ISBN 978-3-8382-1183-1

191 *Igor Torbakov* | After Empire. Nationalist Imagination and Symbolic Politics in Russia and Eurasia in the Twentieth and Twenty-First Century | With a foreword by Serhii Plokhy | ISBN 978-3-8382-1217-3

192 *Aleksandr Burakovskiy* | Jewish-Ukrainian Relations in Late and Post-Soviet Ukraine. Articles, Lectures and Essays from 1986 to 2016 | ISBN 978-3-8382-1210-4

193 *Natalia Shapovalova, Olga Burlyuk (Eds.)* | Civil Society in Post-Euromaidan Ukraine. From Revolution to Consolidation | With a foreword by Richard Youngs | ISBN 978-3-8382-1216-6

194 *Franz Preissler* | Positionsverteidigung, Imperialismus oder Irredentismus? Russland und die „Russischsprachigen", 1991–2015 | ISBN 978-3-8382-1262-3

195 *Marian Madeła* | Der Reformprozess in der Ukraine 2014-2017. Eine Fallstudie zur Reform der öffentlichen Verwaltung | Mit einem Vorwort von Martin Malek | ISBN 978-3-8382-1266-1

196 *Anke Giesen* | „Wie kann denn der Sieger ein Verbrecher sein?" Eine diskursanalytische Untersuchung der russlandweiten Debatte über Konzept und Verstaatlichungsprozess der Lagergedenkstätte „Perm'-36" im Ural | ISBN 978-3-8382-1284-5

197 *Alla Leukavets* | The Integration Policies of Belarus and Ukraine vis-à-vis the EU and Russia. A Comparative Case Study Through the Prism of a Two-Level Game Approach | ISBN 978-3-8382-1247-0

198 *Oksana Kim* | The Development and Challenges of Russian Corporate Governance I. The Roles and Functions of Boards of Directors | With a foreword by Sheila M. Puffer | ISBN 978-3-8382-1287-6

199 *Thomas D. Grant* | International Law and the Post-Soviet Space I. Essays on Chechnya and the Baltic States | With a foreword by Stephen M. Schwebel | ISBN 978-3-8382-1279-1

200 *Thomas D. Grant* | International Law and the Post-Soviet Space II. Essays on Ukraine, Intervention, and Non-Proliferation | ISBN 978-3-8382-1280-7

201 *Slavomír Michálek, Michal Štefansky* | The Age of Fear. The Cold War and Its Influence on Czechoslovakia 1945–1968 | ISBN 978-3-8382-1285-2

202 *Iulia-Sabina Joja* | Romania's Strategic Culture 1990–2014. Continuity and Change in a Post-Communist Country's Evolution of National Interests and Security Policies | With a foreword by Heiko Biehl | ISBN 978-3-8382-1286-9

203 *Andrei Rogatchevski, Yngvar B. Steinholt, Arve Hansen, David-Emil Wickström* | War of Songs. Popular Music and Recent Russia-Ukraine Relations | With a foreword by Artemy Troitsky | ISBN 978-3-8382-1173-2

204 *Maria Lipman (Ed.)* | Russian Voices on Post-Crimea Russia. An Almanac of Counterpoint Essays from 2015–2018 | ISBN 978-3-8382-1251-7

205 *Ksenia Maksimovtsova* | Language Conflicts in Contemporary Estonia, Latvia, and Ukraine. A Comparative Exploration of Discourses in Post-Soviet Russian-Language Digital Media | With a foreword by Ammon Cheskin | ISBN 978-3-8382-1282-1

206 *Michal Vít* | The EU's Impact on Identity Formation in East-Central Europe between 2004 and 2013. Perceptions of the Nation and Europe in Political Parties of the Czech Republic, Poland, and Slovakia | With a foreword by Andrea Pető | ISBN 978-3-8382-1275-3

207 *Per A. Rudling* | Tarnished Heroes. The Organization of Ukrainian Nationalists in the Memory Politics of Post-Soviet Ukraine | ISBN 978-3-8382-0999-9

208 *Kaja Gadowska, Peter Solomon (Eds.)* | Legal Change in Post-Communist States. Progress, Reversions, Explanations | ISBN 978-3-8382-1312-5

209 *Paweł Kowal, Georges Mink, Iwona Reichardt (Eds.)* | Three Revolutions: Mobilization and Change in Contemporary Ukraine I. Theoretical Aspects and Analyses on Religion, Memory, and Identity | ISBN 978-3-8382-1321-7

210 *Paweł Kowal, Georges Mink, Adam Reichardt, Iwona Reichardt (Eds.)* | Three Revolutions: Mobilization and Change in Contemporary Ukraine II. An Oral History of the Revolution on Granite, Orange Revolution, and Revolution of Dignity | ISBN 978-3-8382-1323-1

211 *Li Bennich-Björkman, Sergiy Kurbatov (Eds.)* | When the Future Came. The Collapse of the USSR and the Emergence of National Memory in Post-Soviet History Textbooks | ISBN 978-3-8382-1335-4

212 *Olga R. Gulina* | Migration as a (Geo-)Political Challenge in the Post-Soviet Space. Border Regimes, Policy Choices, Visa Agendas | With a foreword by Nils Muižnieks | ISBN 978-3-8382-1338-5

213 *Sanna Turoma, Kaarina Aitamurto, Slobodanka Vladiv-Glover (Eds.)* | Religion, Expression, and Patriotism in Russia. Essays on Post-Soviet Society and the State. ISBN 978-3-8382-1346-0

214 *Vasif Huseynov* | Geopolitical Rivalries in the "Common Neighborhood". Russia's Conflict with the West, Soft Power, and Neoclassical Realism | With a foreword by Nicholas Ross Smith | ISBN 978-3-8382-1277-7

215 *Mikhail Suslov* | Geopolitical Imagination. Ideology and Utopia in Post-Soviet Russia | With a foreword by Mark Bassin | ISBN 978-3-8382-1361-3

216 *Alexander Etkind, Mikhail Minakov (Eds.)* | Ideology after Union. Political Doctrines, Discourses, and Debates in Post-Soviet Societies | ISBN 978-3-8382-1388-0

217 *Jakob Mischke, Oleksandr Zabirko (Hgg.)* | Protestbewegungen im langen Schatten des Kreml. Aufbruch und Resignation in Russland und der Ukraine | ISBN 978-3-8382-0926-5

218 *Oksana Huss* | How Corruption and Anti-Corruption Policies Sustain Hybrid Regimes. Strategies of Political Domination under Ukraine's Presidents in 1994-2014 | With a foreword by Tobias Debiel and Andrea Gawrich | ISBN 978-3-8382-1430-6

219 *Dmitry Travin, Vladimir Gel'man, Otar Marganiya* | The Russian Path. Ideas, Interests, Institutions, Illusions | With a foreword by Vladimir Ryzhkov | ISBN 978-3-8382-1421-4

220 *Gergana Dimova* | Political Uncertainty. A Comparative Exploration | With a foreword by Todor Yalamov and Rumena Filipova | ISBN 978-3-8382-1385-9

221 *Torben Waschke* | Russland in Transition. Geopolitik zwischen Raum, Identität und Machtinteressen | Mit einem Vorwort von Andreas Dittmann | ISBN 978-3-8382-1480-1

222 *Steven Jobbitt, Zsolt Bottlik, Marton Berki (Eds.)* | Power and Identity in the Post-Soviet Realm. Geographies of Ethnicity and Nationality after 1991 | ISBN 978-3-8382-1399-6

223 *Daria Buteiko* | Erinnerungsort. Ort des Gedenkens, der Erholung oder der Einkehr? Kommunismus-Erinnerung am Beispiel der Gedenkstätte Berliner Mauer sowie des Soloveckij-Klosters und -Museumsparks | ISBN 978-3-8382-1367-5

224 *Olga Bertelsen (Ed.)* | Russian Active Measures. Yesterday, Today, Tomorrow | With a foreword by Jan Goldman | ISBN 978-3-8382-1529-7

225 *David Mandel* | "Optimizing" Higher Education in Russia. University Teachers and their Union "Universitetskaya solidarnost'" | ISBN 978-3-8382-1519-8

226 *Mikhail Minakov, Gwendolyn Sasse, Daria Isachenko (Eds.)* | Post-Soviet Secessionism. Nation-Building and State-Failure after Communism | ISBN 978-3-8382-1538-9

227 *Jakob Hauter (Ed.)* | Civil War? Interstate War? Hybrid War? Dimensions and Interpretations of the Donbas Conflict in 2014–2020 | With a foreword by Andrew Wilson | ISBN 978-3-8382-1383-5

228 *Tima T. Moldogaziev, Gene A. Brewer, J. Edward Kellough (Eds.)* | Public Policy and Politics in Georgia. Lessons from Post-Soviet Transition | With a foreword by Dan Durning | ISBN 978-3-8382-1535-8

229 *Oxana Schmies (Ed.)* | NATO's Enlargement and Russia. A Strategic Challenge in the Past and Future | With a foreword by Vladimir Kara-Murza | ISBN 978-3-8382-1478-8

230 *Christopher Ford* | Ukapisme – Une Gauche perdue. Le marxisme anti-colonial dans la révolution ukrainienne 1917-1925 | Avec une préface de Vincent Présumey | ISBN 978-3-8382-0899-2

231 *Anna Kutkina* | Between Lenin and Bandera. Decommunization and Multivocality in Post-Euromaidan Ukraine | With a foreword by Juri Mykkänen | ISBN 978-3-8382-1506-8

232 *Lincoln E. Flake* | Defending the Faith. The Russian Orthodox Church and the Demise of Religious Pluralism | With a foreword by Peter Martland | ISBN 978-3-8382-1378-1

233 *Nikoloz Samkharadze* | Russia's Recognition of the Independence of Abkhazia and South Ossetia. Analysis of a Deviant Case in Moscow's Foreign Policy | With a foreword by Neil MacFarlane | ISBN 978-3-8382-1414-6

234 *Arve Hansen* | Urban Protest. A Spatial Perspective on Kyiv, Minsk, and Moscow | With a foreword by Julie Wilhelmsen | ISBN 978-3-8382-1495-5

235 *Eleonora Narvselius, Julie Fedor (Eds.)* | Diversity in the East-Central European Borderlands. Memories, Cityscapes, People | ISBN 978-3-8382-1523-5

236 *Regina Elsner* | The Russian Orthodox Church and Modernity. A Historical and Theological Investigation into Eastern Christianity between Unity and Plurality | With a foreword by Mikhail Suslov | ISBN 978-3-8382-1568-6

237 *Bo Petersson* | The Putin Predicament. Problems of Legitimacy and Succession in Russia | With a foreword by J. Paul Goode | ISBN 978-3-8382-1050-6

238 *Jonathan Otto Pohl* | The Years of Great Silence. The Deportation, Special Settlement, and Mobilization into the Labor Army of Ethnic Germans in the USSR, 1941–1955 | ISBN 978-3-8382-1630-0

239 *Mikhail Minakov (Ed.)* | Inventing Majorities. Ideological Creativity in Post-Soviet Societies | ISBN 978-3-8382-1641-6

240 *Robert M. Cutler* | Soviet and Post-Soviet Foreign Policies I. East-South Relations and the Political Economy of the Communist Bloc, 1971–1991 | With a foreword by Roger E. Kanet | ISBN 978-3-8382-1654-3

241 *Izabella Agardi* | On the Verge of History. Life Stories of Rural Women from Serbia, Romania, and Hungary, 1920–2020 | With a foreword by Andrea Pető | ISBN 978-3-8382-1602-7

242 *Sebastian Schäffer (Ed.)* | Ukraine in Central and Eastern Europe. Kyiv's Foreign Affairs and the International Relations of the Post-Communist Region | With a foreword by Pavlo Klimkin and Andreas Umland| ISBN 978-3-8382-1615-7

243 *Volodymyr Dubrovskyi, Kalman Mizsei, Mychailo Wynnyckyj (Eds.)* | Eight Years after the Revolution of Dignity. What Has Changed in Ukraine during 2013–2021? | With a foreword by Yaroslav Hrytsak | ISBN 978-3-8382-1560-0

244 *Rumena Filipova* | Constructing the Limits of Europe Identity and Foreign Policy in Poland, Bulgaria, and Russia since 1989 | With forewords by Harald Wydra and Gergana Yankova-Dimova | ISBN 978-3-8382-1649-2

245 *Oleksandra Keudel* | How Patronal Networks Shape Opportunities for Local Citizen Participation in a Hybrid Regime A Comparative Analysis of Five Cities in Ukraine | With a foreword by Sabine Kropp | ISBN 978-3-8382-1671-3

246 *Jan Claas Behrends, Thomas Lindenberger, Pavel Kolar (Eds.)* | Violence after Stalin Institutions, Practices, and Everyday Life in the Soviet Bloc 1953–1989 | ISBN 978-3-8382-1637-9

247 *Leonid Luks* | Macht und Ohnmacht der Utopien Essays zur Geschichte Russlands im 20. und 21. Jahrhundert | ISBN 978-3-8382-1677-5

248 *Iuliia Barshadska* | Brüssel zwischen Kyjiw und Moskau Das auswärtige Handeln der Europäischen Union im ukrainisch-russischen Konflikt 2014-2019 | Mit einem Vorwort von Olaf Leiße | ISBN 978-3-8382-1667-6

249 *Valentyna Romanova* | Decentralisation and Multilevel Elections in Ukraine Reform Dynamics and Party Politics in 2010–2021 | With a foreword by Kimitaka Matsuzato | ISBN 978-3-8382-1700-0

250 *Alexander Motyl* | National Questions. Theoretical Reflections on Nations and Nationalism in Eastern Europe | ISBN 978-3-8382-1675-1

251 *Marc Dietrich* | A Cosmopolitan Model for Peacebuilding. The Ukrainian Cases of Crimea and the Donbas | ISBN 978-3-8382-1687-4

252 *Eduard Baidaus* | An Unsettled Nation. State-Building, Identity, and Separatism in Post-Soviet Moldova | With forewords by John-Paul Himka and David R. Marples | ISBN 978-3-8382-1582-2

253 *Igor Okunev, Petr Oskolkov (Eds.)* | Transforming the Administrative Matryoshka. The Reform of Autonomous Okrugs in the Russian Federation, 2003–2008 | With a foreword by Vladimir Zorin | ISBN 978-3-8382-1721-5

254 *Winfried Schneider-Deters* | Ukraine's Fateful Years 2013–2019. Vol. I: The Popular Uprising in Winter 2013/2014 | ISBN 978-3-8382-1725-3

255 *Winfried Schneider-Deters* | Ukraine's Fateful Years 2013–2019. Vol. II: The Annexation of Crimea and the War in Donbas | ISBN 978-3-8382-1726-0

256 *Robert M. Cutler* | Soviet and Post-Soviet Russian Foreign Policies II. East-West Relations in Europe and the Political Economy of the Communist Bloc, 1971–1991 | With a foreword by Roger E. Kanet | ISBN 978-3-8382-1727-7

257 *Robert M. Cutler* | Soviet and Post-Soviet Russian Foreign Policies III. East-West Relations in Europe and Eurasia in the Post-Cold War Transition, 1991–2001 | With a foreword by Roger E. Kanet | ISBN 978-3-8382-1728-4

258 *Paweł Kowal, Iwona Reichardt, Kateryna Pryshchepa (Eds.)* | Three Revolutions: Mobilization and Change in Contemporary Ukraine III. Archival Records and Historical Sources on the 1990 Revolution on Granite | ISBN 978-3-8382-1376-7

259 *Mikhail Minakov (Ed.)* | Philosophy Unchained. Developments in Post-Soviet Philosophical Thought. | With a foreword by Christopher Donohue | ISBN 978-3-8382-1768-0

260 *David Dalton* | The Ukrainian Oligarchy After the Euromaidan. How Ukraine's Political Economy Regime Survived the Crisis | With a foreword by Andrew Wilson | ISBN 978-3-8382-1740-6

261 *Andreas Heinemann-Grüder (Ed.)* | Who are the Fighters? Irregular Armed Groups in the Russian-Ukrainian War in 2014–2015 | ISBN 978-3-8382-1777-2

262 *Taras Kuzio (Ed.)* | Russian Disinformation and Western Scholarship. Bias and Prejudice in Journalistic, Expert, and Academic Analyses of East European and Eurasian Affairs | ISBN 978-3-8382-1685-0

263 *Darius Furmonavicius* | LithuaniaTransforms the West. Lithuania's Liberation from Soviet Occupation and the Enlargement of NATO (1988–2022) | With a foreword by Vytautas Landsbergis | ISBN 978-3-8382-1779-6

264 *Dirk Dalberg* | Gegenwartsbeschreibungen und Zukunftsvorstellungen im tschechoslowakischen Dissens (1968-1989). Das politische Denken von Egon Bondy, Miroslav Kusý, Milan Šimečka und Petr Uhl | ISBN 978-3-8382-1318-7

ibidem.*eu*